The Church!

When did it begin?
(And why is that important?)

By Olive and Lloyd Allen

About the cover

On the first page of this book is a picture of a church. Appropriately it is a picture of Bendale Bible Chapel. For over 40 years Bendale has provided a church home for Olive and myself, and the Believers and Elders there have given us comfort and support over the years during many dark times. They have accepted us as fellow Christians despite the fact that they knew that we held some beliefs that differed markedly from those that they held. They have never tried to force us to change. The example of these good people is one that could teach us all. Their gentle discussion with us forms part of the background that caused us to attempt to write down our beliefs and brought this book into being. If any one benefits from these pages then the people of Bendale deserve credit.

Lloyd Allen

ISBN: 978-1-78364-477-3

Publications of the Open Bible Trust and Bible Search Publications Inc. must be in accordance with their evangelical, fundamental and dispensational basis. However, beyond this minimum, writers are free to express whatever beliefs they may have as their own understanding, provided that the aim in so doing is to further the object of The Open Bible Trust and Bible Search Publications Inc. A copy of the doctrinal basis is available from **www.obt.org.uk** or from

The Open Bible Trust
Fordland Mount, Upper Basildon
Reading, RG8 8LU, UK.

TO OUR CHILDREN
so that they may know some of the things
that Mom and Dad believed.

AND TO OUR
GRANDCHILDREN
so that they may know
some of the things that Grandma and
Grandpa believed.

TO HIS GLORY
And God said unto Moses,
"I AM THAT I AM...
Thou shalt say...
I AM hath sent me unto you"
(Exodus 3:14)

About the authors:

Olive Lily Allen was born in London, Ontario, Canada and attended school there. She graduated from the Salvation Army Training College in Toronto and rose to the rank of Captain with the Salvation Army, having served as an officer in various corps. She left the clergy and moved to Toronto where she later met Lloyd. After they were married, she went back as a civilian employee of the Salvation Army, where she worked on various departments, including Overseas Projects, helping to expedite the Army's work in foreign countries.

James Lloyd Allen was born in Toronto, Canada, where he received his lower schooling. He became a photo engraver and became a member of the union. Through Olive's urging, he went back to school at age 45 and graduated when 53 with a Bachelor of Arts degree in Geography and Sociology from the University of Toronto.

Olive and Lloyd met at Peoples Church, in Toronto, where they were married. In 1956 they left Peoples Church and joined with seven friends to start a Sunday School in an area of new subdivisions. This later became Bendale Bible Chapel. However, they both are now retired and live in Scarborough, Ontario. They have three children, who are all active Christians, and seven grand-children. This book has primarily been written for them, so that they can know what their parents, or grand-parents, believe. However, what is said here, for the benefit of their personal family, will be of benefit to the whole family of God.

Contents

PREFACE

God's will for us is contained in the Bible. As faithful servants, it is imperative that we submit our minds to the correction of the Scriptures. Unfortunately, our tendency, even as committed believers, is to look at verses individually and link them together according to our own preconceptions. By quoting random verses out of context it is possible to prove virtually any idea that suits our desires, regardless of how contrary it may be to God's will. This is not to suggest wilful disobedience, but to recognise a weakness in our thought processes. There is also an element of pride involved. It is hard to admit that some of the ideas that we have held so dearly for so long may be wrong. We tend to search the Scriptures for anything that appears to substantiate our own position.

At the same time we cannot casually throw out what we have believed or we would be guilty of being blown about by every wind of doctrine. This would be equally erroneous.

What is needed is a sound thoughtful way of looking at each proposition in context. Michael Penny, in his book *Approaching the Bible*, suggests a way to place each verse in context by asking appropriate questions such as "Who said it?", "Of whom was it said?", "When was it said?", "To when does it relate?", "Where is it about?", "What was the subject involved?", "Why was it said?", and so on. He goes on to illustrate the method in detail. When considering the context, it is necessary to look at both the immediate circumstance, and the remote framework. The latter, the general structure of the Bible, is the subject here.

The Bible is not simply a random collection of wise sayings to be used in isolation. Both the near and remote contexts have bearing on each statement and may modify our understanding of it; i.e. each statement in the Bible needs to be understood in the light of God's complete Word. His Word is at the same time elegant in its simplicity and profound in its complexity. It is like no other book ever written. There is one Person Who is the subject of God's Word; Jesus Christ, the Son of God the Father, glorified by God the Holy Spirit. There is one overriding theme; God's grace and forgiveness extended to man through the sacrificial death of Christ.

As simple as these truths may appear, it took the whole Bible to disclose them to man. God has made them manifest in two stages through two stewardships. The first steward was Israel and the second was, and still is, 'The Church which is the Body of Christ'..... us! Neither stage is complete in itself, nor are they contradictory to each other. Rather they complement each other forming a glorious message of God's love

The beginning of 'The Church which is His Body' represents a change of stewardship; i.e. a change of stewards and a shift in the message that God was giving to man. God committed new responsibilities to man, specifically to us Gentiles, and we need to remember that we are His servants. If we are to be faithful servants, or stewards, we need a clear knowledge of what has been committed to us and for that we need to understand what is set forth in the Scriptures. We cannot impart to others what we do not understand ourselves.

I hope to show that the 'New Stewardship', committed to us by God, is not simply a continuation of the old but is quite distinct, although it shares certain features with the old. The Bible, the Word of God, is our only authority, and pleasing *Him* should be our only goal.

Lloyd Allen

Acknowledgements

Thanks to Michael Penny and his editors who criticized, corrected, edited and in general kept me from publishing confusing and contradicting material, to say nothing of *typos*. How much time and effort did they expend editing, typesetting, proof reading, designing the cover, laying out the table of contents and the long index of quotes? Thanks also to Ron Moore who persuaded me to try and have my scribblings published in the first place.

Part 1

When

DID THE CHURCH BEGIN?

Chapter 1

INTRODUCTION

When one considers all the disunity amongst Christian believers, all of the denominations, all the Church splits, indeed all the suffering, want, quarrelling and hatred and war in our world today, one is tempted to say "Let us stop splitting hairs and get on with the great issues and forget the minor ones." To some extent this is right. We do indeed often major on minor issues and minor on major issues. Often we are more interested in proving our point than in having a genuine interest in truth as such. All too often pride is the true issue, with disastrous results.

One might reasonably ask, "Then why bother writing a book on such an obscure subject as when the church started? Is it not enough that it did start? As Christians should we not get on with living a life that honours Christ and helping the hurting?"

I will try to answer and I ask the reader to be gentle with me. Let me make it clear that this is presented as a personal opinion offered for consideration only. In the Book of Acts chapter 17, Luke is dealing with the journeys of Paul and Silas. They have been in Thessalonica where the Jews rioted. They continue on to Berea and go into the synagogue of the Jews. In verse 11 Luke makes a most pointed statement: "These were more noble than those at Thessalonica, in that they received the word with all readiness of mind, and searched the Scriptures daily, whether these things were so." It is in this Berean spirit that I would ask the reader to consider this thesis. No-one's opinion should be accepted as such, but if it is supported in God's Word then we must accept it, for the Bible is the only authority. If it becomes apparent that it is contrary to the Bible then we owe it to the people holding such an opinion, in love, prayerfully to discuss such contrary evidence with them.

A teacher I once had, said something like "When we take on a noble cause, we need to be careful that we do not forget the single individual or our noble cause can become the end that justifies harm to the individual without our even realising it." I pray to God that He will always make me conscious of the fact that my self-professed "noble cause" must not only give praise to God but also help other individuals to appreciate more fully the wonders of His grace and His revelation to us.

Reasoned

When Jesus "reasoned" with men He spoke with authority, for He was God incarnate, yet He opened the Scriptures and taught from them. When the apostle Paul "reasoned" with men he spoke as one who had received Divine revelation, yet he opened the Scriptures and taught from them. We have neither the authority of Christ nor direct Divine revelation. When we reason we must hold only to the Scriptures, for we have no other ground on which to stand.

The subject of this book is phrased as two questions, "When did the Church start?" and "Why is that important?" I will now state my view on the first question and attempt to justify that view. Then I will attempt to answer the second.

When?

I hold that the Church which is the Body of Christ, the church of today, began at some time after the incidents recorded in Acts 28:25-28. This "church" was revealed to and by the apostle Paul only, in the letters that he wrote after that time. This revelation, along with its implications, constitutes a major part of the work of the Holy Spirit through Paul's later ministry and leads us into all truth (John 14:26). The implications themselves are so vast that I could not begin to deal with them but must restrict myself to only certain general principles.

This view of the church's beginning is at great variance with a generally accepted view that the church began on the Day of Pentecost. There are other views of course, such as an Acts 13 beginning for the church, or the more broadly held opinion that the Church is only an extension or inheritor of Israel's ministries and blessings. This last idea is the underlying concept of the Jehovah's Witness movement and, in varying forms and degrees, is held by many others. These other views will not be dealt with extensively here, but shall be looked at later in this book. However, when we consider differing alternatives, only careful study of the "Word" will clarify matters. There are three Scriptures that can help and guide us.

> *2 Timothy 3:16*: All Scripture is given by inspiration of God, and is profitable for doctrine, for reproof, for *correction*, for instruction in righteousness.

At most, only one of the stated views can be right, but we can only be sure which is *correct* by a careful consideration of the scriptural evidence. We do each other honour by reasoning as fellow believers in the court of God's word. It may be that in so doing we will find further truth that none of us has yet perceived. On the other hand, it would be quite wrong to argue that just because some other person or group, such as the Catholic Church or the Jehovah's Witnesses, holds a particular view that error must be involved. That would be arguing personalities rather than issues. In such cases emotion destroys reason!

There is, in this verse in 2 Timothy, a phrase of immense significance. It says that "All Scripture" is inspired by God, (i.e. God breathed), not just some of it. If this is not so then the Bible is not authoritative and we are left to our own devices. We can then select whatever verse or idea from the Bible that suits our preconceived notions and purposes and simply reject everything else out of hand. Of course most Christians do not go that far but without our even realising it, the idea of grading the Scriptures as being of greater or lesser authority has crept into our thinking. It is the source of much of our theological and denominational differences.

Of particular importance to our present study is the way it affects our view of the New Testament. The *Red Letter Bible*, for instance, by placing undue emphasis on the spoken words of Christ over the rest of Scripture, carries with it the inherent danger of misunderstanding the Gospels and the rest of the Scriptures. It certainly is an advantage to illuminate direct narration for ease of study. This could possibly be better achieved by the simple use of quotation marks as it is in some of the newer translations. After all, the punctuation, and indeed the chapter and verse divisions that we have in our English Bible, were not in the original manuscripts but were only added for convenience. They suit our language and make referencing easy.

At first glance it would seem reasonable to emphasise the spoken words of Christ above all other Scripture, after all He is God Incarnate, but there are problems with this. First, as will be mentioned again, the author of the "other" Scripture is none other than God the Holy Spirit. By suggesting that Christ's spoken words are to be given greater weight, are we not in fact intimating that the words of the Holy Spirit are in some way less reliable?

In the case of any apparent differences in what is taught, we would have the situation in which we would have to be arbiters choosing between the teachings of God the Son and the teachings of God the Holy Spirit! This would be intolerable. God cannot contradict

Himself neither would He leave us with so unclear a message.

Second, it is recorded that Christ wrote only once, and that was in the sand. Men have often speculated as to what He wrote but we do not know for that writing has long since disappeared and it was never, to our knowledge, copied. We are dependent entirely on third party accounts to let us know what Christ said. The usual comparison is between the teaching of Jesus in the four Gospels, written by Matthew, Mark, Luke and John, and the teaching of the apostle Paul in his epistles. We might reason that although God would not contradict Himself, we have two classes of men being used to transcribe Holy Writ. We may reason that since Paul did not actually walk with the Lord and was not taught by Him in His earthly ministry, he might not be as reliable as the other four, and he may have misunderstood the full message of the gospel. However, Luke did not meet Jesus either.

Again, there is a problem with that view. Of all the penmen of the New Testament, only Matthew, John, and Peter were of the twelve who walked with Christ. Humanly speaking, Mark and Luke recorded only oral or written tradition of what Christ said, if we set aside the principle of divine authorship. How can we therefore be certain of the veracity of the records of Christ's spoken teachings in two of the gospels and The Book of Acts? Once we renounce the concept of the verbal inspiration of *the entire* Bible we cannot be sure of the basis of our salvation!

It should be noted that there was indeed a difference between what Christ said in the Gospels and what Paul taught, especially in his later epistles. In his second epistle Peter makes that clear. Chapter 3, verse 15 and 16 says "Bear in mind that our Lord's patience means salvation, just as our dear brother Paul also wrote to you *with the wisdom that God gave him*. He writes the same way in all his letters, speaking in them of these matters. His letters *contain some things that are hard to understand*, which ignorant and unstable people distort, as they do *the other Scriptures*, to their own destruction" (*NIV*).

Peter clearly indicates that Paul wrote of things that he, Peter, was not familiar with. These things must have been different to the oral communications that Christ delivered to Peter and the apostles, otherwise after three years instruction and his experience with the risen Christ, why would they be hard for him to understand? At the same time he confirms the source of Paul's authority. He wrote "with the wisdom that God gave him." Again, he links Paul's writings to "the other scriptures" so that to distort either would bring about one's own destruction.

These distinct teachings of Paul's epistles are in fact the words of the risen and glorified Christ, given through the Holy Spirit. In some instances they are different to our Lord's earthly decrees that were given to the nation of Israel (Romans 15:8), a people under the Mosaic Law. Jesus' own words confirm this when He said, "But when he, the Spirit of truth, is come, he will guide you into all truth" (John 16:13).

It is hoped that in this book, by following the substance of some of the dissimilarities in various portions of God's word, we may come to a clear answer as to the issues that are under discussion.

> *2 Timothy 2:15*: Study to show thyself approved unto God, a workman that needeth not to be ashamed, rightly dividing the word of truth.

> *Philippians 1:10*: That ye may approve things that are excellent.

The term "rightly dividing" is often rendered "rightly handling" but there is implicit in it the idea of cutting asunder: in short, placing the word in its proper context. The literal translation of Philippians 1:10 is the very awkward, "for to prove you the differing" (*The Interlinear Greek-English New Testament*) or more easily stated "prove" or "test the things that differ".

Some may recognise these two principles, "the right division" and "testing things that differ", as two of the laws of bible study laid out in the Scriptures and often quoted and used by those who think of themselves as "dispensationalists". This is true but their prime importance stems from the fact that they are instructions given to us by the risen Christ through the Holy Spirit's use of the apostle Paul as His penman. We must obey Christ in order to be "a workman that needeth not to be ashamed" and so faithfully serve our Lord.

I would however, at this time, like to look at them in a slightly different light. I would like to set aside their status as commandments and look at the nature of some presumptions involved and some of what these ideas may teach concerning "mankind" as God's special creation.

One mistaken presumption we can make is that 'right division' and "testing things that differ" are just two ideas that are part of dispensational teaching. They are clearly not! The scriptural idea of "dispensation" refers to the substance of God's grace and the method of its delivery to man. It can be discovered only in the pages of divine revelation. On the other hand, the other two ideas are integral to the theory of knowledge. They are part of the natural law governing man's thinking instituted by God as Creator. Particularly they are two of the means by which we sort out information to gain understanding on any given subject. While they are indispensable in shedding light on the truth of dispensational teaching, they are as evident outside the Bible as in it.

In Genesis 1:26 we read "And God said, Let us make man in our image," and in verse 31, "And God saw every thing that He made, and behold, it was very good." God then proceeded to speak to man and give him instructions concerning matters that required a rational intellect. No other creature on earth was ever so treated. Animals act by instinct. Man alone can reason. We know that we live in a sin-cursed state, but nonetheless our ability to gain knowledge and our physical being are as much gifts of God as the eternal life that He purchased for us on Calvary. They should be treated with as much respect.

In his book *Evolution or Creation?*, Dr. Arthur C. Custance points out that "man" is not simply a brute beast that "evolved" a mind. He was created as distinct from the beasts as possible in every aspect. He was made a rational, moral being which in its unsullied state could provide a fit tabernacle for the habitation of the Son of God in His incarnation.

In Eden, God immediately assigned to man tasks that required practice of the principles laid out in our two theme verses. He was set to naming the animals. That would involve noting the "differences" and "rightly dividing" them into kinds and species. This is how man always learns. If we cannot differentiate between shades of light we are blind. If we cannot 'rightly divide' slight shades of sound and corresponding meaning, we cannot comprehend language. Consider the following tabulation presented by Dr. Custance in his book:

- Man structures time by composing music.
- Man structures emotion by writing poetry.
- Man structures space by art and architecture.
- Man structures quantity by creating mathematics.
- Man structures events by writing history.
- Man structures his sense of justice by formulating codes of law.

- Man structures social behaviour by custom (which is really the objective of primary education)
- Man structures his religious impulses by liturgy and ritual.
- Man structures his faith and calls it theology.

Man must organise. This is how God created him. We might wish to phrase some of these statements differently but the basic thesis is well taken. Man is a rational being.

We often say in an off-hand fashion, "We need heart knowledge, not head knowledge, if we are to commit our way to the Lord." This is not quite right. "Heart knowledge" refers to emotional commitment and we do indeed need this for we are told to love the Lord. "Head knowledge" suggests intellectual commitment. The two are not mutually exclusive. They are both parts of mental activity and both are needed if we are to serve the Lord effectively.

Ron Moore in his series on *The Worthy Walk*, which appeared in the Newsletter of the Canadian Bible Fellowship, emphasised the idea of "balance". Just such a balance is needed. Emotional commitment alone can lead to fanaticism and so dishonours the Lord. Consider Saul's attacks on the Church. Intellectual knowledge alone can lead to vain imaginations and corruption. Consider those people so mentioned in Romans the first chapter.

By the commitment of His love God has made us able to love Him in return. By the giving of the Bible and the laying out of such principles as 'right division' and "testing things that differ", He has made us able to discover His will for us. By giving us the faculties of a rational mind, so necessary to use these principles, which have been denied to all other living creatures, He has honoured us as His special beloved creation. We may fall short, but by His grace let us strive to use these gifts from Him to honour and serve Him.

It may seem that when we emphasise the idea of "rightly dividing" the Bible that we are preparing to take those parts of Scripture we find useful to our own viewpoint and rejecting those that are not convenient. Quite the reverse is true. The purpose is to see the Bible as God wrote it and not see it through the distortion of our own preconceptions. Anyone who has tried to practise 'right division' has soon learned how flawed their own viewpoint was and has been forced to yield to *correction* by God's word, often to their own chagrin.

There is but one author of the Bible, the Holy Spirit, but it was penned by many people, over many centuries, under many circumstances. It was written to specific people and should be so interpreted. In addition it is progressive, adding truth upon truth. God is sovereign. He has the authority to supersede and change any instruction He chooses if it suits His purpose. Some of these changes will be noted below. Only when we see Scripture in its proper context can we hope to understand what God has for us.

God's book is orderly. It must be considered logically and systematically. When God makes a promise to, or calls, one person or one group, we must differentiate according to context: "For the gifts and calling of God are without repentance" (Romans 11:29). The so-called "contradictions" of the Bible, so gleefully pointed out by non-believers, those not explained by mistranslation or by our mistaken assumptions, fade into nothing when dealt with by the principle of right-division. The genuine differences the Holy Spirit has placed in His Word are not there by accident. He has placed them there to teach us His will by contrasting realities and we ignore them at our peril! We learn as much by contrast as by similarity.

As I have stated, this is presented as a personal view so I have no intention of quoting sources of information other than the Bible itself in matters of substance. I will however refer to other sources (sparingly) for such things as word definitions. The chief aid is the Appendix to *The Companion Bible*.

Chapter 2
DEFINITIONS

There are several words that are critical to these discussions and warrant careful definition. They are "Church", "Dispensation", "Mystery", "Hope", and "Calling". We are all aware of their English meanings and of course they can be used correctly in various ways according to the context. The thesaurus on this computer came up with no less than 16 synonyms for "church", 15 for the word "dispensation", and 5 for "mystery". Of the latter, only *one* for "mystery" matched the scriptural correct usage!

Language is a living thing and changes continually to suit current usage; therefore all words tend to accumulate multiple meanings. When we are studying the Bible, or any other book, we must remember that the author of that book is the one who decides how the word is to be used in that context. To follow other than the author's dictate is to invite total confusion.

In the present case we must remember that the English translation, no matter how excellent, is just that, a translation. The original revelation was in Hebrew, Aramaic and Greek. We must go back to the original, as much as possible, to establish a firm common understanding for intelligent study. Again, we cannot emphasise too much that the *author*, the Holy Spirit, is not the translator.

The following are brief definitions of the words pertinent to this study. They come from the appendices of *The Companion Bible*, along with a few comments that are important to this study.

Church

In appendix 186 of *The Companion Bible*, it will noted that the general meaning of the word "church" (Gr. *ekklesia*) is simply an *assembly*, or a gathering of *called out ones*. In Acts 19:32,41 the same Greek word is rendered assembly and refers to the guild, or "union" of Ephesian craftsmen. Considering this latter use, and the multiple uses of *ekklesia* and its Hebrew equivalent *kahal*, it is evident that the meaning of any particular word or phrase comes not only from the general meaning but also from the particular context.

In the *KJV* the word *ekklesia* is rendered "church" 115 times and "assembly" 3 times. The Hebrew *kahal* is given as "congregation"

86 times, "assembly" 17 times, "company" 17 times and "multitude" 3 times. We know that the Greek and Hebrew words are equivalent since Stephen, speaking to his accusers in Acts 7:38 refers, to "the church (*ekklesia*) in the wilderness" and is clearly talking about the congregation of Israel. Such insistence on detail may appear to be little more than unnecessary niggling, but quite the reverse is true.

This present matter is an excellent case in point. When we study the Bible, and if the word being used is unusual, or if the manner of its use is unusual, we may recognise that there is a problem. We may then go to a dictionary or some other source for help. If, however, we come to the word "church" in our English translation, or any other apparently common word for that matter, we tend to take it for granted that we understand what is being said, but we could be wrong. It is our self-assurance that can lead us astray.

In the vulgar world of our day to day life and language, the word "church" has come to express some ideas that while useful and correct in modern context do not conform to scriptural usage. We may speak of a "church" as a building used by a group as a place in which to congregate and worship. We may speak of a "church" with reference to a national or international organization such as the United Church of Canada, the Roman Catholic Church, or the Salvation Army. These and other definitions will appear in a standard dictionary of the English language but in no way are they helpful in understanding biblical teaching. We must determine the correct meaning of the word by its usage in context.

There are two terms used in modern sociology that may help in understanding more precisely the scriptural terms translated as "church". As noted above, when the Bible uses the word church or its equivalent it always refers to a group of people. When a sociologist deals with groups of people he may categorise them as being either a "collective" or as an "aggregate". The distinction is as follows:

> *An aggregate* - a body of people with a common property, but with no bond.

> A *collective* - a body of people with a common property, but bonded with a common purpose and common norms.

By way of illustration, suppose we are standing by the side of the road and we see a large number of people walking up or down the street in no particular order or direction and with no particular awareness of each other. This group is an "aggregate" as they have the common property of walking on the street but no other factor in common.

While we are standing there we see another group of people. This time they are marching in rank and file. They are dressed in uniform, have rifles over their shoulders. It is clear that this is an army. Like the other group they have a common property. Each soldier may have a specific and distinctive function but they are also bonded by a common purpose and common norms that are more than the aggregate of the individual functions. They are a "collective". They are *called* to a *purpose*. It is not difficult to see why the Ephesians' craft guild is called an *ekklesia*. It is also clear that when the word "church" is used in the Bible it may and does refer to a number of different groups.

Dispensation

Dispensation (Gr. *oikonomia*): literally, administration of a household (e.g. stewardship) Appendix 195 *The Companion Bible*.

This word has some confusion connected with it. It is frequently understood as a time period. Even *The Companion Bible* Appendix 195, 2, presents the heading "The Seven Times or Dispensations", and links *oikonomia* with *chronos* (time, unlimited duration) and *kairos* (a certain limited and definite portion of *chronos*).

If we are to have a better understanding of the word it would seem appropriate to look at the way that the word is used in the Bible. The Greek word *oikonomia* occurs seven times in the New Testament. In the Gospel of Luke it occurs three times, in 16:2-4, in connection with "the parable of the unjust steward", and is always translated "stewardship". Only very obliquely is any idea of a time period related to its usage. The idea of delegated responsibility would appear more relevant.

In 1 Corinthians 9:17 we read of "a dispensation (*oikonomia*) of the gospel" being committed to Paul. This is clearly a call to service or a stewardship. No time frame is even hinted at.

Ephesians 1:10 is interesting in that *oikonomia* is used in conjunction with *kairos*. The verse reads: "That in the *dispensation* of the fulness of *times*". It would appear that the two words must have differing connotations. Since "fulness of *times*" is clearly just what it says, a time period, and the word *dispensation* refers to the idea of an administration or stewardship.

The other two times that *oikonomia* is used are in Ephesians

3:2 and Colossians 1:25. However, since these are essential to the general theme of the article they will not be discussed here but will be dealt with in more depth later.

It may be worthwhile to note the words related to the Greek word *oikonomia* used in the New Testament. *Oikonomeo* is used once, in Luke 16:2, and is translated "be steward" in the *KJV* and "be manager" in the *NIV*. *Oikonomos* occurs 10 times and in the *KJV* is translated "steward", "chamberlain" or "governor". The root word *oikos* occurs 114 times and is almost always translated "house", "household", or "home".

Mystery

Mystery (Gr. *musterion*): "a sacred secret" or something concealed; see Appendix 193 *The Companion Bible*.

Musterion is used 27 times and is always translated as "mystery" in the *KJV*, but that does not mean that the information cannot be known or is beyond knowing. Rather it means that it cannot be known until it is revealed, and then ... it is no longer a secret. God alone has the power and authority to choose how, when, and to whom He will show His secrets. The Scriptures show clearly that only those who come to Him in faith will become privy to an understanding of these secrets when they are revealed. In Matthew 13:11-13 Christ told His apostles that He spoke in parables so that they would understand but that those who came in unbelief would not! Faith does not mean believing "in God", or believing "on God", but "believing God".

Central to the thesis of this book is the idea of a secret hid in God and then, at the time of His choosing delivered to His spokesman by the Holy Spirit. The timing and substance of a particular "mystery", and its significance for us, will be a constant theme. The entire Bible is important but some portions can be key to our greater understanding of God's word by clarifying overall context.

Hope

In the Old Testament the Hebrew words translated as "hope", along with their derivatives, occur many times. In the New Testament two Greek words are used. Those same words are translated by a variety of other English words. Some of the derivative words are opposites, being rendered "no hope" or "folly" or "despair" etc. In our modern use of the word "hope" the idea of "wish" or "wishful thinking" is involved. Somehow implied is uncertainty and doubt. In no case, whether positive or negative, is any doubt involved in the original words. The positive words used are strong words such as "confidence", "secure", "safe", "bold", and "trust".

There is another consideration. In some cases we are dealing with a verb, and in some cases a noun. The verb will likely refer to an act on our part or that of some other person. The noun on the other hand often refers to a *thing hoped for*, the *prospect* or the *ground for that hope*.

Since God is the author of the promises of the Bible, it follows that the "hopes" laid out in Scripture are certain and sure and substantial. For instance, those to whom He promised a kingdom can be assured that they will inherit a real kingdom upon this earth and not some kind of vague spiritualised substitute. We cannot claim what He has promised others, or what we want according to our own will. We can only claim what He has actually promised us, but more on this later.

Calling

Calling, (Gr. *klesis*): in the *KJV* translated 10 times, vocation: 1 time a
    call or invitation.
    (Gr. *kaleo*): to call or salute one by name.

These are two of the words connected with the idea of call or calling in the Scriptures. The primitive thought seems to be accosting a person met. Connected with the various words are such ideas as … summon, name, commission, appoint, be chosen and be called out. The nature and purpose of a calling is of extreme importance.

The "calling" is that portion of God's will that He wishes us to accomplish once we have committed ourselves to His lordship. It is our commission, our grateful service. The Scriptures speak of "the hope of your calling" but we are not called to a hope, we are granted a hope. The "hope" is that state or place of certain future blessing granted by grace according to the love He has for us. It is the gift of a loving Father.

If we connect this back to the fact that the "church" is a congregation of "called out ones" we can see a pattern emerging. We are talking about the stewardship of those people called the "Church which is the body of Christ", which is the church of today.

To sum up

The prime purpose of this exercise has been to clarify the meaning of words as they are used in the Bible, but there is another important reason. Unless the writer makes the reader aware of the way in which he, the writer, intends to use words there will be a breakdown in communications and confusion will result. Other meanings of these important words are perfectly correct in other contexts but in this work these are the meanings that I intend.

Chapter 3
CANONICAL ORDER

The books of the Bible are arranged in what we call canonical order. This refers to the order in which they appear in our present Bibles. It might be worth noting that the word "canon" came from the Greek word *kanna*, a reed, a cane. It means a straight rod, a rule or a standard. What an appropriate term to apply to the Word of God!

They were not always so arranged. The Old Testament was produced over many centuries in Hebrew and of course used by the Jews. At the time of Christ the Septuagint Greek translation was in common use. There is evidence that this is the version of the Scriptures that Christ Himself quoted when He taught in the Temple, thereby putting His seal of approval on it. It can be used to compare the use of Greek and Hebrew words. In A.D. 90 and 118 the councils of Jammia gave final affirmation to the Old Testament canon (39 books).

For the purpose of our present subject, it is perhaps more important to consider the structure and origin of the New Testament. As it was with the Old Testament, so it was with the New, God chose men to transcribe His revelation to man. A problem arose. It was the same basic problem that has arisen repeatedly. Whenever godly men sought to glorify God, usurpers sought to spread confusion.

Earlier we considered the depth of God's love for man in that He created him as a rational, moral being, capable of receiving God's written word. Now we come to another dimension of that love. When He called Abraham and his seed to their special stewardship, He left nothing to chance but carefully prepared them for their role.

We often tend to think of the apostles as simple unlettered fishermen and they are often portrayed as being rather gullible and naive. This does more to emphasise the intellectual arrogance of our society than it does to represent truth. We tend to think that anyone who earns their living with their hands is bound to be somewhat less intellectual. In fact it is probable that the Jews of Christ's time were, as a class, among the most literate people in their world. The very possession of the Old Testament, along with the rabbinical writings which Jewish men in particular had to study and read, insured a high degree of literacy. Because of the abstract nature of the concepts involved, while they were technologically inferior to students of our day, it is probable that they were our equals or superiors in overall literacy.

In the account of Christ's writing on the sand it would be strange if those around Him could not read what He wrote. In fact many, if not most people, could speak more than one language. Aramaic was commonly used in daily life, Hebrew in religious life, particularly in worship and the reading of Scripture (e.g., Luke 4:16-30). The third language of the eastern Roman Empire was Greek and there is evidence that even orthodox Jews used Greek in everyday dealings with each other. For more detail on "How we got our Bible", see *Christian History* Issue 43 [Vol. XIII, No. 3].

Romans 3:1-2 says, "What advantage then hath the Jew? or what profit is there in circumcision? Much every way: chiefly, because that to them were committed the oracles of God." In this we see the love of God for us displayed. The commitment of "the oracles of God" to the Jew was no random act. It represented centuries of preparation during which God controlled their history so that at the appropriate time they might provide a fitting tool for His purpose, the display of His love to us.

Compare the tradition of literacy of Israel with the experience of my people the Celts. The heathen Druidic priesthood forbade the Celts from recording anything in written form, presumably so that they could keep the control of knowledge and the people in their own hands. As a result any insights they might have had have long since been lost in the mists of time. On the other hand the record of God's word has come down to us unblemished in spite of all the efforts of ungodly men to prevent it.

We know that there were many other accounts written of the events surrounding the Lord aside from those preserved in Holy Writ. Luke 1:1-2 reads, "Many have undertaken to draw up an account of the things that have been fulfilled among us, just as they were handed down to us by those who from the first were eye-witnesses and servants of the word" (*NIV*).

Early Christians were profoundly interested in, collected and distributed such material and continued to write more (see John 21:25, 2 Timothy 4:13, and Revelation 1:1). In total there must have been a mass of written material in the possession of the various churches. Much of it would have been good, legitimate communications between godly men, pastoral letters, historical accounts, commentaries and so on, and of course including the twenty-seven books that we now recognise as the New Testament. There were, on the other hand, large quantities of writings that were clearly not apostolic. Just as false teachers went about from church to church causing trouble with fraudulent teaching, even so fraudulent texts were produced.

There were more than 20 spurious gospels produced, including the *Gospel of Nicodemus*, and the *Arabic Gospel of the Infancy*. There were other books like *The Shepherd of Hermas, The Wisdom of Solomon, and The Revelation of Peter*. One book, *The Gospel of Thomas*, is illustrative. Some of its teaching can only be viewed as bizarre. It is a mixture of authentic sayings of Jesus and Gnostic teaching. For example in it Peter is represented as saying "Let Mary leave us, for women are not worthy of life." To which Jesus replies "I myself shall lead her in order to make her male, so that she too may become a living spirit resembling you males. For every woman who will make herself male will enter the kingdom of heaven." Little wonder that The Gospel of Thomas was rejected!

Early Christians were continually under attack. False teachers and false Scriptures abounded as they do in our day. The three foundational truths were and are under constant attack. They are:

1. The identity and authority of God's divine revelation.

2. The divinity and authority of Christ Jesus as co-equal with God the Father, and God the Holy Spirit.

3. The complete and exclusive efficacy of Christ's sacrifice on behalf of mankind as a means of salvation, salvation by grace *alone*.

This third issue was the central factor in the Protestant Reformation. Although it had been a constant matter of debate through the ages, it came to a head at that time. The other two could not wait that long. Marcion (A.D. 85-160) taught that there were two Gods, the harsh Old Testament Creator God, and the loving New Testament God, and rejected the Old Testament and any New Testament references that suggested that they were the same God. Origen (A.D. 185-254) taught that Jesus was not as divine as the Father and dealt with the Scriptures as allegorical and not to be considered literally.

Athanasius, the Egyptian bishop of Alexandria, stood firm on the Divinity of Christ, in spite of repeated persecution and exile imposed on him. His enemies were the followers of Arius who taught that Jesus was a created being, neither of the same substance as God nor equal with Him.

Amid all this welter of confused writings it became evident that it would be necessary for Christians to declare exactly what the canon of Scripture should be. They needed a "straight rod", a standard. If we are to follow the good example of the Bereans and, to paraphrase Acts 17:11, "with all readiness of mind, search the Scriptures daily, whether these things are so", we need to know which writings we can trust. In A.D. 367, after his return from another exile, the faithful Athanasius wrote his most important annual letter to the church. In it was contained his list of 27 writings that marked for the first time that a church leader identified the very books Christians today call the New Testament.

In A.D. 397 the Council of Carthage established the orthodox New Testament canon. In about A.D. 400 Jerome translated the Bible from Greek into Latin, the *Vulgate* (or common language) translation. Those in the western half of the Roman Empire, who could read Latin, could then read the Bible for themselves.

Since then there have been on-going efforts not only to translate the Bible into as many languages as possible but, where necessary, to up-date those translations as the current languages change. Such is the case with our English translations. This does not imply criticism of our older versions such as the *KJV*, but as older manuscripts are found and become available and as the English words evolve in meaning, it becomes necessary to re-translate so that the Bible student can have a rendering that is closer to the original manuscripts.

We must understand that it was God's sovereign will to communicate His love to us in Greek and Hebrew. He placed on us the responsibility of diligently seeking His message to us through that medium.

The early Christians gave us an invaluable gift when they established the canon of Scripture. They told us what to study but not *how* to study. That is left to us to discover by earnest effort and prayerful diligence. They did give us some help however. They began the process of right division. Some of the old manuscripts were written in Greek in capital letters without breaks between words, and there were a number of contractions. Imagine if the opening verse of Mark's Gospel were written as follows:

THBEGINNINGOTHGOSPELOJESUSXTHSONOGOD.

The first step was to divide the letters into separate words. By adding verse and chapter breaks and more punctuation, the process was carried along. The addition of chapter and verse numbers is a widely accepted format that allows ease of reference and cross-reference. The result was a text that is in the form that we are more accustomed to dealing with. It must be remembered, however, that the Bible is not a single book but something like a whole library of books.

This textual division must not be thought of as being in itself authoritative since it was not part of the original manuscripts but was added later for convenience and clarity's sake. There are instances where verse and chapter breaks come in the middle of a thought but noting the context will prevent any problem. The Protestant Old Testament is identical in contents with the Hebrew Bible but the books are arranged and divided differently.

The material in the Hebrew canon is divided into 24 books and in 3 divisions: The Law, The Prophets, and The Writings. The Protestant Old Testament has the same material divided into 39 books and 4 divisions: Law, History, Poetry and Wisdom, Prophecy. The Catholic Old Testament adds other Hebrew writings that were not part of the Hebrew cannon.

Chapter 4
HISTORICAL ORDER

We have been considering the canonical order of the books of God's word. When we refer back, however, to a verse quoted earlier, 2 Timothy 2:15, it becomes clear that simply reading the Bible is not enough. We are told to *study* to show ourselves approved unto God. Simply learning the Bible by rote and memorising verses, while valuable, is not study. If we are to be obedient to God's will we must put in the effort and study as rigorously as possible.

Christianity is called an "historic" faith. This is entirely true. Other of man's religions tend to be mystical, magical, or animistic. In Christ, God entered personally and directly into history, into time and space. He took on the form of man, lived as a man, spoke to men as a man, and, as the Son of Man, died for all, so that those who accept His death as a sacrifice for their sins, can be given everlasting life. We need no mystical powers to receive and understand His message. He reached down to us on our level and through the prophets and the apostles spoke to us in our own form of speech.

Romans 3:2, speaking of Israel, says that "to them were committed the oracles of God". In Isaiah 28:13 we read "But the word of the Lord was to them precept upon precept, precept upon precept; line upon line, line upon line; here a little, and there a little." This is how the word was given to them and how through them it is given to us. This is how we teach our own children in school. We do not start in kindergarten with a course in trigonometry then proceed to university culminating with 2 x 2 = 4. There is a reasonable sequential pattern to any development of knowledge. It is true of the Bible when we study it, and just as true of the manner that God revealed his will to us. There is a historical pattern that must be understood if we are to gain a sound grasp of His will for us.

The "historical order", unlike the "canonical order", is not quite so apparent, nor does it correspond exactly. The historical order deals with the order in which the books were written, rather than the way they appear in the Bible, but this does not tell the whole story. Ecclesiastes 3:1 says, "To every thing there is a season, and a time to every purpose under the heaven." I hope to make clear the importance of this to our study as this book continues.

The first book to be written is presumed to be Job but it does not affect the issues that we are pursuing here. A quick review of overall biblical history could be useful at this point. Initially God created the heavens and the earth. Then:

1. At some point God created the spiritual beings.
2. Satan and his host rebelled. We don't know when.
3. God created Adam and Eve and placed them in the garden.
4. They fell and were cast out of the garden.
5. God maintained a faithful remnant but dealt with individuals such as Seth, Enoch and Noah.
6. Men proved unfaithful, on the whole, and the result was the flood.
7. God chose a man, Abraham and his seed, to be His witness on earth and made a covenant with them.
8. 430 years later through Moses He gave them the Law.
9. From that time till almost 400 years before Christ, God inspired various men to write the books that we now call the Old Testament.
10. At God's appointed time Christ was born.
11. Christ commenced His earthly ministry and chose Twelve Apostles to represent the twelve tribes of Israel, the descendants of Abraham, to whom He had given the promise.
12. Christ was crucified, buried, resurrected, walked with His disciples again for a while and then ascended into heaven.
13. The gospel was preached by the Apostles, and others, some of whom wrote the books of the New Testament.
14. The Apostle Paul was saved and became the Apostle to the Gentiles.
15. Paul preached and wrote seven books of the New Testament. (I consider Hebrews as Pauline.)
16. Paul first preached to the Jews until finally, after two warnings under the inspiration of the Holy Spirit, he told the nation that they were set aside after which the gospel would go to the Gentiles. (Acts 28:28)
17. After this time Paul wrote seven more books.

This review implies a number of things. First, that God dealt with different people at different times in different manners. He walked with Adam in the garden. He appeared to Abraham as an angel. He spoke to Moses from the burning bush and in a cloud on Sinai, and to Israel through tablets of stone. He speaks to all men now through His written word, but we must realise that at no given time in the past, until the completion of the Bible, was His whole revelation known to men. God spoke to each generation in terms that they could understand. Before Sinai, Israel could not know the law. While God always saved men by grace, until the crucifixion even the apostles did not understand about Christ's sacrifice and the gospel of grace.

We must conclude that if we are to understand the Bible, when we study any given passage, we must not assume knowledge that had not yet been made known at the time the passage was written. We must try to understand it as the person involved would have understood it at that time and in their circumstances.

Second, the term "The New Testament" itself presents us with a problem. In the canon of Scripture, we understand it to mean those books written after Christ's earthly ministry and dealing with the period just before His birth and through the ministry of the apostles. In that context it is acceptable. As we have observed, neither the Old Testament nor the New Testament consisted as books as such, but rather collections of writings. The Old, being the Hebrew canon, was written in Hebrew, and the New, never having been accepted by the Jews, was written in Greek.

The problem is that the word "testament" means a covenant or a will. Hebrews 9:16-17 states, "For where a testament is, there must also of necessity be the death of the testator. For a testament is of force after men are dead: otherwise it is of no strength at all while the testator liveth."

Since Christ was alive during the events recorded in all the four Gospels, apart from the short passages between His death and resurrection, it follows that at that time the Old Covenant or Testament was in force and not the New. The understanding as to what the "New Testament" is, when it came into effect and to whom it was given, is extremely important to the subject under consideration.

This leads to a third point. The date of the writing of a book, while important, may be considered as less important in some instances than the date of the events recorded. One must appraise all of the relevant evidence available in order to determine relative significant values. Both factors must be considered.

In all instances, except for prophecy, books must be written *after* the event recorded and described. This is obvious with regard to historical material. In regard to doctrinal subjects we find a different story. A change in doctrine indicates a change in God's instructions to man. When God through His servant says "You are no longer under *law* but under *grace*" we should listen. In such a case a book is apt to display a distinct pattern and the dating of its writing, compared with the sequence of events involved, will teach us much.

However, it should be noted that under both Law and Grace, man was always saved by God's grace, by man's faith being counted for righteousness. By grace God gave the Law of Moses as a guide to the people of Israel. By grace He guides us through the indwelling of His Holy Spirit and through His written Word. What was Law for them is profitable for us as reproof, correction and instructions in righteousness (2 Timothy 3:16). Here we see a change in His dealings with His chosen servants.

Since the question "When did the Church start?" is in essence a question of timing or "history", this aspect of study warrants great care. This matter, which in other studies would not be significant, becomes quite important.

There is one more item that I would like to enter under the heading of Historical Order. It is as follows:

Paul's Epistles in chronological order.

Before Acts 28:28	After Acts 28:28
Galatians	Ephesians
1 Thessalonians	Colossians
2 Thessalonians	Philemon
Hebrews	Philippians
1 Corinthians	1 Timothy
2 Corinthians	Titus
Romans	2 Timothy

Chapter 5
ACTS 28:28

Near the beginning of this book I stated that I held that the Church of today began at a time after the events recorded in Acts 28:25-28. So far most of this book has been devoted to generalised material. It is time to bring these generalizations to bear on the specific subject. It is true that no single verse in the Bible is sufficient to build a doctrine on and to attempt to do so is extremely foolhardy. A single verse may however be the key to understanding others. Such is the case here.

The Holy Bible records points in history when God's dealings with man undergo momentous change, the expulsion from Eden, the choosing of Abraham, the birth of our Lord, are examples. Such a point came with Paul's actions in Rome.

The Book of Acts ends with the record of Paul calling together "the chief of the Jews" in order to witness to them concerning Christ. They were willing to listen.

> *Acts 28:23-29*: And when they had appointed him a day, there came many to him into his lodging; to whom he expounded and testified the kingdom of God, persuading them concerning Jesus, both out of the Law of Moses, and out of the prophets, from morning till evening. And some believed the things which were spoken, and some believed not. And when they agreed not among themselves, they departed, after Paul had spoken one word, Well spoke the Holy Spirit by Isaiah the prophet to our fathers, Saying, Go to this people, and say, Hearing ye shall hear, and shall not understand; and seeing ye shall see, and not perceive: For the heart of this people is waxed gross, and their ears are dull of hearing, and their eyes have they closed; lest they should see with their eyes, and hear with their ears, and understand with their heart, and should be converted, and I should heal them. *Be it known therefore to you, that the salvation of God is sent to the Gentiles, and they will hear it.* And when he had said these words, the Jews departed, and had great disputing among themselves."

Throughout the Scriptures, up to this point, the Jews, since their calling out from the nations, had always been in a place of pre-eminence, and Paul, even while he was the apostle to the uncircumcision, followed the same principle during the period covered by the Acts of the Apostles. Up until this time Paul, under the direction of the Holy Spirit, had always gone to the "Jew first" and then to the Gentile. However, after this the Jew no longer held that first ranking position in Paul's ministry.

Look carefully and the inescapable conclusion is that it was not Paul setting Israel aside but God. The quote from Isaiah in Acts 28:26-27 indicates that God knew that Israel would reject their Messiah (Isaiah 6:9-10). God had warned them before. Earlier, when Paul and Barnabas were in Antioch in Pisidia, they went into the synagogue on two Sabbath days and taught Christ from the Old Testament beginning with the words "Men of Israel, and ye that fear God give audience" (Acts 13:16). Again the Jew came first. The Gentile was in a secondary position. He carefully taught Christ to them step by step, stressing that they had crucified their Messiah. When some Gentiles accepted Christ we read:

> *Acts 13:45-47:* But when the Jews saw the multitudes, they were filled with envy, and spoke against those things which were uttered by Paul, contradicting and blaspheming. Then Paul and Barnabas became bold, and said, "It was necessary that the word of God should first be spoken to you: but seeing ye reject it, and judge yourselves unworthy of everlasting life, lo, we turn to the Gentiles. For so hath the Lord commanded us, saying, `I have set thee to be a light of the Gentiles, that thou shouldest be for salvation to the ends of the earth.'"

There is a notable difference between the two events. At Antioch after Paul and Barnabas had warned the Jews that they, (Paul and Barnabas), were about to turn away from Israel and turn to the Gentiles, (Acts 13:46) they immediately reminded them that God had chosen them, the Jews, to be "a light of the Gentiles". The believers, including Paul, continued to deal with the Jews as the nation of God's choosing right up to the declaration in Rome. It is interesting that the Antioch statement was "*We turn* to the Gentiles", and the apostles left the city in disgust. In Rome the words were "the salvation of God is *sent* to the Gentiles" implying that it was now God's determination and not theirs. After Rome the whole character of revelation is different. This is a statement that is very sweeping and it will of course need to be substantiated with an abundance of evidence if it is to be accepted. What follows is an attempt to provide just such evidence so that the reader can be the judge.

Acts 28:28 is in effect a sign-post marking the end of one dispensation (stewardship) and the beginning of another. It is for this reason that the above listing of the Pauline Epistles was presented under the "Before Acts 28:28" and "After Acts 28:28" headings. If the contention is correct then the substance of the two bodies of Pauline revelation will differ, bearing in mind that the author is in fact the Holy Spirit and not Paul. Since Paul only is called "the apostle to the Gentiles (un-circumcision)", it follows that the non-Pauline books must relate to the stewardship of Israel; that is "the circumcision".

I have, in a cavalier manner, used the term "it follows". I have assumed that the proposition that I am making, that "an apostleship to a different group of people bespeaks of a different message", is obvious and will be clear to anyone. Such may, of course, not be the case. In the next chapter I intend to examine some assumptions we generally make about God, and their possible influence on my position, and compare a series of pairs of verses from different books of the Bible to illustrate the real differences in the messages.

Chapter 6
PAIRS TO COMPARE

Might God not choose different apostles as being more capable to reach differing groups yet have them deliver the same message?

God did exactly that! When God called Paul on the road to Damascus, He had him declare essentially the same message that the other apostles and writers of the New Testament uttered. At the same time, when Ananias feared Saul, we read in Acts 9:15 that the Lord said to him, "Go: for he is a chosen vessel to me, to bear my name before the Gentiles, and kings, and the children of Israel". Initially Paul was sent to the children of Israel and to the Gentiles of the Acts period, those who were to be grafted into Israel (Romans 11:11-17). It was only after God set Israel aside after the events of Acts 28:25-28 that the substance of Paul's message to those Gentiles changed.

Since God is the same "yesterday, today and forever" would not the Bible message to all people be the same? Otherwise, would that not suggest inconsistency on God's part?

It is indisputably true that God is the same yesterday, today and forever in character. However, His nature is vital and responsive not static. In the Garden of Eden He walked with Adam and Eve but ceased when sin entered. In Noah's time we read "And the Lord repented that he had made man on the earth, and grieved him at his heart ..... But Noah found grace in the eyes of the Lord" (Genesis 6:6,8). These and many other changes took place but all within the foreknowledge of God. Only to man in his ignorance does it seem strange.

When God chose to alter His dealings with man it was completely within His authority to do so. It does not in any way compromise the eternal consistency of His person or the certainty of His just will or the abundance of His love, etc. If we somehow feel that this is not fair, that He ought to treat us all the same or in accordance with our preconceived notions, then let us consider the parable in Matthew chapter 20 concerning the workers in the vineyard. In this parable Christ compares the kingdom of heaven to a householder who hires workers to tend his vineyard. They were hired at different times of the day, therefore worked different lengths of time, and yet at the end of the day, were paid the same amount. The ones that had worked all day protested that they ought to be paid proportionally to the amount of time they had worked. The householder's answer came in verses 13 to 15.

> *Matthew 20:13-15:* But he answered one of them, and said, Friend, I do thee no wrong: didst thou not agree with me for a penny? Take that which is thine, and depart: I will give to this last, even as to thee. *Is it not lawful for me to do what I will with my own?* Is thine eye evil, because I am good? (*KJV*)

The context of this parable is a section of the gospel in which Christ is teaching the disciples about the kingdom promised to the nation of Israel. In the preceding verses He tells the Twelve that they will sit on the thrones of the twelve tribes of Israel. In the following verses, when the mother of James and John asked Christ for special honours for her sons, He tells her that some things are not even in His power to decide but only in the Father's.

With the parable itself, Christ was preparing His followers for things to happen in the kingdom that they, as Jews, would not have been prepared for, nor would have approved of. Israel had been God's nation yet God would in latter times bless Gentiles along with the Nation without subjecting them to the same long service discipline as Israel.

The key verse for us at this point is the italicised portion of verse 15; "Is it not lawful for me to do what I will with my own?" It is clear that God will accomplish whatever He says He will do. It is also clear that He has both the authority and the ability to deal with and to use different people in different ways in the accomplishment of His overall plan. His actions do not need to fit our preconceived notions. None of this in any way suggests inconsistency on His part. *He is* Lord! Through the Bible there is unity of underlying teaching but many differing individuals and groups are chosen to fulfil various parts His purpose. We need to know what God expects of us, both as individuals and as groups, and how we fit into His purpose!

Earlier I mentioned the use of the terms "New Testament" and "Old Testament" as logical divisions of the Bible in canonical terms. It is necessary before continuing to differentiate three rather than two groups of writings in the Bible and to define some special terms to be used. Some may be uncomfortable with this, but it is much easier to have agreed upon reference terms than to continually go into lengthy explanations each time a change of venue arises. I ask the reader to accept my terminology at least for this study, but I am aware that my three divisions cannot be considered as having any more authority than the two way division used in the "Canon", since neither exists in the original manuscripts.

The three portions of Scripture are not mutually exclusive in that there are many common threads of truth between the three. This exercise, however, is more than just a convenience. It is an attempt to obey the commandment of 2 Timothy 2:15 to "rightly divide the word of truth". As one continues on this line of study it becomes clear that there are in fact distinct shifts in God's dealings with "man" between these three bodies of truth.

The terms to be used are as follows:

The Old Testament or *Old Covenant*: Beginning with the books of Moses and the promise to Eve, and based on the Abrahamic covenant, it carries on to include that portion of the Gospels up until the time of the crucifixion.

The New Testament or *New Covenant*: The subject of prophecy in the Old Testament, offered by Christ during His earthly ministry, re-offered after his resurrection during the time covered by the Acts of the Apostles, and the subject of all the canonical New Testament except Paul's last seven epistles. It is also based on the Abrahamic covenant.

We shall also be using the following terms:

The New Dispensation (Stewardship) or *Body Truth*: This Body Truth, concerning 'The Church which is the Body of Christ', is **not** the subject of prophecy nor is there any promise involved about the Messianic Kingdom. It is found only in those books of the Bible that Paul wrote after his Roman imprisonment of Acts 28:28. Christ kept it secret during His earthly ministry and during the period of time covered by the Acts of the Apostles It was revealed to the Apostle Paul after Acts 28:25-27 and is contained in the last seven letters he wrote: Ephesians, Philippians, Colossians, 1 & 2 Timothy, Titus, Philemon.

Kingdom Truth: Since the first two of the above relate to the Abrahamic Covenant and both ultimately promise that the Nation of Israel is to be the inheritor of an earthly Messianic Kingdom under Christ, they are often referred to jointly as

Kingdom truth.

The Nation: When the word Nation is used and capitalised it will refer to the natural descendants of Abraham, Isaac and Jacob, and not some spiritualised entity, unless so stated, and be equivalent to the name Israel.

The Body: When the word "Body" is used and capitalised it will refer to 'The Church which is the Body of Christ', which is, in my understanding, the church of today, the one which is the subject of this book.

It is also true that whether "Old" or "New Covenant", "Kingdom" or "Body", there is but one Christ over all, one sacrifice sufficient for all, and one grace of God that saves us all. We are all called to live a life that honours our Lord. The Mosaic Law is no longer valid as law of ordinance but through all times and in all dispensations God's righteous values are as valid as ever. In Ecclesiastes 12:13 we read, "Let us hear the conclusion of the whole matter: Fear God, and keep his commandments: for this is the whole duty of man."

If we are to "keep his commandments" we must not only seek to understand and honour the constants that run through the Bible but also to learn and honour the differences.

In the previous section of this book I mentioned three assumptions regarding the orderliness of God's word and that the internal evidence of the word itself must establish the differences and pattern of substance. We can start that process by comparing pairs of verses.

Let us compare two verses that on the surface appear to be outright contradictions of one another. The non-believer might well say that they show the inconsistency and indeed the un-reliability of the Bible. The first is from the Old Testament, from the books of the law. The second is from that portion of the Scriptures that I have labelled "Body Truth", the prison epistles.

Deuteronomy 6:25: And this shall be our *righteousness*, if we observe to do all these commandments before the Lord our God, as He hath commanded us.

Titus 3:5: Not by works of *righteousness* which we have done but according to His mercy He saved us, by the washing of regeneration, and the renewing of the Holy Ghost.

If there were not some kind of underlying difference in the context in which these two verses are found then we would indeed have a problem. The first one clearly is concerned with "our *righteousness*". Works are of prime importance. Our standing before God depends on our observance of commandments. The second verse reads, "Not by works of *righteousness* which we have done".

When placed back in context, we realise that in Deuteronomy God was addressing the Nation of Israel through Moses and in Titus he was addressing The Body through Paul, they make perfect sense. The one was under Law and the other was under grace. The requirements for salvation were not the same. Under grace salvation is simply the gift of God's mercy. The Jews on the other hand were required by God to follow an intricate system of commandments and practise an elaborate routine of rituals in order to please Him. In both cases it is God's grace that saves but the added burden of the Law was placed on the Jews. It was needed for their special ministry, but more on this point later.

[Now there is a certain circularity about my reasoning here. I have started to illustrate the identity of various bodies of truth in the Word by comparing a pair of verses. I showed that these verses possessed different values and then proceeded to justify the apparent contradiction by identifying them with the very bodies of truth that I intended to illustrate in the first place. Our western idea of logic does not allow for circular reasoning but perhaps our western idea of logic is not always as efficient as we would like to suppose. Does a square peg fit a round hole? Perhaps a somewhat circular logic is needed to study a circular system.]

A great many Christians would easily accept the idea of a difference in teaching between the Old and New Testaments. The two verses quoted are just the beginning. As has been mentioned, the picture of a severe and judgemental God of the Old Testament is so different from the God of love and forgiveness of the New Testament that Marcion mistakenly concluded that there must be two Gods. I doubt that anyone today would be so foolish as to go to that extreme. One factor involved in the developing vision of God in the Bible is the principle of progressive revelation. God did not tell us all about Himself all at once, neither did He tell us all about His plans for us all at once. Perhaps if Marcion had understood this, he might not have been so quick to jump to a wrong conclusion.

Let me make it clear. While I believe in "progressive revelation" *within* the Bible, I do not accept the idea that there is now any further direct Divine revelation being given today. The Bible is the complete word of God. All we need to know this side of eternity is within its pages! All other supposed wisdom must conform to the "Word of God" or it is false.

People tend to have a great deal more difficulty in coming to grips with differences between Christ's teaching in His earthly ministry and what Paul recorded under the direction of the Holy Spirit. On the face of it the differences can be startling. Consider the following:

> *Matthew 19:16-17*: And, behold, one came and said unto Him, Good Master, what good thing shall I do, that I may have eternal life? ... but if thou wilt enter into life, keep the commandments. (See also Mark 10:17-27 Luke 18:18-27 Luke 10:25-28.)

> *Ephesians 2:8-9*: For by grace are you saved through faith; and that not of yourselves: it is the gift of God. Not of works lest any man should boast.

In the portion of Scripture quoted from Matthew, and in the three other references accompanying it, Christ is asked, "what good thing shall I do, that I may have eternal life?" The issue is clearly salvation and the answer is to keep the law and do good works. You must do something! Paul's statement in Ephesians is just as clearly the opposite of what Christ said as possible, good works in his statement are *not* what lead to salvation. I don't know of any kind of temporising or spiritualising that can explain this incongruity away. Either these two teachings contradict each other and one must be wrong, or some more reasonable answer must be found. As has been pointed out before, if they contradict each other then one portion of the Bible is unreliable and must be rejected. In such a case we are left to sit in judgement between the pronouncements of God the Son and God the Holy Spirit.

The *NIV* renders 2 Peter 1:20-21 thus: "Above all, you must understand that no prophecy of Scripture came about by the prophet's own interpretation. For prophecy never had its origin in the will of man, but men spoke from God as they were carried along by the Holy Spirit." Given this, it follows that any pattern, or set of patterns, that appears in the Word must originate with God and not with man. We are not free to interpret in such a way as to accommodate our own wishes, desires or opinions but must, if we are to honour God, seek to trace and understand those patterns that He has ordained.

We have considered two pairs of verses and marked differences have been noted between the two verses in each pair. If we now arrange those same four verses in two alternate groupings labelled "A" and "B", a new order emerges.

Group "A"

> *Deuteronomy 6:25*: And this shall be our *righteousness*, if we observe to do all these commandments before the Lord our God, as He hath commanded us.

> *Matthew 19:16-17*: And, behold, one came and said onto Him, Good Master, what good thing shall I do, that I may have eternal life? ..... but if thou wilt enter into life, keep the commandments.

Group "B"

> *Titus 3:5*: Not by works of *righteousness* which we have done but according to His mercy He saved us, by the washing of regeneration, and the renewing of the Holy Ghost.

> *Ephesians 2:8-9*: For by grace are you saved through faith; and that not of yourselves: it is the gift of God. Not of works lest any man should boast.

Now, within each pair of verses there is complete harmony. In the "Group A" examples, while one is from the Old Testament and the other is from the New Testament, both *insist on* the law of commandments (*works*) as a necessary part of salvation. The "Group B" pair is drawn from what I have labelled "Body Truth". Both *deny* *"works"* as a necessary requirement for salvation. God's dealings with man have undergone a dramatic change.

Since Galatians 3:24 tells us "the law was our schoolmaster to bring us to Christ, that we might be justified by faith", it would be reasonable to assume that once Christ came the law would no longer be required. If that were the case then Christ's words in Matthew 19 would be difficult to understand. However, such is not the case.

In Matthew 5:17 Christ Himself said "Think not that I am come to destroy the law, or the prophets: I am not come to destroy, but to fulfil." Christ actually strengthened the law. The law forbade adultery but Christ said that the mere thought of adultery was morally the equivalent to the act. The full impact of Christ's strengthening of the law's requirements can be felt in those verses following the quote from Matthew 5:17.

> *Matthew 5:18-22*: For verily I say to you, Till heaven and earth pass, one jot or one tittle shall in no wise pass from the law, till all be fulfilled. Whosoever therefore shall break one of these least commandments, and shall teach men so, he shall be called the least in the kingdom of heaven: but whoever shall do and teach them, the same shall be called great in the kingdom of heaven. For I say to you, That except your righteousness shall exceed the righteousness of the scribes and Pharisees, ye shall in no way enter into the kingdom of heaven. Ye have heard that it was said to them of old time, Thou shalt not kill; and whoever shall kill shall be in danger of the judgment: But I say to you, That whoever is angry with his brother without a cause shall be in danger of the judgment: and whoever shall say to his brother, Raca, shall be in danger of the council: but whoever shall say, Thou fool, shall be in danger of hell fire.

The Pharisees taught and insisted on the practice of the letter of the law which is clearly in agreement with the statement of Deuteronomy 6:25. Verse 20 quoted above, with other verses, indicates that Christ demanded a more stringent obedience to both the letter and the spirit of the law. This is at total variance with the "Group B" teaching.

The teaching of Paul under the guidance of the Holy Spirit represented by these verses, of "salvation by grace, through faith, without works" has been grossly misunderstood and misrepresented over the years. Many have taken this to be licence. They have thought that as long as they went through some ritual of confessing and professing Christ as Saviour, without also recognising Him as Lord and Master, that this freed them of any further responsibility. They then could go on to any gross conduct that pleased and it would be covered by grace. A cynic might call this "buying fire insurance". Once you buy the policy, you no longer need to practise safety. Insurance will replace your loss.

Nothing could be more incorrect. Such an attitude is just an evasion of responsibility. We are indeed saved by grace alone but God requires us to exercise "faith" before that "grace" is credited to us for salvation. "Faith" as I have previously stated means "believing God". God not only told us about how He will save us but also what He has saved us for and what He expects of us once we are saved (Ephesians 2:10-11). For us to accept what is useful to ourselves, and not *all* He says, is not faith but simple selfishness and shows contempt for God and His love.

Chapter 7
THE OLD COVENANT AND THE MESSIAH

Before considering the "New Dispensation" or the "New Stewardship" and salvation by grace alone, it is desirable to study the nature of the "Old Covenant", the "New Covenant" and Christ's relationship to each of them. Later consideration must be given to the distinction between the "New Covenant" and the "New Stewardship" of Ephesians, the latter of which is a basic element distinguishing what I call "Body Truth".

It would be beyond the objectives of this study to go too extensively into the covenants of the Old Testament. Those covenants are a study in themselves, and are worthy of separate effort. Only some of the points directly relevant to our purpose will be considered.

Very early God covenanted with mankind with a promise that foreshadowed redemption. Even as our first parents were being driven from the garden, God prepared the way for the healing of the rift between God and man and restoration of the Edenic rule of peace and love. In Genesis 3:15 we read "And I will put enmity between thee and the woman, and between thy seed and her seed; it shall bruise thy head, and thou shalt bruise his heel." Please notice that this is an unconditional covenant, a one-sided covenant dependent only upon God. Usually we think of a covenant as being an agreement between two parties in which there is a responsibility to be fulfilled by both participants in order for the agreement to be completed. This covenant was a promise made by God. It concerned the woman and her seed. It was to be fulfilled through Abraham in the person of Christ. It was a unilateral determination by God and did not depend on man's compliance. God had decided to redeem man and by this act to glorify Christ. It is not the only unconditional, one-sided covenant.

During that long time covered by the first eleven chapters of Genesis, we read that God preserved the line from which the Messiah was to come. I scarcely need to point out that it was not in any way due to the obedience or faithfulness of man, but rather in spite of him, that this was achieved.

In chapter twelve God tells us of the choosing of the man through whose family God's Edenic promise would come.

Genesis 12:1-3: Now the Lord had said to Abram, Depart from thy country, and from thy kindred, and from thy father's house, to a land that I will show thee: And I will make of thee a great nation, and I will bless thee, and make thy name great; and thou shalt be a blessing: And I will bless them that bless thee, and curse him that curseth thee: and in thee shall all families of the earth be blessed.

This covenant did have a requirement attached to it. It was a promise to Abram and not his seed. Abram had to act, and he did. The promise could not be affected by the behaviour of the seed. It became a certainty.

In Genesis 15 God renewed and expanded the covenant outlining the extent of Abram's inheritance. At a time when Abram and his wife Sarai were, by human standards, too old to have children, we read:

Genesis 15:4-6: And, behold, the word of the Lord came to him, saying, This shall not be thine heir; but he that shall come forth out of thy own loins shall be thine heir. And he brought him forth abroad, and said, Look now toward heaven, and count the stars, if thou art able to number them: and he said to him, So shall thy seed be. And he believed in the Lord; and he counted it to him for righteousness.

The text tells us that God then allowed Abram to fall into a deep sleep and God made His declaration about the future of Abram's seed. Abram being asleep could therefore not respond to this portion of the covenant. Even though this latter was about the seed, the whole covenant was made with Abram and, in his act of faith in verse 6, he fulfilled all that was required of him. This became a covenant of one, God's unfailing promise to Abram. Genesis 17 extends the covenant.

Genesis 17:5-6: Neither shall thy name any more be called Abram, but thy name shall be Abraham; for a father of many nations have I made thee. And I will make thee exceedingly fruitful, and I will make nations of thee, and kings shall proceed from thee.

Thus the promise of the Messianic kingdom begins to take shape. On Abraham and his heirs was now laid the requirement of circumcision.

Abraham obeyed but those who followed were not always so faithful. In Genesis 28:12-15, God identified Jacob's descendants as the legitimate inheritors of God's assurances to Abraham.

Four hundred years after the Abrahamic covenants had been made, God added the law through Moses and gave them the Mosaic Covenant.

> *Exodus 19:5-6*: Now therefore if ye will obey my voice indeed, and keep my covenant, then ye shall be a peculiar treasure unto me above all people; for all the earth is mine: And ye shall be unto me a kingdom of priests, and an holy nation. These are the words which thou shalt speak unto the children of *Israel*.

This does no more than sketch God's plans and covenants in the Old Testament. There is very much more but this is enough for our consideration. The covenant in Genesis 3 unquestionably referred to Jesus the Christ. However, it was so unencumbered, having no specifics (such as references to manner, time, nation, or Messiahship), that the way was clear for Christ to be the Saviour of all mankind without regard to any other factor. He was to be the victor over Satan! Christ was to be the way and only by His grace can man see God.

The covenants did become more specific. God chose a man and a nation from amongst the nations. The coming Messiah was not only to be Saviour of the Nation and the nations, but also King of the Nation, Israel (2 Samuel 7). Further, concerning the Nation, consider again the words of the Mosaic covenant in Exodus 19:6: "And ye shall be unto me a kingdom of priests, and an holy nation. These are the words which thou shalt speak unto the children of *Israel*."

Through Moses the royal priesthood was promised to Israel but it was a very conditional promise. The Law had been added. Christ was the Saviour of the world and in His sacrifice on Calvary and His resurrection He fulfilled that task, but in His earthly ministry He had additional responsibilities to perform for the Father. Paul declares in Romans 15:8, "Now I say that Jesus Christ was a minister of the circumcision for the truth of God, to confirm the promises made to the fathers". This is why Jesus said "Think not that I am come to destroy the law, or the prophets: I am not come to destroy, but to fulfil." He was both their King and the Guarantor of the promises. He had to lead them in the fulfilment of the requirements of the covenants. He was their Lord but also their leader. All that was required of them was to obey and accept Him as their King and the Kingdom would be established. While Christ was alive they were under the rules of the Old Covenant, and living under expectation of the fulfilment of that Old Covenant.

Israel, however, failed. In spite of the mass of instruction in the Law and the clear teaching represented by the two verses from Deuteronomy and Matthew already considered, that adherence was necessary for God's blessing to be fulfilled. The Nation gave only nominal adherence to the letter of the Law and almost none to the spirit of the Law. They were so much like us in their fallibility that it is clear that God's purpose in choosing them, to be the example people, was so that He could show His great love and mercy to us no matter how much we fail Him.

They not only rejected their King but they crucified Him, yet on that very cross He prayed, "Father forgive them. They know not what they do." They were forgiven. Those who call the Jews "Christ killers", and seek to reject and punish them for that reason, should remember that they are forgiven of that sin. Such people should also remember the admonition to "judge not lest thou be judged". We are in fact more guilty then they. They had only the revelation of the Old Testament. We claim to have more in that we have both Old and New. From those who have been given much, much is expected.

In terms of the covenant we come to a problem that is outlined in Galatians Chapter 3.

Galatians 3:16-21: Now to Abraham and his seed were the promises made. He saith not, And to seeds, as of many; but as one, And to thy seed, which is Christ. And this I say, that the covenant, that was confirmed before by God in Christ, the law, which was four hundred and thirty years after, cannot set aside, that it should make the promise of no effect. For if the inheritance is by the law, it is no more by promise: but God gave it to Abraham by promise. What purpose then serveth the law? It was added because of transgressions, till the seed should come to whom the promise was made; and angels in the hand of a mediator ordained it. Now a mediator is not a mediator of one, but God is one. Is the law then against the promises of God? By no means: for if there had been a law given which could give life, verily righteousness should have been by the law.

God had promised Abraham, Isaac, and Jacob that:

> a) I will make of thee a great nation. [Genesis 12:2]
> b) In thee shall all the families of the earth be blessed. [Genesis 12:3]
> c) I will make nations of thee, and kings shall proceed from thee. [Genesis 17:6]
> d) A promised land would be given. [Genesis 15:18-21]
> e) Covenants passed on to Isaac to Jacob (Israel). [Genesis 28:1-4]
> f) Many more details not necessary to mention here.

While the Law of Moses could not bring life, it still carried with it the promise, "And ye shall be unto me a kingdom of priests, and an holy nation."

So many promises were made to Abraham and his seed, many more than I have recounted here! Because of his faith God had counted Abraham righteous. "And this I say, that the covenant, that was confirmed before by God in Christ, the law, which was four hundred and thirty years after, cannot set aside, that it should make the promise of no effect." God is faithful and will be true to His part of the covenant, for Abraham, in spite of his failings, fulfilled his responsibilities.

The problem lies in the fact that the covenants were made "to Abraham *and his seed*". God was bound by His own faithful word to righteous Abraham but what about his seed? They were not faithful. They rejected the prophets and killed the Son. How could God fulfil His covenants to faithful Abraham without rewarding the faithless seed? How could He deny the blessings to the faithless seed without breaking His word to faithful Abraham, especially since the covenants had been "confirmed before by God in Christ"? Remember, while a covenant is always between two parties, it is not always the case that both parties must fulfil some duty in order for the obligation to be valid. Responsible parents, by virtue of their parenthood, are in a covenant relationship with their children to care for their children as long as they are in a helpless state, Such parents will continue to love a child even when that child rebels. Such a condition can be called a covenant of one, for the child's part is simply to be the child, which is something that is not of the child's choice or volition.

There are several alternatives that can and have been suggested. One is that "the promised kingdom" is in fact not a literal kingdom but a spiritual one and so the kingdom will come when Christ truly reigns in the hearts of believers. This way Abraham's spiritual seed could be blessed while his natural, unfaithful seed could safely be cut off. Under this scenario, if there ever was a literal kingdom promised, it was forfeited when Israel rebelled. Now at least, the very idea of a literal kingdom is redundant. In that case, perhaps, the over 150 mentions of the kingdom in the New Testament have no substance!

Why do we so easily set aside God's chosen people Israel and consider ourselves to be all-important? A serious problem arises with doing this. If such a central theme of the Old and New Testaments can be so easily spiritualised out of existence, then are all the promises to us only figurative? Perhaps the promise of eternal life is just a trick to keep us in line. If we start spiritualising the Scriptures at will, it becomes increasingly difficult to decide which parts of the Bible are real and literal, and which parts are figurative only. We then become arbiters, sitting in judgement on God's word.

Of the Old Testament covenant recipients we have considered Abraham, Isaac, and Jacob. These are all very important but David and the promises to him are in some ways key to our understanding. Saul was Israel's choice as king but David was a man of God's choosing. Consider the following quotes connected with the Davidic covenant and on your own look at the passages in which they are found.

> *2 Samuel 7:16-17*: And thy house and thy kingdom shall be established forever before thee: thy throne shall be established forever. According to all these words, and according to all this vision, so did Nathan speak to David.

> *2 Samuel 23:1,5*: Now these are the last words of David. David the son of Jesse said, and the man who was raised on high, the anointed of the God of Jacob, and the sweet psalmist of Israel, said ... yet he hath made with me an everlasting covenant.

> *Psalm 89:3-4,24,35-36*: I have made a covenant with my chosen, I have sworn to David my servant, Thy seed will I establish for ever, and build up thy throne to all generations ... I have found David my servant; with my holy oil have I anointed him ... My covenant will I not break, nor alter the thing that hath gone out of my lips. Once have I sworn by my

holiness that I will not lie to David. His seed shall endure forever, and his throne as the sun before me.

Isaiah 55:3: Incline your ear, and come to me: hear, and your soul shall live; and I will make an everlasting covenant with you, even the sure mercies of David.

Jeremiah 33:20-21,26: Thus saith the Lord; If ye can break my covenant of the day, and my covenant of the night, so that there should not be day and night in their season; Then also may my covenant be broken with David my servant, that he should not have a son to reign upon his throne; and with the Levites the priests, my ministers ... will I cast away the seed of Jacob, and David my servant, so that I will not take any of his seed to be rulers over the seed of Abraham, Isaac, and Jacob: for I will cause their captives to return, and have mercy on them.

Luke 1:31-33: And, behold, thou shalt conceive in thy womb, and bring forth a son, and shalt call his name *Jesus*. He shall be great, and shall be called the Son of the Highest: and the Lord God shall give to him the throne of his father David: And he shall reign over the house of Jacob for ever; and of his kingdom there shall be no end.

Acts 2:30: Therefore being a prophet, and knowing that God had sworn to him with an oath, that from the fruit of his loins, according to the flesh, he would raise up Christ to sit on his throne.

Now if the Bible is in fact God's word and His word is true then we must agree that these verses, along with a host of other evidence, indicate that this Jesus is the Christ, the Messiah, the very real King that will sit on the real throne of his father David in a Messianic kingdom on this earth.

Clearly God had made an *everlasting* covenant with David; that if God should break His covenant with day and night, then "he should not have a son to reign upon his throne". Only if day and night should cease, only "Then will I cast away the seed of Jacob, and David my servant". And so He speaks of "the *sure* mercies of David". David, on his part, rested in the certainty of God's word. God repeated His vow over and over. This was all reaffirmed in the New Testament in the verses quoted and many others. Christ was to sit on the throne of His father David. The literal Messiahship of Christ seems clear. What is questioned is the identity of His subjects. Note that the terms of the Davidic covenant are simply refinements of the earlier covenants and that nothing essentially new has been added.

In the light of the foregoing, the idea of a purely spiritual kingdom is not easily sustainable. However, some suggest that the Israel of promise can be thought of as "spiritual Israel". While it was true in the case of Christ that He was literally "from the fruit of his loins, according to the flesh," that is David's literal descendant, could not Abraham's spiritual seed be the successors to natural Israel? In fact, something like this has been a widely held view.

The Jehovah's Witnesses believe that literal Israel has been disinherited because of disobedience and that they, the Witnesses, have been granted the kingdom in their stead. This is of course why they call their meeting places 'Kingdom Halls'. They expect to spend eternity on a paradise like world in God's kingdom on earth. The variations on this theme are endless.

Some true and good Christians believe that 'the Church is spiritual Israel'. The Roman Catholic doctrine of 'apostolic succession' is one variation and the Pentecostal teaching that "Whatever was available to the apostles is available to the believer today" is another. Some, on the other hand, think that Israel will be restored and share a thousand year Messianic kingdom with the 'Christians', while others think that only those Jews who as individuals become Christians will be saved to that kingdom. To cover all the diversity of thought would be impossible and unnecessary. Each set of ideas has its own set of adherents and apologists, who are both honest and intelligent, and far more able to present their case than I am. It is not my desire to criticise others but to present my own view for consideration. I have simply presented these other interpretations so that contrast will help us focus better.

That the patriarchs of old expected that God would again walk on earth and that they would be present with Him in some future time, even after their own death, can be seen from the magnificat of Job.

> *Job 19:25-27*: I know that my Redeemer lives, and that in the end he will stand upon the earth. And after my skin has been destroyed, yet in my flesh I will see God; I myself will see him with my own eyes - I, and not another. How my heart

yearns within me! (*NIV*)

There is nothing in this that suggests anything other than a future physical presence on earth. It must surely be referring to resurrection at the time of the Messianic kingdom. Speaking of the same period, consider Christ's words to the apostles contained in the following verses:

> *Matthew 19:27-28*: Then answered Peter and said to him, Behold, we have forsaken all, and followed thee; what shall we have therefore? And Jesus said to them, Verily I say to you, That ye who have followed me, in the regeneration when the Son of man shall sit on the throne of his glory, ye also shall sit upon twelve thrones, judging the twelve tribes of Israel.

> *Luke 22:28-30*: Ye are they who have continued with me in my temptations. And I appoint to you a kingdom, as my Father hath appointed to me; That ye may eat and drink at my table in my kingdom, and sit on thrones judging the twelve tribes of Israel.

In these words Christ not only links the kingdom to the Nation of Israel but also links the Twelve Apostles to the Nation. They are to "sit upon twelve thrones, judging the twelve tribes of Israel". The idea that Israel and the Gentiles could be joint heirs is totally foreign to this context and for that matter there is no mention of heaven or anything like it.

It is clear that Christ has in mind a kingdom in which the Nation is central. The church which is the Body of Christ, simply does not fit this pattern. It is not made up of twelve tribes. The Body is not structured in a hierarchical form so that there could not be any thrones to sit upon. The members of the Body are all equal, and are joint heirs with Christ (Ephesians 3:6).

When we consider the expectations of the followers of Christ we can see that they accepted the idea of resurrection to a real kingdom on earth just as we are describing, and in agreement with Job's hope. The idea of being seated in the heavenlies in Christ, which is promised to the members of the Body, was foreign to them. John chapter 11 tells us about the resurrection of Lazarus.

John 11:23-25: Jesus saith to her, Thy brother shall rise again. Martha saith to him, I know that he shall rise again in the resurrection at the last day. Jesus said to her, I am the resurrection, and the life: he that believeth in me, though he were dead, yet shall he live:

Upon her declaration of faith He gave her a foretaste of the future blessing. He raised her brother. Had Israel likewise accepted their Messiah the kingdom could have been established then and there and all Israel would have been raised.

If we look at all the Scripture that we have quoted about the covenants, along with all the other material not considered, especially that pertaining to the kingdom, we come up with a structure for that kingdom something like the following:

- The Lord Jesus Christ as King and absolute ruler, the Messiah, the chosen one of Israel.
- The Twelve Apostles as His delegates ruling on the thrones of the twelve tribes of Israel carrying out His wishes.
- The Nation of Israel (the twelve tribes) serving God as "a kingdom of priests, and an holy Nation" standing between the Messiah and the Gentiles and governing them.
- The Gentile Nations living in peace and blessedness because of Christ's rule through the Stewardship of Abraham's seed. (And in thee shall all families of the earth be blessed, Genesis 12:3.)

This describes Christ's position and office in the kingdom. However, it does not explain why there was a need for a kingdom or why God the Father wanted the Son to fill this function or what was to be accomplished by the whole exercise. If the Bible is essentially God's love letter to us and a blueprint for our salvation, then why would it not make sense for God simply to take all individual believers to heaven and scrap the world? We are often told that there is no good in material things so would it be any loss?

God did not have to make the covenants with "the fathers" to include a kingdom but then He did not have to save us. We are His creations and He owes us nothing and He owed Israel nothing. He would have been justified in dispensing with the whole human race since its very existence is dependent on the word of His power. Without His grace we would not have been created in the first place.

There is no moral power greater than He to sit in judgement on His actions. God is just and loving, not because He must be but because He wills to be so.

Because God is just and loving, He commended His love to us in that while we were yet sinners Christ died for us. This does not explain the need for an earthly Messianic kingdom. We could say that He chose the Nation to give us an example of His love and to teach His faithfulness to those who serve Him. He could have done that just as well through individuals without the promise of a kingdom. It would appear that there will be, in God's reckoning, a special value in the existence of the kingdom itself, quite apart from and in addition to its usefulness to man's salvation.

We may find some hints if we go back to creation. If we look again at Genesis 1:31: "And God saw every thing that He made, and behold, it was *very good*." Contrary to what we often think, God did value this whole creation of His and not just mankind. In Genesis 3 after rebuking Adam for his sin God makes the sad statement in verse 17, "cursed is the ground for thy sake". His beautiful creation had been soiled by Satan's rebellion and Adam's disobedience. God had made this beautiful world and given Adam the care of it. Adam was to be caretaker of it and the federal head of mankind. Instead, Adam had believed a lie and rejected God's instructions. His stewardship came to an end and he was ejected from the garden.

So far in this section Christ has been looked at as the Son of Abraham and as the Son of David, as Messiah, the King of Israel. Now it would be profitable to look at Him as the Son of Adam. He is both the Son of God and He is often referred to in Scripture as the Son of man. The name Adam also means "man". In the third chapter of Luke there appears a genealogy of Christ Jesus. It ends in verse 38 with the words:

> Who was [the son] of Enos, who was [the son] of Seth, who was [the son] of Adam, who was [the son] of God.

The Holy Spirit took great pains to assure us as to whose [son] Jesus was. His Father was God. Through Mary He was "the son of Adam, who was the son of God." Adam was the son of God in that he was created by God and so had no earthly father and came directly from God. This person who came from God and was uniquely blessed by God, failed God. Satan had corrupted man and the whole of creation suffered. Lucifer (Satan), who sought to be equal with God, had dishonoured God. To his eventual doom he had entered into a battle that he will eventually lose to the true Son of God. The covenant of Genesis 3:15 about "the seed of the woman" followed.

Study the following selected verses and the ensuing table.

Romans 5:14: Nevertheless death reigned from Adam to Moses, even over them that had not sinned after the similitude of Adam's transgression, who is the figure of him that was to come.

1 Corinthians 15:21-22,45-47: For since by man came death, by man came also the resurrection of the dead. For as in Adam all die, even so in Christ shall all be made alive ... And so it is written, The first man Adam was made a living soul; the last Adam was made a living spirit ... However that was not first which is spiritual, but that which is natural; and afterward that which is spiritual. The first man is from the earth, earthy: the second man the Lord from heaven.

And about the last days:

Isaiah 2:1-2: The word that Isaiah the son of Amoz saw concerning Judah and Jerusalem. And it shall come to pass in the last days, that the mountain of the Lord's house shall be established on the top of the mountains, and shall be exalted above the hills; and all nations shall flow to it.

Isaiah 11:1,6,9: And there shall come forth a rod out of the stem of Jesse, and a Branch shall grow out of his roots ... The wolf also shall dwell with the lamb, and the leopard shall lie down with the kid; and the calf and the young lion and the fatling together; and a little child shall lead them ... They shall not hurt nor destroy in all my holy mountain: for the earth shall be full of the knowledge of the Lord, as the waters cover the sea.

Micah 4:2-4: And many nations shall come, and say, Come, and let us go up to the mountain of the Lord, and to the house of the God of Jacob; and he will teach us of his ways, and we will walk in his paths: for the law shall go forth from Zion, and the word of the Lord from Jerusalem. And he shall judge among many people, and rebuke strong nations afar off; and they shall beat their swords into ploughshares, and their spears into pruning hooks: nation shall not lift up a sword against nation, neither shall they learn war any more. But they shall sit every man under his vine and under his fig tree; and none shall make them afraid: for the mouth of the Lord of hosts hath spoken it.

The pattern:

> The first Adam - sinful
> > The last Adam - sinless
> The first Adam - mankind damned
> > The last Adam - mankind saved
> The first Adam - came death
> > The last Adam - came resurrection
> The first Adam - God blasphemed
> > The last Adam - God honoured
> The first Adam - the earth cursed
> > The last Adam - the earth restored

Summary

In Eden God walked with Adam. Since the Bible tells us in John 6:46 "Not that any man hath seen the Father, save he who is from God, he hath seen the Father", we can reasonably assume that it was God the Son who walked there in the Garden. Since the first Adam failed, the last Adam had to take his place as the federal head of mankind. The covenants of restoration were given to Eve and her seed, to be fulfilled through the literal seed of Abraham, the Nation and the Nation's "Chosen One", the Messiah. Since Adam's Lordship was over the material world, which God declared to be good, the last Adam's Lordship had to include Lordship over the material world if His task was to be meaningful.

God the Son by His own divine will gave the promises and declared, "My covenant will I not break, nor alter the thing that hath gone out of my lips." He, by that same will, became the Holy One of Israel, the Christ of God, Jesus, "for he shall save his people from their sins" (Matthew 1:21). He was the Giver of the promises and the Guarantor of those same promises. He was the Creator of the world, including the paradise of Eden, and the Redeemer of that same paradise. He gave the throne to David and was the seed of David who was to sit on that throne. We may be the spiritual seed of faithful Abraham but we are not the seed of David. David's kingdom was real. His throne was over a Nation. We are not a nation. We are left with the same problem. How could Christ fulfil His promise to faithful Abraham and sit on the throne of David over literal Israel without ruling over a faithless seed? The answer is found in the New Covenant.

Chapter 8

THE NEW COVENANT AND THE MESSIAH

Near the end of the Old Testament revelation the prophet Jeremiah arose within the Nation. Through him God proclaimed the promise of a New Covenant. The following quote from Jeremiah 31 is from the *NIV*. I chose this version because the visual effect of the layout adds force to emphasise God's clear statements. Please note the phrase in italics that is repeated so frequently.

(27-28) "The days are coming," *declares the Lord*, "when
      I will plant the house of Israel and the house
      of Judah with the offspring of men and of
      animals. Just as I watched over them to
      uproot and tear down, and to overthrow, destroy
      and bring disaster, so I will watch over them
      to build and to plant," *declares the Lord*.

(29) "In those days people will no longer say,
      'The fathers have eaten sour grapes,
      and the children's teeth are set on edge.'
(30) Instead, everyone will die for his own sin;
      whoever eats sour grapes -
      his own teeth will be set on edge.

(31) "The time is coming," *declares the Lord*,
      "when I will make a new covenant
      with the house of Israel
      and with the house of Judah.
(32) It will not be like the covenant
      I made with their forefathers
      when I took them by the hand
      to lead them out of Egypt,
      because they broke my covenant,
      though I was a husband to them,"
            declares the Lord.
(33) "This is the covenant that I will make
      with the house of Israel

after that time," *declares the Lord.*
"I will put my law in their minds
and write it on their hearts.
I will be their God,
and they will be my people.

(34) No longer will a man teach his neighbour,
or a man his brother, saying,
'Know the Lord,'
because they will all know me,
from the least of them to the greatest,"
declares the Lord.
"For I will forgive their wickedness
and will remember their sins no more."

(35) *This is what the Lord says,*
he who appoints the sun to shine by day,
who decrees the moon and stars to shine by night,
who stirs up the sea so that its waves roar -
the Lord Almighty is his name:

(36) "Only if these decrees vanish from my sight,"
declares the Lord,
"will the descendants of Israel ever cease
to be a nation before me."

(37) *This is what the Lord says:*
"Only if the heavens above can be measured
and the foundations of the earth below be searched out
will I reject all the descendants of Israel
because of all they have done," *declares the Lord.*

(38-40) "The days are coming," *declares the Lord,* "when
this city will be rebuilt for me from the Tower
of Hananel to the Corner Gate. The measuring
line will stretch from there straight to the
hill of Gareb and then turn to Goah. The
whole valley where dead bodies and ashes are
thrown, and all the terraces out to the Kidron
Valley on the east as far as the corner of the
Horse Gate, will be holy to the Lord. The city
will never again be uprooted or demolished."

The Lord God is our Creator. He knows all about our weaknesses. When He made the Old Covenant with Israel, He was well aware that the Nation would fail. He had an alternative plan in mind, the New Covenant. In this way He could keep His word to faithful Abraham and still take into account Israel's unfaithfulness.

An overwhelming feature of the New Covenant is the fact that in 14 verses the phrases "*declares the Lord*" or "*This is what the Lord says*" are used 11 times. To question or deny anything in these statements is to question or deny the surety of God's word. Whatever God says He will do, He will do. Consider verse 31:

> "The time is coming," *declares the Lord*,
> "when I will make a new covenant
> with the house of Israel
> and with the house of Judah."

Yet in spite of the clear statement of verse 31, some Christians tend to think that the New Covenant is with us Gentiles, 'The Church which is the Body of Christ'. Let us remember that this revelation came through Jeremiah, a prophet of the Nation to the Nation! There is no suggestion of a spiritual Israel nor would it make any sense for it to be anything other than literal Israel. Those to whom the promise was given could not have understood anything other than themselves as a real Nation; otherwise God would have been deceiving them. This is not God's way.

In verse 32 He makes it clear that He knew and expected them to break their covenant with Him and goes on to state that He will make a New Covenant in spite of their unfaithfulness.

In verses 33-34 He states the nature of the new promise. He will now ensure all the requirements of both parties are fulfilled. It is "grace" towards Israel. No longer will the Law be on tablets of stone, but instead it will be in their minds and on their hearts. They will be faithful. Now God can keep His promise to faithful Abraham and David, and have the Chosen One sitting on David's throne over a faithful Israel.

In verses 35-37, God gives Israel the assurance that as long as the sun, the moon and the stars shine, and the sea waves roar, they will remain "a nation before me". We can no longer say that because they sinned they are finished in God's plans. That issue is taken care of in the New Covenant. They are without doubt set-aside for the time being as God's premiere Nation, but by His own infallible word He *declared* that they are still there in His plans. He will restore them even as He brought them back from captivity. They are *Lo ammi*, not my people, but they will be called *Ammi*, my people. ("It shall be said unto them, *Ye* are the sons of the living God", Hosea 1:10.)

I mentioned, when investigating the relationship between the Messiah and the covenants, that it would be useful to include the position of the Apostles as well. When we consider the years of Christ's earthly ministry, teaching those men whom He chose to be His chief representatives to Israel, we should give full weight to the reality that He constantly expounded the Old Testament canon to them. Time and again He spoke to them of the promised kingdom and presented Himself as their King. He was the promised Messiah. They were, as Jews, familiar with the Scriptures from their youth. It was a part of the very fabric of their life.

He never suggested that there would not be a real kingdom. As already mentioned, He promised the Twelve Apostles a very prominent place in it. Their questions to Him, and the statements of faith such as that of Martha, showed that they understood that He was their King and that in keeping with Job's hope they too would be resurrected to His kingdom. He would not have allowed them to keep on believing this if it were not so. His statement of John 8:58 (Jesus said to them, "Verily, verily, I say to you, Before Abraham was, I am") connects Him not only to Abraham but also to all the various covenants and prophecies of the Old Testament, since it is a claim to divinity (compare with Exodus 3:14). This, therefore, identifies Him as the Promiser and their promised Messiah. His very existence confirmed all their hopes.

I find it amazing when modern scholars suggest that the disciples and apostles were quite lacking in understanding in all these matters while they, the modern scholars, know so much more. "When the Bible says kingdom it did not really mean a real kingdom, and when it says that Israel will inherit this kingdom it really meant the church!" For my part, if I must choose between the modern scholar and those men whom Christ personally chose and instructed, then I will choose the Apostles.

There are two things that happened during Christ's ministry that are of particular importance to our present study. The first is the fact that when Christ sent the apostles out to evangelise in Matthew 10:5-6. He told them "Do not go among the Gentiles ... go rather to the lost sheep of the house of Israel." And to the Canaanite woman in Matthew 15:24 "he answered and said, I am not sent but to the lost sheep of the house of Israel". These statements are in full conformity with the Old Covenant concept that the Messiah would come to rule the Nation and that the Nation would become a royal priesthood, the conduit through which the blessings of God would be distributed to the Gentiles (note: "and in thee shall all families of the earth be blessed" Genesis 12:3). The Old Covenant was still in effect. Christ made no attempt to contact or make immediate provision for the Gentile nations. His *earthly* ministry was to *The Nation*.

The second event was what we usually call the "last supper". To understand the significance of what took place in the upper room we need to look at the wider context.

We learn the details of the event in Matthew 26, Mark 14, and Luke 22. It is worth noting that "The Gospel According to John", while recording events that took place in the upper room, ignores the bread and the wine. It records the treachery of Judas, the failure of Peter, and the promise of the Comforter. It also tells of Christ washing the feet of the Apostles and instructing them to do the same for each other. Most modern Christians largely set this latter ritual aside even though it has the same authority as the "breaking of bread" practice. The fact that John does not mention the bread and wine fits into the pattern of a gospel that presents Jesus not as the "Son of Man" but as the Christ (Messiah) of Israel and as the Son of God, as God Himself (John 20:31).

The accounts of the Last Supper in all three of the synoptic gospels begin with the mention of the coming of the time of the Passover. Christ expresses a desire to eat the feast with them. They ask Him where He wishes to eat it. He sends them to Jerusalem with elaborate instructions about how to find and obtain use of the upper room.

Luke 22 has relevant passages that reasonably summarise most of the points of interest that we need to consider:

> *Luke 22:12-20,29-30*: And he shall show you a large upper room furnished: there make ready. And they went, and found as he had said to them: and they made ready the *Passover*. And when the hour was come, he sat down, and the Twelve Apostles with him. And he said to them, I have earnestly desired to eat this *Passover* with you before I suffer: For I say to you, I will not any more eat of it, until it shall be fulfilled in the kingdom of God. And he took the cup, and gave thanks, and said, Take this, and share it among yourselves: For I say

to you, I will not drink of the fruit of the vine, until the kingdom of God shall come. And he took bread, and gave thanks, and broke it, and gave to them, saying, This is my body which is given for you: this do in remembrance of me. Likewise also the cup after supper, saying, This cup is the new testament in my blood, which is shed for you ... And I appoint to you a kingdom, as my Father hath appointed to me; That ye may eat and drink at my table in my kingdom, and sit on thrones judging the twelve tribes of Israel.

The *Passover* was established in the books of the Law but it would be too time consuming to go into all the Scripture involved. To see a thorough study of the Passover in relation to the Lord's Supper read the book *Think On These Things* by Ernest Streets and look at chapter 5 entitled "The Lord's Table". Pastor Streets quotes Rabbi Gamaliel who was a contemporary of Christ and the apostle Paul for the order of service and meaning of the 14 elements of the Passover feast of that time and clearly illustrates that the actions of Christ were consistent with the elements of that feast.

The first time we read of Jesus partaking in the feast of the Passover was in Luke 2:41-42 when He went with his parents to Jerusalem. Now, knowing that He was about to be crucified, He wanted to have this last Passover with His disciples (v 15). It was normal to celebrate the feast in Jerusalem whenever possible and when away from the city it ended with the cry by all present "next year in Jerusalem", hence the location of the Last Supper.

It would seem to be redundant to keep repeating the point that the event that took place in the upper room was the Passover feast, a distinctly Jewish occasion. In the light, however, of the fact that this is so widely taken as not very important I feel that it is beneficial to dwell on the matter since it will vitally alter our understanding of its doctrinal significance. Let us ponder over a number of points:

1. According to Christ's instructions the apostles made ready the Passover. (v 13)

2. Christ called it the Passover and stated that He would not eat it again "until it shall be fulfilled *in the "kingdom of God"*. (v 16)

3. The host was Jesus the Messiah of the Nation. (Romans 15:8)

4.	Those present were the Twelve Apostles, obviously all Jews (v 14). Only a circumcised person could be present at the Passover feast, a Jew or a proselyte.

5.	The first act of the Passover was the taking of the first cup of wine, the "cup of sanctification" - followed by the ceremonial washing of hands. In the sixth act, the second cup, the "Cup of salvation or redemption" was taken. At one of these points He said, "I will not drink of the fruit of the vine, until *the kingdom of God shall come.*" (v 18)

6.	Judas partook of the *sop* and then left to betray the Lord. The *sop* was the seventh element of the feast consisting of herbs dipped in nut paste along with unleavened bread representing the bitterness of bondage in Egypt. (John 13:26-30)

7.	The third event of the feast had been the breaking in two of the middle one of the three especially prepared unleavened cakes. They were hidden by the president of the feast, usually under a cushion to represent Israel and Judah in captivity. The actual meal had followed the sop and now as the meal was finishing, the broken loaf was recovered and divided with those present (event #9). This depicted the Nation's release from bondage. Thus those present partook of the redemption. At this point Jesus added meaning to the ceremony and altered its application. Now it was His broken body that would in future redeem the Nation that was symbolised by the broken bread (Matthew 26:26, Mark 14:22, Luke 22:19). His body was the anti-type of the manna, the bread of life that had sustained the Nation.

8.	Next came possibly the most significant act (event # 10). The third cup, "of blessing" was then taken. To the Rabbis this represented the life-giving water from the rock (Exodus 17). Now that rock was Christ and the water symbolic of His life-giving spirit. The words He spoke are so pivotal that they must be repeated here.

Matthew 26:28: For this is my blood of the *new testament* which is shed for many for the remission of sin.

Mark 14:23-24: And he took the cup, and when he had given thanks, he gave it to them: and they all drank of it. And he said to them, This is my blood of the *new testament,* which is shed for many.

Luke 22:20: Likewise also the cup after supper, saying, This cup is the *new testament* in my blood, which is shed for you.

The *NIV* translates "new testament" as "new *covenant*" which is quite right. Here we have the Messiah of the Jews speaking to twelve Jews, at a strictly Jewish Passover feast, in Jerusalem, declaring, "This is my blood of the *new covenant"*. These men were well aware of the promise of Jeremiah 31. God had promised to make a "new covenant" with Israel and Judah. Now the blood of the Lord was to be the guarantee of that covenant. They still did not know quite how this was to be accomplished but they believed Him.   He repeatedly made it clear what this feast was about. He bound this feast to the Kingdom.

1.   He would not eat the Passover again until "it shall be fulfilled in *the kingdom of God"*. This could only refer to the Passover meal since He did eat "boiled fish and honeycomb" with them after the resurrection. (Luke 24:42-43)

2.   He would not drink the fruit of the vine till the *"kingdom shall come".*

3.   He appointed them to *a kingdom* in which they would judge the twelve tribes of Israel. (vs 29-30)

4.   He additionally told them that they would continue to eat and drink at His table in the *messianic kingdom.*

There is no suggestion of the church which is The Body of Christ, much less any spiritual Israel. Only among the literal descendants of Abraham are there twelve tribes. He was speaking of exactly the kind of real kingdom that they had always been taught to expect. They understood well what He was saying and they were correct in that understanding.

The very last question that they asked the Lord before His ascension shows what they understood and expected. His answer confirms that they were right. After 40 days of instruction from the risen Christ, they asked:

> *Acts 1:6-7*: Lord, wilt thou at this time restore again the kingdom to Israel? And he said to them, It is not for you to know the times or the seasons, which the Father hath put in his own power.

Their firm belief was that, just as He had promised, He would bring about the Messianic kingdom and that literal Israel would be restored to its proper place under His rule. The question was "When?" not, "Would it happen?" At this point Christ had a perfect opportunity to put them straight if it was not to be. He did no such thing. He only told them that they were not to know the time. Since there was a time that they could not know, by implication it follows that the event itself *would* take place. It is unthinkable that a loving Christ would deceive them, if the kingdom had been set aside at that time.

The Apostle Paul, when he was reasoning with the Jewish believers, wrote in Hebrews 8:8, "he saith, Behold, the days come, saith the Lord when I will make a new covenant with the house of *Israel* and with the house of *Judah*." Paul continues to repeat the complete New Covenant as still valid. This book was written during the period covered by the Book of Acts but before Acts 28:28. The indication is that at that time God was still dealing with the Nation in terms of the restored kingdom. He was not dealing with the Church which is the Body of Christ.

Summary

The Old Testament carries a single thread through it. From the "fall" of Adam right through to the crucifixion of our Lord, the constant theme has been Satan's battle to maintain Lordship over God's creation, to be the god of this world, versus God's determined plan to give the Son His proper place as ruler of the heavenly kingdom over His own creation. For all the apparent twists and turns through the recorded history in the Scriptures one thing is clear, God maintained the royal line. Seth took the place of Abel. Noah was saved out of the flood. Abraham was called out from among the idolaters of Ur. Jacob was preserved from the famine and went into Egypt. In spite of Egypt, Assyria, Babylon, the Medo-Persians, Greece and Rome, Christ was born in God's time. He was born into the Nation of God's choosing, over which He was to rule as Messiah.

God will not only restore the kingdom to Israel, but He will also restore Israel to their King. By the Old Covenant God offered the restoration but that covenant was weak because of man's sinful nature. Christ offered the kingdom but Israel refused their King. As He approached the end of His earthly ministry, He used this last Passover to teach them in a graphic manner that God had guaranteed the New Covenant, which was a better covenant because He, Christ, would make it come to pass. His body was broken for Israel's redemption and His blood was the guarantee of its effectiveness.

When Christ observed His first Passover, it had been a memorial to the exodus from Egypt and God's gift of the kingdom to Israel of old, the redemption from slavery, the Old Covenant.

When Christ observed His last Passover it was to become an everlasting memorial to His sacrificial death and the redemption of the Nation to the certainty of the Messianic kingdom.

When the apostles asked their question, "Lord, wilt thou at this time restore again the kingdom to Israel?" they were not only correct in asking the question but they determined the whole subject matter of the Book of Acts and the period covered by that book. They understood better than most of us about the covenants and the kingdom and had acknowledged Him as their king. We need to rethink many of our doctrinal presumptions in the light of that very important question, since effectively, although not in so many words, Christ's answer was "Yes, I will in the Father's own time".

Chapter 9

CHRIST AND THE APOSTLES

We need to remember that whatever was said or written in the Bible was not said in a vacuum nor was it all directed *to* us. It is quite true that whatever was spoken or written was *for* us and is, as the Scriptures state, "profitable" for us in many ways. None the less, when Christ, or anyone else spoke, it was to people who were actually there and if we are to understand the full meaning of what they were saying we must seek to comprehend what it meant to them under their circumstances. Otherwise, if we do not do this, we are in danger of taking the words out of context. The result can be an interpretation that suits our purpose but not necessarily what God intended.

When Christ entered into His ministry, when He called His apostles, walked with them and taught them, not one word of the New Testament had been written. The apostles knew nothing about "the church which is called the Body of Christ". They understood things as Jews steeped in the teachings and traditions of the Old Testament and of Israel. If we are to understand what went on, we must set aside our assumptions based on our knowledge of what was revealed later and try to view events from their perspective. It is true that there were some things written later that enlighten us on what happened earlier and help to clarify the teaching. However, we must be careful not to read into events, things that were not there at the time.

In Mark 1:4 we read, "John was baptising in the wilderness, and preaching the baptism of repentance for the remission of sins." And in Acts 13:24, "John having first preached before his coming the baptism of repentance to all the people of Israel." In the light of these two verses it is sometimes difficult to understand the event recorded in Matthew 3.

Matthew 3:13-17: Then cometh Jesus from Galilee to Jordan to John, to be baptised by him. But John forbad him, saying, I have need to be baptised by thee, and comest thou to me? And Jesus answering said to him, Permit it to be so now: for thus it is fitting for us to *fulfil all righteousness*. Then he consented to him. And Jesus, when he was baptised, went up immediately out of the water: and, lo, the heavens were opened to him, and he saw the Spirit of God descending like a dove, and lighting upon him: And lo a voice from heaven, saying, This is my beloved Son, in whom I am well pleased.

Why was Christ baptised?

The usual reasons given for water baptism today are:

1. To follow Christ's example in obedience.

2. To thereby identify with Him.

3. To symbolise His death and resurrection.

4. As an outward sign of an inward committal to Him.

None of these reasons can reasonably apply to Christ's own water baptism. He had not yet died or been resurrected and He did not need to symbolise what He would actually do. His real actions were the only signs He needed. Or were they? What did He mean by "it is fitting for us to *fulfil all righteousness*"?

Consider John's baptism. When John started his ministry, people were angry at his accusations concerning their sin and the need for repentance but it would seem that the ritual itself did not surprise them. They apparently understood it. At that time it could not have had any of the connotations that are ascribed to water baptism today. Christ had not even started His ministry let alone been crucified, buried, and resurrected. The rite must have had a reasonable meaning to them that was in full accord with their experience and practice as Jews and people of that time and culture. Otherwise they would have been more confused than angry. They fully understood what John was saying.

If we look back at what Exodus 29 tells us about the consecration of the Aaronic priesthood we find the words:

> *Exodus 29:1,4*: And this is the thing that thou shalt do to them to hallow them, to minister to me in the priest's office ... And Aaron and his sons thou shalt bring to the door of the tabernacle of the congregation, and shalt wash them with water.

It is clear that the ceremonial cleansing from sin had been a part of the preparation for the Jewish priesthood for centuries and had been quite familiar to the people. It did not start with John or with Christ's earthly ministry. As a ceremony for the priests, the Jews could gladly accept it. When John told them that they actually needed to repent from sins and that they were a sinful people they became vengeful and angry.

John's baptism was "the baptism of repentance for the remission of sins." and it was "the baptism of repentance to all the people of Israel". He told them "prepare ye the way of the Lord" (Matthew 3:3). Did Christ have sins that He needed to repent of? Was He simply another Jew? There were better reasons for His baptism than any that have been suggested so far.

Let us remember that according to the covenants, the whole Nation of Israel was to serve God as a nation of priests and kings. It would be necessary for them to repent of their sins, receive forgiveness from God, and to be ceremonially cleansed with water in preparation for priestly service, just as Aaron had been. It was to prepare for just this situation that John was sent. Baptism was the ceremonial cleansing! Jesus was their Messiah. He was to be their King and their High Priest. Had they accepted Him, their destiny would have been fulfilled and the Kingdom would have come. They needed to be ready, but they were not. The Law had failed because of their weakness of the flesh. More evidence is found in the book of Hebrews chapter 7:

> *Hebrews 7:11-17*: If therefore perfection were by the Levitical priesthood, (for under it the people received the law,) what further need was there that another priest should rise after the order of Melchisedek, and not be called after the order of Aaron? For the priesthood being changed, there is made of necessity a change also of the law. For he of whom these things are spoken pertaineth to another tribe, of which no man gave attendance at the altar. For it is evident that our Lord sprang from Judah; of which tribe Moses spoke nothing concerning priesthood. And it is yet far more evident: for that after the similitude of Melchisedek there ariseth another priest, who is made, not after the law of a carnal commandment, but after the power of an endless life. For he testifieth, Thou art a priest forever after the order of Melchisedek.

Earlier reference was made to the fact that Christ was called "a minister of the circumcision ... to confirm the promises made to the fathers". He Himself said "Think not that I am come to destroy the law

... but to fulfil". Christ was to fulfil the "Law" yet in Hebrews we are told that it was necessary to change the law. It was true that the Levitical priesthood had fallen short of its responsibilities but it was not done away with. Instead, a higher priesthood was introduced that would augment them.

The difficulty was that Christ was of the tribe of Judah and not of the tribe of Levi. Under law only a Levite could be a priest. This was not a right but a requirement and responsibility under the distribution of the inheritance at the time of the acquisition of the Promised Land. Joseph's sons received a double portion and Levi none. In return, Levi's seed became the priests and all Israel was required to support them through tithes.

A "priest" is not a person who stands between God and the unbeliever but between God and the believer. The Levites under 'normal' conditions would be advocates before God for a believing Israel. If the Nation were to become a Nation of priests and kings, the Law would have to be altered to accommodate a wider priesthood. The priesthood takes precedence over the law since under the priesthood the people received the law. They did not receive the priesthood by the Law, but the Law laid down the manner of dealing with the priests and provided parameters for its existence. It is these parameters that were changed. The new priesthood, after the order of Melchisedek, was not only to be wider but superior and more powerful.

Christ was to be the first and highest of the new order. While He had changed the Law, He had not done away with it. In all His life He followed not only the letter but also the spirit of the Law. Now He entered into His ministry by following the ritual requirements of entering the new priesthood. This is what He meant by "to fulfil all righteousness". By this act He not only confirmed the law but He also identified himself with the Nation as their promised Messiah.

The wonder is that Christ chose to do things in this manner. He had the power to do whatever He wished. The power of an endless life resides in Him. He is God yet He chose to teach us by example. It is the measure of His love and grace to mankind. He laid no requirement on man that He was not willing to submit to Himself. He came unto His own and lived as one of His own - an Israelite.

From Israel's standpoint all this still had to be confirmed. That confirmation occurred and is recorded in Matthew 3:16-17. The Spirit of God descended and declared, "This is my beloved Son, in whom I am well pleased". Throughout the Old Testament, prophecies had been made, and throughout the New, the phrase "That it might be fulfilled" is repeated. By these signs God identified His servants and their ministries. The patriarchs received their covenants with signs. Moses received the law and led the Nation out of bondage with the accompaniment of many signs and wonders. Whether by signs that were prophecies fulfilled, or by supernatural events, God always used such events to declare Israel to be His chosen people and the instrument through which He would reveal His will to man.

It should be mentioned that miracles in the Bible were always related to the Nation and its ministry. They confirmed a teaching or a teacher. When Christ raised Lazarus He could have as easily raised all the dead people in the land at the same time but that would not have served His greater purposes. He did not raise Lazarus because of his friend's faith, (Lazarus was dead and could have no faith) but because the act would help Him, Jesus, to be revealed as the Christ. It was clear that all that are in Christ will be raised at the resurrection in any event and that all whom He raised during His earthly ministry died later, so the miracle was not in itself the object of God's purpose.

When Christ was born, His birth was heralded by many signs and now, at the beginning of His ministry, His baptism, a divine sign, the sign of the dove, heralded Him as Messiah.

It may seem a long way between discussing signs, the apostles, the manner in which Christ dealt with them, and the question of when the Church, the Body of Christ, started. It is, however, necessary to distinguish the difference between God's revelation to, and purpose for Israel and His revelation to, and purpose for the Body of Christ. They are not the same. His love for all men is the same but His purpose is not. Christ is Lord of all but the Twelve Apostles are intimately connected with Israel. They are apostles to the circumcision, to Israel. If we can find a point at which what He taught them, and how He dealt with them, differs substantially from what the Holy Spirit teaches us in the last Pauline epistles, where the Church which is the Body of Christ is declared, then we have our starting point. We must find out exactly what He taught them and whether it applies to us. As I pointed out, many believe that whatever was available to the apostles is available to us today. If that were true then Pentecost would indeed be the beginning of the Church, that is to say, right after the death and resurrection of the Testator, but it is not. The gospel to the circumcision is not identical to the gospel of grace.

There are many scriptures that make clear just how vital signs were, especially to the Jews. Consider a few. When writing to the Corinthians about the simple message of salvation by the power of the cross of Christ, Paul said in 1 Corinthians 1:22-23 "the Jews require a sign, and the Greeks seek wisdom: But we preach Christ crucified, to the Jews a stumbling block, and to the Greeks foolishness". The Greeks did require wisdom, and Paul offered it to them. Look at Paul's Mars Hill address (Acts 17:22-34). The Jews did require a sign.

> *Matthew 12:38*: Then certain of the scribes and of the Pharisees answered, saying, Master, we would see a sign from thee.

> *Matthew 16:1*: The Pharisees also and the Sadducees came, and tempting desired him that he would show them a sign from heaven.

The answer in both cases was a curt "and there shall no sign be given to it, but the sign of the prophet Jonah", for these men were only looking for a reason to find fault. They did not want to believe.

Again, in John 2:18-19, they asked for a sign. He had taken a scourge and driven the money changers out of the temple and "Then answered the Jews and said to him, What sign showest thou to us, seeing that thou doest these things? Jesus answered and said to them, Destroy this temple, and in three days I will raise it up." This time He gave them a sign for He was referring to His resurrection but they did not believe and their disbelief condemned them.

Christ understood their need for a sign, for He was their Creator, and when they needed one He provided one. A rich man came to Him asking for his ailing son who was on the point of death and Christ said "Except ye see signs and wonders, ye will not believe" (John 4:48). The man believed and his son was healed.

His life on earth, particularly the years of His ministry, is marked by fulfilled prophecies, signs, wonders, and miracles. We tend to be overawed by what we perceive as a supernatural event. We think of a miracle as a kind of magic that is contrary to nature. In fact a miracle is an act of the Creator God using His creation to declare His purpose. We might think of a verse quoted before from a parable used in another context, Matthew 20:15 "Is it not lawful for me to do what I will with my own?" A miracle is not 'supernatural' but '*super-natural*'. As Paul said in Acts 17:28, "For in him we live, and move, and have our being; as certain also of your own poets have said, For we are also his offspring." The Apostle John summed it all up when he wrote:

John 20:30-31: And many other signs truly did Jesus in the presence of his disciples, which are not written in this book: But these are written, that ye may believe that Jesus is the Christ, the Son of God; and that believing ye may have life through his name.

Christ came not only to live but to die. It was necessary for Him to prepare His disciples to take His place after his ascension, and to rule over the twelve tribes of Israel in the coming Kingdom. He promised them that they would. To these ends He gave them special instructions and powers that would be for them alone. When we think that we are the inheritors of all that was given to the twelve and that we have all their powers, we fall into doctrinal error.

Let us look at some of the instructions Christ gave the Apostles before His crucifixion.

Matthew 10:1,5-8: And when he had called to him his twelve disciples, he gave them power against unclean spirits, to cast them out, and to heal all manner of sickness and all manner of disease ..... These twelve Jesus sent forth, and commanded them, saying, Go not into the way of the Gentiles, and enter ye not into any city of the Samaritans: But go rather to the lost sheep of the house of Israel. And as ye go, proclaim, saying, The kingdom of heaven is at hand. Heal the sick, cleanse the lepers, raise the dead, cast out demons: freely ye have received, freely give.

Parallel passages occur in Mark 6:7-13 and Luke 9:1-6. In Luke 10:1-12 He appointed Seventy more to go out and minister. There are three other notable portions of Scripture from before the cross that describe instructions the Lord gave the apostles and some of the accompanying powers that were granted. When Peter gave his confession of Christ's identity the Lord made a marvellous statement:

Matthew 16:18-20: And I say also to thee, That thou art Peter, and upon this rock I will build my church; and the gates of hell shall not prevail against it. And I will give to thee the keys of the kingdom of heaven: and whatever thou shalt bind on earth shall be bound in heaven: and whatever thou shalt loose on earth shall be loosed in heaven. Then he charged his disciples that they should tell no man that he was Jesus the

Christ.

Similar powers were granted later:

> *Matthew 18:18-20*: Verily I say to you, Whatever ye shall
> bind on earth shall be bound in heaven: and whatever ye shall
> loose on earth shall be loosed in heaven. Again I say to you,
> That if two of you shall agree on earth concerning any thing
> that they shall ask, it shall be done for them by my Father who
> is in heaven. For where two or three are assembled in my
> name, there am I in the midst of them.

In the Upper Room, just before He was to leave them, He spoke words
that began with "Let not your heart be troubled: ye believe in God,
believe also in me." Now He was not sending them on a limited
mission, as before, but He was preparing them for His absence. He
was giving them authority that He knew they would soon need. He
now added some very powerful words:

> *John 14:11-15*: Believe me that I am in the Father, and the
> Father in me: or else believe me for the very works' sake.
> Verily, verily, I say to you, He that believeth on me, the works
> that I do shall he do also; and greater works than these shall he
> do; because I go to my Father. And whatever ye shall ask in
> my name, that will I do, that the Father may be glorified in the
> Son. If ye shall ask any thing in my name, I will do it. If ye
> love me, keep my commandments.

Many honestly think that all these powers granted to the apostles are
for us today, but can we justifiably claim the powers without the
restrictions? We proclaim salvation full and free to all who believe.
They were to proclaim the kingdom of heaven. Since they were to rule
in that kingdom, could it be other than the Messianic kingdom that is
meant, considering that they were told *not* to go to the Gentiles? They
were told to go rather to the lost sheep of the house of Israel. The
instructions were explicit. It is doubtful that any today would go only
to Jews and not to Gentiles. Just as Christ's miraculous signs identified
Him as the Messiah, even so His deputies, the under-kings of the
Kingdom, needed similar identification.

Again in John 14 He gives the reason for the works (the
signs), so that they may believe. Then he told them that they would do

the same kind of works and greater "because I go to my Father". Later in the Acts period it became evident that they did do such works. It is useful to list, from these passages, points that were relevant for the disciples:

1. Go to Israel only.

2. Do not go to Gentiles.

3. Proclaim kingdom of heaven.

4. Tell no one He was the Christ.

5. He will build His church on Peter's confession.

6. Receive Keys of kingdom of heaven.

7. Heal the sick.

8. Raise the dead.

9. Cast out demons.

10. Whatever ye shall bind on earth shall be bound in heaven:

11. Whatever ye shall loose on earth shall be loosed in heaven.

12. Two or three gathered in Christ's name Christ is there.

13. If two agree on earth, it will be done by the Father.

14. If ye shall ask any thing in my name, I will do it.

15. If ye love me, keep my commandments.

The first four points raise some interesting questions. We need to question why they were told to go only to the Jews and not the Gentiles? And why, if they were told to proclaim the kingdom of heaven, were they told to tell no one that Jesus was the Christ, the Messiah King? God's purpose in the first place, according to the covenants, was not to bless Israel only but that through Israel's seed all of the nations of the earth would be blessed. All these being so, why not go to the Gentiles and why not proclaim Israel's king as Saviour of the world? The answer lies in the timing and a principle that appears in Romans 2 very clearly:

> *Romans 2:9-10*: Tribulation and anguish, upon every soul of man that doeth evil, of the Jew first, and also of the Greek; But glory, honour, and peace, to every man that worketh good, to the Jew first, and also to the Greek:

God is a God of order. All things happen in accordance with God's plan and schedule. Christ was born in God's chosen time and place, regardless of the attempts of Herod to intervene. The Scriptures were delivered to man in God's chosen time and place, regardless of Pharaoh's or anyone's hostility. God's principle of "to the Jew first, and also to the Greek" can be seen in practice throughout the Scriptures, from Genesis 12 to Acts 28:28. Throughout that time, the Jew was God's chosen vehicle to reach man. This is one of the keys to understanding the vast majority of God's word in context. It is the key to understanding the main questions of this book.

In this case, Christ was still preparing Israel for its ministry. The time had not yet come for the message to go out to the Gentiles - "the Jew first". Later the apostles would be told both to go to the Gentiles and to proclaim Him as Messiah. It does not follow that all the things directed towards Israel or to the apostles would ultimately be granted to all Christians.

Point five speaks of Christ building His "church" on Peter's confession that Jesus was the Christ, the Son of the living God. The confession of Jesus Christ as our Divine Lord is the basis of salvation for all who are redeemed. In this limited sense the word "church" could apply to all believers but, as has been pointed out earlier under definitions, there are a number of distinct churches mentioned in the Bible.

Point six speaks of Peter receiving the Keys to the "kingdom of heaven". Often the terms "*church*" and "*kingdom of heaven*" are viewed as being more or less synonymous with each other and with the "Body of Christ" which exists today. Considering that Christ had told the twelve in Luke 22:29, "And I appoint to you a kingdom", it would seem reasonable to assume that the "kingdom of heaven" was the one in which they would rule, that is the Messianic kingdom. This "kingdom" is an *ekklesia* of called out ones and in that sense a "church", but that does not make it the "Church which is the Body of Christ", nor does it make Peter the first leader appointed to establish the church of today as Christ's vicar. Neither does it follow that we are the inheritors of all the powers, gifts and positions granted to Israel or the Twelve Apostles.

An understanding of a word in any given case depends on context. To phrase it another way, consider the word "church". In Matthew 16:18 it refers to the assembly of those called to the "Kingdom", whereas in Colossians 1:18 it refers to "The Body of Christ". However, in Ephesians 1:10 we read "That in the dispensation of the fulness of times he might gather in one all things in Christ". When God brings about this future condition the distinction between the "Kingdom" and the "Church which is the Body of Christ" may well become blurred. However, at this present time, and certainly when the Bible was written, the people of the Kingdom and the people of the Body were two distinct groups or churches, called to different destinies and service. Until those callings and service are completed, each church must remain separate and seek to follow its own place in God's will according to the careful instructions of God's word. The mere use of the word "church" does not indicate the "Body", but more of this later.

Summing these two points up it would seem that while the word "church" of Matthew 16:18 could be broadly understood, the term "kingdom of heaven" of the following verse is more exclusive and specific to the Nation of Israel and its calling. The powers granted were awarded to facilitate the establishment of that kingdom and should not be construed as applying to all believers.

It is clear that during the time of the events recorded during the Book of Acts the Apostles did in fact heal the sick, raise the dead, and cast out demons and by those deeds they succeeded in establishing themselves as Christ's representatives. Considering that their ultimate mission was to the Nation of Israel, and not to preach today's gospel in which the Jew has no priority, it is hard to see why we would need the same powers.

Aside from the fact that we are told that the Jew required a sign, the apostles needed similar spectacular evidence to establish that their authority came from Christ. They could not appeal to the authority of the New Testament, since it had not yet been written and they were themselves the subjects of much of its content. This is not true of us. They could not appeal to the Old Testament alone since the object of their ministry was to affirm, by fulfilled prophecy and wonders, that Jesus was the Christ, the promised Messiah, and that they were His accredited representatives.

By contrast our sole authority resides in appeal to the completed revelation of God through His word the Bible. According to the Bible the day will come in the end times when those who are the enemies of Christ will do wonders. Even today many supposedly supernatural acts are performed that are contrary to scriptural teaching. Given choice, certainty lies in God's word alone.

The first nine elements of the list that we have presented instruct the apostles about their mission and by signs confirmed their identity as Christ's servants and verified the mission itself. It is all preparatory. From point ten onward something different is added. The emphasis shifts from identity to authority.

These twelve were clearly told that they would rule as under-kings over the twelve tribes of Israel in the coming kingdom. For this task they needed administrative authority. Signs were not enough. They needed the power to rule and make executive decisions. They needed to be able to make "binding" decisions, and that is exactly the power that Christ conferred on them. They were told that whatever they bound or loosed on earth would be bound or loosed in heaven. God delegated divine authority to them. They were not told to pray about a matter but to make decisions and He would make it so.

Point twelve is a restatement of Matthew 18:20. Look at that verse again:

> *Matthew 18:20*: For where two or three are assembled in my name, there am I in the midst of them.

The usual understanding of this verse with variations is applied to Christians today. We tend to think of it as a call to go to church or gather as a corporate group in order to gain some type of status before God and have His presence with us. There is a problem. If I am in Christ and He in me, is He not with me even when I am alone? Do I really need to be with other believers in order to be assured of the presence of God with me? It is without question needful for us to gather together as a "church" to support one another as members of His "Body" and to praise Him. But this verse has a special connotation in context that does not apply to us.

Let us remember that the Jew as a member of the Nation was in a radically different relationship to God than we are as members of

His Body. Their standing before God depended on their individual submission to the statutes and ordinances of the Law and their genetic descent from Abraham. A priest had to be a son of Levi. The royal line was Judah's. Grace came to them through the Law and the covenants to Abraham's "seed". We become members of his Body through grace alone as individuals without reference to lineage.

God chose to meet with His ancient people in ways that are not His will today. He met with them as a Nation in specific places. There was the tabernacle and then the temple. He led them visibly through the wilderness in a cloud by day and in a pillar of fire by night. He appeared as strangers to Abraham and as a dove at Christ's baptism. At Pentecost, after this promise, He appeared to the assembled disciples as a rushing wind and again as flames of fire.

The Twelve were in effect to be God's cabinet in the kingdom. They were to have delegated authority. They needed to know that when they met and decided on anything, they had assurance of His approval and power: hence His promise of His presence when they were about His business. They were promised, "If two agree on earth, it will be done by the Father." Again, "If ye shall ask any thing in my name, I will do it." We never gather with their kind of authority.

This last statement and some others that I have made will strike some as being erroneous. At first glance the doctrine of apostolic succession in any form would appear reasonable. Since Christ granted these powers to His followers and they died, would it not seem needful that those powers should pass on to others? God made promises to, and covenants with the patriarchs and fulfilled them in their seed. Why should this not be true of the apostles also? The difference is that those earlier agreements were made with the patriarchs *and* their seed. The apostles were themselves to rule. No mention was made of their seed.

Had Israel accepted their Messiah then the Kingdom would have been established at that time and the Twelve would have taken their place on the thrones of the twelve tribes. They still will for He is the resurrection and the life. They themselves will rule and not others. The promised Messianic kingdom has been set in abeyance and not permanently set aside. God's word is certain and sure! Since they will rule there is no reason to pass on their unique authority to others. We have a different calling not tied to Israel or its need for signs.

After the cross the resurrected Christ instructed them further and granted them more powers. It is evident that Christ did not consider power enough. Knowledge of the Word was necessary for the proper administration of that power. These chosen men were to be provided with all that was necessary to be His representatives on earth and in the coming Kingdom.

> *Luke 24:44-47*: And he said to them, These are the words which I spoke to you, while I was yet with you, that all things must be fulfilled, which were written in the Law of Moses, and in the prophets, and in the psalms, concerning me. Then he opened their understanding, *that they might understand the Scriptures*, And said to them, Thus it is written, and thus it was necessary for Christ to suffer, and to rise from the dead the third day: And that repentance and remission of sins should be preached in his name among all nations, beginning at Jerusalem.

If the apostles, having walked in the flesh with Christ, and been instructed by Him in person, and having been eye witnesses to the crucifixion and the resurrection still needed to *understand the Scriptures*, how much more do we need to submit our thinking to the instruction of the Word? We need constantly to reassess our views to make sure that what we believe is of God and not from our own self-will. Notice that while they were to preach among all nations, they were to begin at Jerusalem, and go to "the Jew first" (see also Acts 1:8). Look at the powers and signs that He now gave them. First consider:

> *John 20:23*: Whose sins ye remit, they are remitted to them; and whose sins ye retain, they are retained.

Now truly they had the power to judge the Nation! Whatever they bound would be bound. Whatever they decided would stand as God's judgement. They no longer simply had to pray for the people, although they still could, they could under God's own authority, decide the fate of the tribes.

A passage at the end of the Gospel of Mark caps the question of the position and ministry of the apostles as Messiah's representatives.

> *Mark 16:14-20*: Afterward he appeared to the eleven as they sat eating, and upbraided them with their unbelief and hardness of heart, because they believed not them who had

seen him after he was risen. And he said to them, Go ye into all the world, and preach the gospel to every creature. He that believeth and is baptised shall be saved; but he that believeth not shall be damned. And these signs shall follow them that believe; In my name shall they cast out demons; they shall speak in new languages; They shall take up serpents; and if they drink any deadly thing, it shall not hurt them; they shall lay hands on the sick, and they shall recover. So then after the Lord had spoken to them, he was received up into heaven, and sat on the right hand of God. And they went forth, and preached every where, the Lord working with them, and *confirming the word with signs following.* Amen.

Verses 15 and 16 instruct them to continue with the purpose to which He had called them, which was to preach repentance from sin to the Nation, and to the dispersed of Israel scattered throughout the nations. They were to proclaim Christ Jesus as the Messiah, the Son of God, and were to baptise individual Jews in preparation for the coming priesthood.

Then in verses 17 and 18 He told them of truly spectacular signs that would follow them.

1.   In my name shall they cast out demons;

2.   they shall speak in new languages;

3.   they shall take up serpents;

4.   if they drink any deadly thing, it shall not hurt them;

5. they shall lay hands on the sick, and they shall recover.

In verse 20 they obeyed and Christ proved faithful to His assurance of support.

If any of us were inheritors of the apostles we should be able to forgive sin or condemn people, heal the sick, raise the dead, and do all the things they could. That would include picking up serpents or drinking any deadly thing without hurt. The power to bind or loose should reside in us and not be just a matter of praying about it. There is a catch however. We would need also to be Jews and be divided according to tribe.

Just before He was taken up to heaven, Christ again stated His will for them: "But ye shall receive power, after the Holy Spirit is come upon you: and ye shall be witnesses to me both in Jerusalem, and in all Judaea, and in Samaria, and to the uttermost part of the earth" (Acts 1:8). Once more it was the Jew first, and even the Jews of the dispersion, those scattered to the uttermost parts of the earth, had precedence over the Gentiles.

Mark 16:14 contains the phrase "Afterward he appeared to the eleven". The stance that I have taken depends for its integrity on there being Twelve Apostles, not eleven, to match the twelve tribes. Peter and the disciples addressed the problem as they waited in the upper room before the Day of Pentecost. In Acts Chapter 1 he addressed the assembled believers:

> *Acts 1:21-26*: Wherefore of these men who accompanied us all the time that the Lord Jesus went in and out among us, Beginning from the baptism of John, to that same day that he was taken up from us, must one be ordained to be a witness with us of his resurrection. And they appointed two, Joseph called Barsabbas, who was surnamed Justus, and Matthias. And they prayed, and said, Thou, Lord, who knowest the hearts of all men, show which of these two thou hast chosen, That he may take part of this ministry and apostleship, from which Judas by transgression fell, that he might go to his own place. And they gave forth their lots; and the lot fell upon Matthias; and he was numbered with the eleven apostles.

This action on the part of the Apostles is the first recorded act under the administrative authority that God had granted them. Some students have mistakenly thought that the Apostles were wrong in what they did. Paul is taken to be the correct replacement for Judas. Paul himself makes clear that he is an apostle to the un-circumcision whereas the twelve were apostles to the circumcision. They needed to re-establish the Twelve as the kingdom was still the promised hope. They had been given the authority to bind the matter on earth with the clear promise that it would then be bound in heaven.

Theirs still were the "keys of the kingdom". Their instructions had not changed from when Christ declared to them earlier.

> *Matthew 10:6-7*: But go rather to the lost sheep of the house of Israel. And as ye go, proclaim, saying, The kingdom of heaven

is at hand.

By their actions the Apostles showed that they understood both their calling and the authority Christ had granted them and established themselves as His vicars on earth. Their modern critics have shown little such understanding.

The Messiah had been rejected. The king had been crucified but on the cross Christ had uttered the immortal words, "Father, forgive them; for they know not what they do" (Luke 23:34). Again the grace of God was extended to rebellious people. In spite of His rejection Christ sent His disciples out to offer the kingdom to Abraham's seed once more.

The next great event after the choosing of Matthias was the Day of Pentecost. Tradition teaches that this marks the birthday of the Church of today. If that were so, then there should be a marked change in the disciples' ministry. The signs and miracles should cease or they should be present today, if we are inheritors of all things Jewish. In the next chapters I intend to look at the Day of Pentecost, the times of the Book of Acts, the books written during that period, and the Pauline books written afterwards to see just where the changes took place.

Chapter 10

THE DAY OF PENETCOST

It is easy to understand why the Day of Pentecost is regarded generally as the "birthday" of the Church. The events that took place that day were, to say the least, spectacular. The disciples' numbers, short weeks ago, had dwindled to very few and even those were possessed by discouragement and doubt. Now the assembled group were all filled with the Holy Spirit and began to speak in other languages "and the same day there were added to them about three thousand souls". If a spectacular event is a sure sign that God's administration to man is changing then this day would qualify.

Earlier, in Chapter 2, I spoke of the idea of "dispensation" (Gr. *oikonomia*). The literal meaning given was "administration of a household". This is simple to illustrate. As a Canadian living in Ontario, I am under a different administration to those people living in Quebec. Quebec provincial law is based, so I understand, on the Napoleonic Code. Ontario's law descends from British common law, as does American law. Despite the similarities I do not live under American ordinances, and would not even if they were exactly the same. If I emigrated to the U.S.A., I would cease to be controlled by the laws of Ontario or Canada. In very broad terms a change of "dispensation" in the Bible refers to a point at which God institutes a new "household" with new rules, resulting in new conditions and patterns of behaviour.

It is important for me to know which province and nation I live in and have my citizenship in, otherwise I would not be able to fulfil my responsibilities properly. I owe both my government and my fellow citizens that much for the help and protection they render to me. How much more do I owe my fellow believers and, most of all, my God to try to understand what God's expectations are for me? Without Him I would have nothing and be nothing. I could get on without my country but not without my God.

When people say that the Church began at Pentecost, they infer that there was a change of "dispensation". A new order is assumed to have come into being. The Church supplanted Israel and "Grace" supplanted the "Mosaic Law". I do not hold to this concept. There is too much evidence that the basic historic order did not change. Israel was still God's Chosen People. They were still being offered the Kingdom in spite of their rejection and killing of their

King. The Law was still in effect. Gentiles were still subservient to Israel. They were being grafted into Israel only to provoke the Nation into believing.

Let us look back on some of the material considered so far. When Adam and Eve were cast out of the Garden, God promised that the Seed of the woman would defeat Satan. Much later God chose Abraham and his seed to be the instrument through which the promised Seed would be born into the world. He covenanted with Abraham that his seed would receive an everlasting kingdom and confirmed it through Isaac, Jacob and David. Abraham believed God so God counted his faith for righteousness. Because Abraham fulfilled his part of the covenant, God's sure word became a certainty in spite of the future failure of the children of Israel. To cover the Nation's failure God promised the New Covenant which is a Covenant of grace since He guaranteed both sides of the covenant. He will be their God and they will be His people. He will write the law on their hearts. Christ came unto His own and was rejected by them, yet the New Covenant still stood. He was nailed to the cross. When Pilate sought to release Christ, "Then answered all the people, and said, His blood be on us, and on our children" (Matthew 27:25).

By human standards this should have ended it. After God had time and again forgiven the Nation's rebellion and had restored them to a place of blessing, they killed His Son! This was the final insult, the final rejection. Not so!! God is a God of love and grace. Christ is God incarnate. On the very cross of shame we hear those glorious words, "Then said Jesus, *Father, forgive them; for they know not what they do* ..... And the people stood beholding. And the rulers also with them derided him, saying, He saved others; let him save himself, if he be the Christ, the chosen of God" (Luke 23:34-35). His own people stood there literally hating Him to death, and He forgave them. After His resurrection, when the apostles inquired as to whether He would at that time restore the kingdom to Israel, it was because of this forgiveness on the cross that He was able to tell them only that they could not know the time. The covenant was still being offered to the Nation. Israel was still first in God's plans.

"The Day of Pentecost" was a pivotal day in the record of God's dealing with man. It is important that we understand it thoroughly.

Christ had promised the Apostles that He would send the Holy Spirit to help them. In John 15:26 we read "But when the Comforter is come, whom I will send to you from the Father, even the Spirit of truth, who proceedeth from the Father, he shall testify concerning me." After the resurrection, just after He told them that the time of the restoration of the kingdom to Israel was in the Father's own power, He disclosed to them "But ye shall receive power, after the Holy Spirit is come upon you" (Acts 1:8). In Luke 24:49 He gave them explicit instructions on the matter: "And, behold, I send the promise of my Father upon you: but tarry ye in the city of Jerusalem, until ye are endued with power from on high."

Before Pentecost the Apostles had authority. They chose Matthias as the twelfth apostle but now with the coming of the Holy Spirit they gained full power. The account of the Day of Pentecost takes the entire second chapter of the Book of Acts. I will refer only to those parts necessary to this present study as they are needed. For a clear understanding it would be best to read the chapter through carefully. Verse numbers used in this chapter will be from Acts 2 unless otherwise indicated.

The chapter begins with the fulfilment of Christ's promise of sending the Holy Spirit, accompanied by dramatic signs both of sight and sound. There was the sound of wind and the sight of tongues of fire; "And they were all filled with the Holy Spirit, and began to speak in other languages, as the Spirit gave them utterance" (v 4). Notice that these were not unknown tongues that had to be interpreted, but were languages of those who heard; "every man heard them speak in his own language" (v 6).

There are a number of aspects relating to this sign that can both confuse and enlighten us. We might ask why it was necessary to have people hear the words in their own language. It would seem reasonable to assume that any group of individuals met together in Jerusalem at what must surely be a 'religious' gathering would all have some competence in a common language. Yet this sign was given. The heart of the incident lay not in the need for the people to be reasoned with in their own speech but as verses 7 and 8 state, "Behold, are not all these who speak Galileans? And how do we hear every man in our own language, in which we were born?" They each heard the same things in different languages! It was exactly the kind of sign that the Jews needed. It fits with all that has been spoken of through this book.

It may appear strange to connect again this sign to the Jews in the light of the fact that in addition to Galilee, 16 other countries and nationalities are mentioned. At first glance this fact would seem to indicate that both Jews and Gentiles were present, giving some weight to the opinion that this was the birthday of the Church. There is textual evidence in this chapter and elsewhere to indicate otherwise.

All the people present were of the Jewish faith. In verse 5 we read, "And there were dwelling at Jerusalem Jews, devout men, from every nation under heaven." In verse 10, the phrase "Jews and Proselytes" is used. A "Proselyte" is a person who is not racially a Jew but has come to worship and accept the God of the Jews and become a Jew in faith. His acceptance into the Nation was not absolute. He was Jewish religiously but in a subservient position.

It is not at all surprising that in verse 11 we read of them saying, "we hear them speak in our languages". The "Jews, devout men, from every nation", were Jews of the dispersion. Israel and Judah had long since been taken into captivity. Only a remnant out of the tribes had returned at the restoration. The rest were scattered through the Gentile nations. Most foreign Jews had a desire to make a pilgrimage to Israel and particularly to Jerusalem. This was made clear, as mentioned before, with the intoning of the cry, "Next year in Jerusalem" at the end of the feast of the Passover by exiled Jews. Like their modern day counterparts, the scattered Jews adopted the culture and language of the nation in which they were born. A Jew born in Toronto would likely speak English: one born in Quebec, French. German Jews speak German. Egyptian Jews speak Egyptian, and Romans, Italian. Whatever nation or area a person is born in, the language of that place becomes for them "our own language, in which we were born". It is clear that these were *all Jews*. That they were from other countries and had other languages as their native tongue does not change their Jewishness. They were not Gentiles.

As important as it is to understand that there were only Jews present, that by itself does *not* establish the idea that what took place was not the institution of the Church which is the Body of Christ. Theoretically the "Church" could have begun with only Jews, and Gentiles could have been added later. Other factors must be considered before coming to any conclusion.

When the onlookers mocked the speaking in tongues as a sign of drunkenness, rather than a sign from the Lord, Peter stood up and addressed the assembly. Notice first that he stood "up with the eleven". This affirms that the Twelve were considered to be restored to full strength. Matthias was accepted as the legitimate successor to Judas. Nowhere in the Bible is there any suggestion that there was to be any other replacement of apostles. The promise was that this Twelve would rule on the tribal thrones. There was no mention of their seed, spiritual or genetic.

The manner, tone, and substance of Peter's address was that of an apostle to the circumcision rebuking the Nation and urging them to repent of their sin and accept their Messiah. He appealed to Old Testament prophecy. He quoted David's words and experience as being authoritative to prove that Jesus was the Christ. This was never done in the last seven Pauline books where the "Church" is made known. It would not have been important to Gentiles. Paul in Romans 9:5 makes this clear. Speaking of the Israelites he says "Whose are the fathers," the "fathers" being the patriarchs of the Nation; Abraham, Isaac, Jacob and his sons, David and all those forebears that the Jews looked back on and honoured. David is only mentioned once in the latter Pauline epistles (2 Timothy 2:8). None of the other "fathers" are mentioned at all in these latter letters.

As Peter began to speak, his salutation was to "Ye men of Judaea, and all ye that dwell at Jerusalem" (v 14). He went on to declare that the events that had just taken place [the tongues of fire and the prophecies in foreign languages] were in keeping with the prophecies of the prophet Joel, clearly related to the nation of Israel. It did not refer to the Gentiles, nor would the Gentiles even know of the prophecy or understand the significance of such a miracle. Peter was following in the footsteps of John the Baptist, calling the Nation to repentance, proclaiming Jesus to be the Christ, the King of Israel, their Messiah, and preparing the way for the establishment of the promised Kingdom.

Let us remember again that the last thing that the apostles asked the Lord was whether He would restore the kingdom to Israel *at this time.* That was after the cross, so any thought that the cross had cancelled out that prospect of the coming kingdom is not valid. There is nothing to indicate that this was not still paramount on the disciples' minds these few days later. Every item in Peter's speech worked towards this end. Peter, like the rest of the apostles, had been time and again told to go and proclaim, "The kingdom of heaven is at hand". He had received no new revelation. Israel had not yet been set aside. The very idea of a new "stewardship" had not even been mentioned! Peter was doing exactly what he had been told to do.

The full strength of the passage can be felt by an examination of the following excerpts from the chapter.

Acts 2:22,25,30,32,36,38-39,41: Ye men of Israel, hear these words; Jesus of Nazareth, a man approved by God among you by miracles and wonders and signs, which God did by Him in the midst of you, as ye yourselves also know ... For David speaketh concerning him, I saw the Lord always before my face ... Therefore being a prophet, and knowing that God had sworn to him with an oath, that from the fruit of his loins, according to the flesh, *he would raise up Christ to sit on his throne* ...This Jesus hath God raised up, of which we all are witnesses ... Therefore let all the house of Israel know assuredly, that God hath made that same Jesus, whom ye have crucified, both Lord and Christ ... Then Peter said to them, Repent ye, and each one of you be baptised in the name of Jesus Christ for the remission of sins. For the promise is to you, and to your children, and to all that are afar off, (Jews, and Jews of the dispersion) ... Then they that gladly received his word were baptised: and the same day there were added to them about three thousand souls.

The entire tenor of this speech was parallel to the message of John's introduction of Christ at His baptism. John was called to go ahead of Christ and prepare the way for His reception as Messiah according to the Old Covenant. However, the Nation had rejected the Lord. Now, grace upon grace, Peter was called to offer the kingdom to the Nation under the New Covenant.

Through all the verses of Acts 2, both those quoted and those not quoted, Israel and things related to Israel and the kingdom are constantly present. "Ye men of Judaea" (v 14), "Ye men of Israel" (v 22), "David" (The fathers) (vs 25,29,34), Joel's prophecy (v 16), baptism for repentance and remission from sin, Christ to sit on David's throne, "the promise is to you" (v 39), all of these things mark this event as a re-offering of the kingdom *to Israel*. With regard to the quote from verse 39, Paul in Romans 9:4 writes, "Israelites; to whom pertain the adoption ... and the promises." This is why I have identified those addressed as "Jews, and Jews of the dispersion".

There is no mention of the Gentiles or of the breaking down of the middle wall of partition in Acts 2. There is no suggestion of co-equality between Jew and Gentile. This does not mean that there is no place ultimately for the Gentile in God's kingdom programme, since it had always been the truth that in the seed of Abraham all the nations of the earth would be blessed. Christ Himself made clear what the order of events was when He spoke to the Samaritan woman in John 4:22 and said, "Ye worship ye know not what: we know what we worship: for salvation is from the Jews" or "out from the Jews". As long as the Messianic kingdom was preached, the Jew had a place of pre-eminence. The Nation had first to accept its king and only then would they become the royal priesthood, stewards of God's administration of a redeemed earth.

There is not one single thing in all the record of the Day of Pentecost, or the events following it to the end of chapter two, that suggests the establishment of the Church which is the Body of Christ. There are two items that can, however, confuse us. Verse 41 states, "and the same day there were added *to them* about three thousand souls" and verse 47, "And the Lord added to the *church* daily such as should be saved." We might reasonably ask, "Does not the '*them*' of verse 41, and the '*church*' of verse 47, indicate the church of today?" My answer would be a decided "No!" Under the heading "Definitions" I made clear that the word "church" (*ekklesia*) can refer to any assembly of people called out for a purpose. Again in Acts 7:38 the "church" referred to is the congregation of Israel. The '*them*' simply means those gathered in the *one place*. Given the forms of address and the subject matter it would appear reasonable to believe that the *church* was a group called out to proclaim the re-offering of the kingdom, again distinctly Jewish.

If this is not the birthday of the "Church, the body of Christ" we need to consider the nature of the disciples' ministry during the Acts period, including Paul's teaching during that time, the hallmarks of the gospel for today, and the differences between the two bodies of truth. Further we need to see the reason that Acts 28:28 should be considered the changeover point, and why there should be any change-over of dispensations. Is not God's kingdom enough?

Chapter 11

THE CHURCH IN THE ACTS PERIOD
The Jew; The Gentile; The Law; Paul; Christ.

Historical order now becomes critical. The events and teaching in the Book of Acts must be considered in concert with the teaching of the other books written at the same time and under the same influence. While not all of the writers of the New Testament books were apostles they were all disciples within the community of the Acts period. There was a harmony of teaching among them. "And they, continuing daily with one accord in the temple ..... with gladness and singleness of heart" (Acts 2:46).

Let us again think of the last question that the disciples asked the Lord just before His ascension. "Lord wilt Thou at this time restore again the kingdom to Israel?" (Acts 1:6). The subject of the "kingdom" can be seen underlying all of the ministry of God's servants including the apostle Paul up until the statement of Acts 28:28. Many modern students, in all sincerity, have suggested that Peter and the Apostles did not understand what was going on. They should not have asked about the kingdom. Peter should not have been surprised at the call to go to the house of Cornelius just because he was a Gentile. Viewed from this point, both the question of the Apostles and Peter's behaviour come across as arrogant and proud, if not racist.

If, however, we look at the position of the apostles from their viewpoint, a different picture appears. For about two thousand years, the Nation of Israel had been promised that they as Abraham's seed would inherit a kingdom from God. Christ did not deny that. In fact, He lamented over the people: "O Jerusalem, Jerusalem, thou that killest the prophets, and stonest them who are sent to thee, how often would I have gathered thy children, even as a hen gathereth her chickens under her wings, and ye would not!" (Matthew 23:37). He still loved them. Time and again He commanded His followers to go to the lost sheep of the House of Israel and preach that the kingdom of heaven was at hand. He had spoken to them of the "keys of the kingdom", and promised them personally that they should receive a kingdom and rule on the thrones of the twelve tribes. At the last Passover He had told them to remember Him till they sat again with Him in His kingdom.

On the other hand, we know about the "Church which is the Body of Christ" from the later Pauline books. Let us not read back into the Apostles' experience knowledge of the Church that they could not possibly have had since it had not at that time been revealed. They had not been commissioned to preach the gospel of grace but the coming Messianic kingdom and the baptism of repentance, for the remission of sins. That they did. They were all under the influence of the Abrahamic Covenant and the New Covenant, in short, prophecy.

After Acts 28:28 there is a complete change of teaching. A change of God's household administration is marked not by some dramatic event but by the introduction of a new purpose, a new message, a new administrator, and a new hope. It will be necessary to set this new teaching of the new administration aside until the next chapter and concentrate on defining the substance of the "Kingdom" teaching of the Acts period.

A thorough study of the Book of Acts, with the "Kingdom" truth in mind, would be useful but is not possible at this time. That would fill another book, without exhausting the subject. We must be content with looking at a limited number of key matters.

Consider the position of the Jew. The promises concerning rule in the kingdom began to take place in embryonic form. Within the assembly of believers Peter and the apostles gradually became a hierarchy. Repeatedly Peter and the leadership in Jerusalem ruled in matters of doctrine and practice. When Peter found Ananias and Sapphira guilty of lying to God they were struck dead but not by the hand of man. As Christ had promised, the disciples had bound a matter and God had sealed the matter. Where believers went, miracles and signs went. The Jew required miraculous signs (1 Corinthians 1:22).

Of deep significance was the nature of the thrust of the disciples' ministry and the identity of the people addressed. Again and again the call was for Israel to repent and acknowledge the Messiah. They were accused of killing the prophets and the Lord. The theme was that if they, the Jews, repented that the blessing of the kingdom would be fulfilled. Note Peter's statement of Acts 3:25: "Ye are the children of the prophets, and of the covenant which God made with our fathers, saying to Abraham, And in thy seed shall all the kindreds of the earth be blessed." Peter addressed "Ye men of Israel", and "Ye rulers of the people, and elders of Israel". Stephen began his address to the high priest with "Men, brethren, and fathers, hearken; The God of glory appeared to our father Abraham, when he was in Mesopotamia" (Acts 7:2).

The Book of Hebrews was obviously written to the Jews of the dispersion. The Book of James begins with "to the twelve tribes scattered abroad" (James 1:1). Throughout the Acts period there was continual reference to the history of the "Nation", to the "fathers" to the "covenants" and to the "promises". All of this fits perfectly with Romans 9.

> *Romans 9:4-5*: Who are Israelites; to whom pertain the adoption, and the glory, and the covenants, and the giving of the law, and the service of God, and the promises; Whose are the fathers, and from whom according to the flesh Christ came, who is over all, God blessed for ever.

Remember again the teaching of Romans 2, "the Jew first and also the Greek", and the commission of Acts 1:8 "But ye shall receive power, after the Holy Spirit is come upon you: and ye shall be witnesses to me both in Jerusalem, and in all Judaea, and in Samaria, and to the uttermost part of the earth."

These are but a few of the references we could follow up. Along with those mentioned in earlier chapters and many others that must be left to the reader, one fact becomes clear. The Jew is not only to be considered first in time, (the disciples must start their mission in Jerusalem) but God gave them primacy of place in all His plans for the kingdom. There was no equality. The Jew ranked higher. The kingdom was the prime subject of prophecy and the Jew was central to the fulfilment of that prophecy. When speaking to the woman of Samaria in John 4, in response to her statement, "I know that Messiah cometh, who is called Christ", He replied, "I that speak to thee am he." In this He associated Himself with the Nation and the coming kingdom as the King.

He went further and placed Israel, from whom He came according to the flesh, and to whom He came as His own people, into the centre of His kingdom mission with the words to her, "for salvation is of the Jews" (John 4:22).

In the Messianic kingdom, the apostles and Israel will hold the same relative position as the sons of Aaron and the Levitic priesthood held in ancient Israel. The old order was established under the Old Covenant. The new order will draw its strength from the New Covenant. The whole Nation will, by God's grace, become a royal priesthood. Just as the Levites stood between God and believing Israel, receiving and passing down God's judgements to the Nation, even so, the *Nation* of Israel will receive and pass down the Messiah's judgements to all the other *Nations*.

Peter and the disciples understood this. They understood that first the Nation had to repent and receive their King. Only then would the kingdom be established and the Gentile Nations be brought under the rule of Messiah. The peace of Eden would again be seen on earth. It was not surprising, given this understanding, that Peter was shocked that God told him to go and preach to the Gentile Cornelius. He had previously been told to go only to the Jews and without warning this totally new instruction was given. Much to Peter's credit, once God told him what to do he set aside his life-long convictions as to the primacy of Israel and obeyed. Would that we were so responsive to God's word. The reason for the Gentiles being reached out of the established order became plain later, but it did not in any way represent the institution of the Church, The Body of Christ.

Later at the "Council of Jerusalem" Peter referred to this incident when he addressed the assembly with the words, "Men, brethren, ye know that a good while ago God made choice among us, that the Gentiles by my mouth should hear the word of the gospel, and believe" (Acts 15:7). As an aside, the Ethiopian eunuch was not a Gentile. When Philip came upon him, he was returning from Jerusalem where he had gone to worship and he was reading the Old Testament. He was either a Jew of the dispersion or quite possibly a proselyte, considering his lack of understanding of the Bible.

There were others going out preaching to Gentiles and seeing many of them saved without such direct instructions. In Acts chapter 11 we read:

> *Acts 11:19-21*: Now they who were dispersed upon the persecution that arose about Stephen travelled as far as Phenice, and Cyprus, and Antioch, preaching the word to none but to the Jews only. And some of them were men of Cyprus and Cyrene, who, when they had come to Antioch, spoke to the Grecians, preaching the Lord Jesus. And the hand of the Lord was with them: and a great number believed, and turned to the Lord.

Some have thought that this action by the Cypriot believers represented a broadening of thought towards Gentiles and a step away from racism. This in their thinking was the beginning of the "Church's" reaching out to the world. This was not the case. Just because Gentiles are won does not make that church the Body of Christ. Paul tells us that this was all in accordance with prophecy.

> *Romans 10:19*: But I say, Did not Israel know? First Moses saith, I will provoke you to jealousy by them that are no people, and by a foolish nation I will anger you.

More will be studied on this point further down.

It is in the fifteenth chapter of the Book of Acts that we find the account of what we call the Council of Jerusalem. This is well after the Day of Pentecost. If the "Church", the Body of Christ, started at Pentecost then the Mosaic Law and circumcision should have long since ceased to be an issue. They were not. Notice first that there was a matter that required judgement and what happened.

> *Acts 15:6*: And the apostles and elders came together to consider of this matter.

The apostles were clearly considered authoritative enough to make judgement on the matter. Once they did, their judgement was accepted as final. The question for judgement was stated in verse 5:

> *Acts 15:5*: But there rose certain of the sect of the Pharisees who believed, saying, That it was needful to circumcise them [the believing Gentiles], and to command them [the believing Gentiles] to keep the Law of Moses.

We know that the "them" was the Gentiles because of the repeated reference to the Gentiles in the discussions and the fact that the final decision was clearly sent to them. Furthermore there was no suggestion that the Jews were in any way released from their ancient stewardship. They still strictly kept the Law. They were keeping fit to be the royal priesthood.

It was James who rendered the decision. Look at his words.

> *Acts 15:13-20*: James answered, saying, Men, brethren, hearken to me: Simeon hath declared how God at the first visited the Gentiles, to take from among them a people for his name. And to this agree the words of the prophets; as it is written, After this I will return, and will build again the tabernacle of David, which is fallen down; and I will build

again its ruins, and I will set it up: That the rest of men may seek after the Lord, and all the Gentiles, upon whom my name is called, saith the Lord, who doeth all these things. Known to God are all his works from the beginning of the world. Wherefore my judgment is, that we trouble not them, who from among the Gentiles are turned to God: But that we write to them, that they abstain from pollutions of idols, and from immorality, and from things strangled, and from blood.

The phrase in this decision by James, "and will build again the tabernacle of David", is evidence that the Apostles still held the lively hope of the restoration of the kingdom to Israel based on Christ's endorsement of the New Covenant, given at the Last Supper, and through His blood on the cross. As was mentioned above, this same James addressed his Epistle to "the twelve tribes" so it becomes evident that his energies were aimed at the restoration and not at the proclamation of a new gospel or the establishment of a new entity called the Body of Christ.

James' further statement, concerning the rebuilding of the tabernacle of David, that it is necessary so that the Gentiles could "seek after the Lord", is fully supported by prophecy. This is surely New Covenant material. The Gentiles were not considered equals with the Jews. They were not required to become proselytes as they would under the Old Covenant and abide by the Law of Moses and the ordinance of circumcision. They were placed under a very limited form of law, with just four rules to follow, it being considered too much to expect them to abide by the complete legal code since even the Jews could not bear the full weight of the Law.

It was always part of prophecy that the Gentiles should share in Israel's blessings, but they were *Israel's* blessings. The Gentiles were in themselves without hope. The presence of Gentiles in what we might call the "church of the kingdom", or the great congregation of Israel, does not suggest that what was being formed was the church of today, the Body of Christ.

Chapter 11 of the Book of Romans makes this clear and it also explains why Gentiles were being saved at that point rather than after Israel accepted the Messiah and the kingdom was established with its royal priesthood. In that chapter Paul speaks of his own status as an Israelite. He reminds his readers how Elijah and David lamented over Israel's unfaithfulness. Then he goes on to make some very enlightening statements.

Romans 11:11: I say then, Have they stumbled that they [the Jews] should fall? By no means: but rather through their fall salvation is come to the Gentiles, to provoke them [the Jews] to jealousy. [My bracket inserts.]

This is it, the Gentiles were at this time being saved in order to provoke the Jews and make them stop and realise that they should perhaps look again at Jesus as the promised Messiah. He carries on:

Romans 11:13-14: For I speak to you Gentiles, inasmuch as I am the apostle of the Gentiles, I magnify my office: If by any means I may provoke to jealousy them who are my flesh, [the Jews] and may save some of them.

Then he issues a warning to the Gentiles and forcefully reminds them of their secondary position to Israel.

Romans 11:17-24: And if some of the branches be broken off, and thou, being a wild olive tree, wast grafted in among them, and with them partakest of the root and fatness of the olive tree; Boast not against the branches. But if thou boastest, thou bearest not the root, but the root thee. Thou wilt say then, The branches were broken off, that I might be grafted in. Well; because of unbelief they were broken off, and thou standest by faith. Be not highminded, but fear: For if God spared not the natural branches, take heed lest he also spare not thee. Behold therefore the goodness and severity of God: on them who fell, severity; but toward thee, goodness, if thou shalt continue in his goodness: otherwise thou also shalt be cut off. And they also, if they abide not still in unbelief, shall be grafted in: for God is able to graft them in again. For if thou wast cut out of the olive tree which is wild by nature, and wast grafted contrary to nature into a good olive tree: how much more shall these, which are the natural branches, be grafted into their own olive tree?

The message is plain, both from God and Paul. In spite of the fact that Paul was chosen as the Apostle to the Gentiles, Israel was God's people at that time regardless of their past unfaithfulness. The root is the root out of Jesse (Isaiah 11:10). The vine and its natural branches are the Jews. The wild olive branches, the Gentiles, have been grafted in to encourage the vine to produce more fruit and can easily be cut out again if they give way to pride. The wild branches receive nourishment from the vine and not the other way around.

Modern man, being immersed in the doctrine of 'my rights', may find difficulty with this. The natural reaction will be that God really should treat us as equals and not show partiality this way. Perhaps it should teach us two things. Firstly, that God is the creator and we are the creatures. His will is sovereign. All we have and are is His. Let us be reminded again of the verse "Is it not lawful for me to do what I will with my own?" (Matthew 20:15). Secondly, it should teach us something about the grace of God. In spite of their unfaithfulness He defended His ancient people and said:

> Romans 11:26-29: And so all Israel shall be saved: as it is written, There shall come out of Zion the Deliverer, and shall turn away ungodliness from Jacob: For this is my covenant to them, when I shall take away their sins. As concerning the gospel, they are enemies for your sakes: but as concerning the election, they are beloved for the fathers' sakes. *For the gifts and calling of God are without repentance.*

He had not yet set them aside, even temporarily. He still had a remnant and would work with them and eventually redeem the Nation.

During the Acts period the Nation of Israel, even though it rejected its King, still accepted the Mosaic Law as binding, at least in principle if not always in spirit. The believing Gentiles were relieved of most of this responsibility by the Jewish leadership of the Acts church (Acts 15). If God's calling is without repentance, and the kingdom was still being offered, and God had promised that he would "put his law in their minds and write it on their hearts", then we need to search the Scriptures to see just how important the Law was to those Jews who had in fact accepted Christ as their King and Lord. This is particularly true of the Apostle Paul, since it is the contention of this book that Paul was commissioned to make known to mankind the gospel of grace, and the church which is the Body of Christ.

Peter, even though he was chosen to be the first to reach out to a Gentile, he never fully lost his hesitancy about fellowshipping with Gentiles, especially in the presence of Jews. He feared offending the Jews (Galatians 2:11-21). Paul was just the opposite. He revelled in his office as apostle to the Gentiles. In spite of this, he longed to see his own people won for the Lord. Whenever he entered a town or city, the first place he went was the synagogue. Each Sabbath he went into the synagogue, opened the Scriptures, and preached from them. This would be the Septuagint translation of Hebrew Scriptures. He preached Christ to the people as Son of God, Messiah and King. Paul expressed his view in Romans 11:1: "I say then, Hath God cast away his people? By no means." This was long after Pentecost.

It was true that the Gentiles were not required to obey the law but Paul himself, at this time, both followed the Law and encouraged the Jewish believers to do likewise. In Acts 21 we read of Paul's return from Caesarea to Jerusalem and his report to the elders. They were thrilled by his report of his success among the Gentiles. Then they brought up a problem that had arisen and presented a solution that would solve it.

> *Acts 21:20-24,26*: They glorified the Lord, and said to him, Thou seest, brother, how many thousands of *Jews* there are who believe; *and they are all zealous of the law*: And they are informed concerning thee, that thou teachest all the Jews who are among the Gentiles to forsake Moses, saying that they ought not to circumcise their children, neither to walk after the customs. What is it therefore? the multitude must needs come together: for they will hear that thou art come. Do therefore this that we say to thee: We have four men who have a vow on them; Take them and purify thyself with them, and pay their expenses that they may shave their heads: and all may know that those things, of which they were informed concerning thee, are nothing; *but that thou thyself also walkest orderly, and keepest the law* ... Then Paul took the men, and the next day purifying himself with them entered into the temple, to signify the accomplishment of the days of purification, until an offering should be offered for every one of them.

It is evident that at this time Paul was not only keeping the Law but also doing all he could to encourage the Jews to do likewise. One might reasonably question why he did so. From other passages such as Romans 15:1, "We then that are strong ought to bear the infirmities of the weak, and not to please ourselves" and Romans 14:20-23, where he compares the dietary laws as secondary to faith, we might conclude that adherence to the Law is just a question of not offending a weaker brother. In 1 Corinthians 8 we read:

1 Corinthians 8:8-9: But food commendeth us not to God: for neither, if we eat, are we the better; neither, if we eat not, are we the worse. But take heed lest by any means this liberty of yours should become a stumblingblock to them that are weak.

In 1 Corinthians 9 he says plainly:

1 Corinthians 9:20: And to the Jews I became as a Jew, that I might gain the Jews; to them that are under the law, as under the law, that I might gain them that are under the law.

Note, however, that while he realised that the spirit of the Law, is more important than the letter of the Law, and he himself felt that he was free from its restrictions, he still regarded the Jews as "those that are under the law". The fact that he placed himself under the Law, out of love for his kin and the desire to win them, did not alter the fact that he recognised their position as inheritors of the kingdom under the New Covenant. Both motivations were present, love for his people and preaching the kingdom as prophesied.

Even when Paul was taken before the authorities he still maintained his respect for the Law. He called Ananias "thou whitewashed wall" for acting contrary to the Law. So far as we know there was no believing Jew present to offend so that his behaviour must have been a natural response. When he found out that Ananias was the high priest he apologised for his own actions as being unscriptural and, therefore, contrary to Law (Acts 23).

After his appearance before Ananias, Paul was held as a prisoner and subjected to a series of trials before various officials. Eventually he was sent to Rome as a prisoner where the events of Acts 28 took place. There was no further historical record in Scripture of his or the other Apostles' activities, other than those inferred indirectly in the later Pauline epistles.

Some of his statements to his various inquisitors substantively reflect and summarise the character of the gospel he was preaching and bear comparison with the gospel of grace as taught in his later epistles. The difference between the two gospels is of great consequence in our understanding of God's word and requires our faithful contemplation.

Before Felix Paul said, "But this I confess to thee ... I worship the God of my fathers, believing all things which are written in the law and in the prophets" (Acts 24:14).

However, before long Felix was replaced in office by Porcius Festus. There followed a series of interviews and Paul said to Festus:

> *Acts 25:8*: Neither against the law of the Jews, neither against the temple, nor yet against Caesar, have I committed any offence.

At the request of King Agrippa he was brought up before Agrippa and Festus for questioning. Bear in mind that this was at a point well on in his ministry so that it represented in a real way a summary of what his message had been.

> *Acts 26:19-23*: Upon which, O king Agrippa, I was not disobedient to the heavenly vision: But showed first to them of Damascus, and at Jerusalem, and throughout all the region of Judaea, and then to the Gentiles, that they should repent and turn to God, and do works fit for repentance. For these causes the Jews caught me in the temple, and went about to kill me. Having therefore obtained help from God, I continue to this day, testifying both to small and great, *saying no other things than those which the prophets and Moses did say should come:* That Christ should suffer, and that he should be the first that should rise from the dead, and should show light to *the people, **and to** the Gentiles*.

After this interview Paul could have been freed but, since he had appealed to Caesar as a Roman citizen, he was sent under guard to Rome. Some incidents that took place during the journey are of special interest. During the sea voyage to Rome the ship foundered on Malta. We read this amazing description of what happened.

> *Acts 28:2-6*: And the barbarous people showed us no little kindness: for they kindled a fire, and received us every one, because of the present rain, and because of the cold. And when Paul had gathered a bundle of sticks, and laid them on the fire, there came a viper out of the heat, and fastened on his hand. And when the barbarians saw the animal hang on his hand, they said among themselves, No doubt this man is a murderer, whom, though he hath escaped the sea, yet justice alloweth not to live. And he shook off the animal into the fire, and felt no harm. Yet they looked when he should have

swelled, or fallen down dead suddenly: but after they had looked a great while, and saw no harm come to him, they changed their minds, and said that he was a god.

From there he went to Rome. Following his usual practice, even though he was a prisoner with a Roman soldier to guard him, he immediately called the leaders of the Roman Jewish community together to witness to them, rather than to the Roman Christians; (note: the Jew first). He told them about his imprisonment and the reason for his calling them together.

> *Acts 28:20*: For this cause therefore have I called for you, to see you, and to speak with you: *because that for the hope of Israel I am bound with this chain.*

They agreed to hear him and at the appointed day came to his house.

> *Acts 28:23*: to whom he expounded and testified *the kingdom of God*, persuading them concerning Jesus, both out of *the law Moses*, and out of *the prophets*, from morning till evening.

As a group they refused to accept Jesus as their King, their Lord, their Christ (the Messiah). They represented the last group that the Holy Spirit, through Paul, would offer the kingdom to at that time. In the future God will resurrect the dry bones of the Nation and take the redeemed people to Himself, but for now He set them aside! Had they as a valid remnant received their King then the kingdom might well have been brought into being then, at that time. As it was, God delivered His sentence on them in Paul's words.

> *Acts 28:28*: Be it known therefore to you, that the salvation of God is sent to the Gentiles, and they will hear it.

Again we come back to the verse that I have described as central to my thesis. Before going on let us look at some of the points in the last set of quotes. Remember, this is Paul describing his own position up to this juncture; i.e. at that time.

Before Felix
  •   Believed in the *law* and the *prophets*.

Before Festus
- Committed no offence against the *law of the Jews* or the *temple*.

Before Festus and Agrippa
- Taught works for repentance - law, starting after Damascus with Jerusalem, Judea, and only then to the Gentiles, the same pattern repeated again.
- *Saying no other things other than those that the prophets and Moses said should come:*
- That Christ should show the light to *the people* (Israel), and to *the Gentiles*.

Before the barbarous people
- Bit by a poisonous serpent without harm as the Lord promised to His apostles, a sign of the kingdom gospel.

Before the Jews in Rome
- B*ecause that for the hope of Israel I am bound with this chain.*
- He expounded *the kingdom of God*, out of the Law of Moses, and *the prophets*.

Summary

Through all of these last quotes, as through the whole book of Acts, some thoughts are repeated over and over again. There is continual reference to the Law, (called the Law of Moses or the Law of the Jews), the prophets, especially Moses, the fathers, the promises, the kingdom, and Jesus as King or Messiah. We are told that all these things pertain to the "circumcision" or the Jew. We are told salvation is of or from the Jew. The Jew first is emphasised and sometimes the followers are told to go only to the lost sheep of the House of Israel. It is Israel's blessings that the Gentiles are to share in.

John the Baptist cried in the wilderness "Repent ye: for the *kingdom* of heaven is at hand." Christ offered Himself as King when He declared, "The kingdom of heaven is at hand." On the Day of Pentecost Peter reminded "Ye men of Israel" that Christ was to sit on the throne of David. Now Paul, the apostle unto the uncircumcision, repeats the same teaching. He said that everything he taught was simply the subject of prophecy. There was nothing essentially new. He also said that he was bound "for the hope of Israel".

The hope of Israel was the kingdom restored, the Messianic rule of the Christ. This was the central subject of prophecy and the object of the promises. Abraham had been promised that all the nations would be blessed in his seed and he looked forward to the coming of the New Jerusalem. David was guaranteed that one would sit on his throne in perpetuity. The Old Covenant had offered the kingdom. The New Covenant had assured it, in spite of the unfaithfulness of the Nation. With these notable statements Paul declares that his teaching was one with what had been taught before.

At the beginning of this book I stated that I would attempt to show that the "Church" of today did not start at Pentecost but rather at some point at or after the end of the Book of Acts. It is my contention that Paul was the instrument through which God revealed a new gospel and a new stewardship, or 'dispensation', to man. As I stated earlier, it seems reasonable that a truly new administration must involve a new purpose, a new message and a new administrator. One other element should be present: God should call it a new dispensation (stewardship). The defining of such a major element of Scripture should not simply be decided on arbitrarily by men, no matter how noble the intent is or how respected the person or group making the decision is.

If my contention is correct then none of the four requirements of a New Stewardship are present in the Acts period, but only the marks of the Old and New Covenants. The events of the Day of Pentecost are dramatic in themselves, but that does not indicate a change in teaching. Rather it represents a fulfilment of prophecy, one more in a series of signs designed to affirm to the Jews the authority of the Apostles as stewards of the Kingdom.

Test the four requirements that I have postulated as they apply to the five items listed in the title of this chapter.

The Jew

Since Abraham's summons from Ur, Abraham's seed, the Israelites, were chosen of God to be the stewards of the Old Dispensation. They had been promised both a kingdom and that the Chosen One of Israel would occupy David's throne in perpetuity. God promised that the kingdom would be restored in spite of Israel's disobedience, by the giving of the New Covenant. Christ came as a minister to Israel to confirm the promises. Christ sent His followers to the Jews only, and then to the Jews first. He had declared that salvation is of the Jew!

On the Day of Pentecost Peter addressed the Jews and reiterated the promises concerning the kingdom. Nothing on the Day of Pentecost suggests a change in the status of the Jew.

After Pentecost the Christian Jews became the governing body of the Acts church. Appeals were made for rulings on doctrine and practice to Jerusalem. The Jew was still in a superior position in all ways. The council of Jerusalem confirmed the Jews' position. Paul constantly reaffirmed the Jew's position by always going to the Jews and the synagogue first whenever he entered a city. And even in almost the last act recorded before the Jews were finally set aside, he declares that it was for the hope of Israel that he was bound.

To the very end of the Acts period the status of Israel had not changed from what it was in the Old Testament. Paul and the Apostles, as affirmed by Paul's own statement, taught nothing but what was prophesied by Moses and the prophets. Israel was still the administrator of God's grace as the future royal priesthood. The message of God's grace through faith, with works following, had not changed. The purpose was still the restoration of God's rule on earth through the kingdom. The Scriptures do not say that the church of Acts is the instrument of a New Stewardship.

The Gentile

God's will was always that all mankind would be brought back to Himself in love. Even before the calling of Abraham, God had possessed a witness on earth of individuals who served and worshipped Him; Seth, Noah, Enoch, Melchisedek, and others, who witnessed to His grace. When He chose Abraham and his seed He changed only His administrator, not His love for all the Nations. The seed of Abraham were to be *the* Nation amongst the Nations. Gentiles could always, by submission to Israel, become proselytes and share in Israel's blessing.

At Pentecost the Gentiles were not even mentioned. The giving of power was intended to equip Israel as a royal priesthood to reach the Nations, enabling them to reach out to the Gentiles with God's blessing as they were supposed to do. Peter's speech was a re-offering of the kingdom to Israel, not a beginning of a new body or a Gentile church.

After Pentecost Gentiles were saved by being grafted into

Israel, which is basically nothing new. Gentiles were still not God's stewards in today's sense. In spite of the fact that Peter recognised God's blessing on the Gentiles he still was nervous in their presence. Until Acts 28:28 the Gentiles were second to the Jews and God had not sent His salvation to the Gentiles independently of the Jews. Pentecost did not change either the position of the Jews or the Gentiles before God.

The Law

The Law was given at Sinai to Israel. It was given in addition to the Abrahamic Covenant. Jews, in order to receive God's blessing, had to submit to God's Lordship and obey the Law: not one or the other but both. It had to be in spirit, not only in the letter of the Law. There had to be a willing obedience; salvation by grace followed by the works of the Law. At Pentecost there was no suggestion of release from the Law for Israel. There was only a reminder of the prophecies and assurance of their fulfilment through Messiah Christ Jesus. The Law was intended to lead men to Christ.

After Pentecost the Law still held sway over Israel. Such ordinances as the feast of the Passover are to be continued in Christ's presence even in the future Messianic kingdom. The full weight of the Law was never imposed as a requirement on the Gentiles. Paul under the direction of the apostles still, as a Jew, practised the Law in his own life and recognised its need for the Jews. Pentecost had not changed the purpose, the message or the administrator of the law. God had not done away with Law as an integral part of that Stewardship.

Paul

In Philippians 3 Paul described his state before his Damascus road conversion.

> *Philippians 3:4-6*: Though I might also have confidence in the flesh. If any other man thinketh that he hath reason to trust in the flesh, I more: Circumcised the eighth day, of the stock of Israel, of the tribe of Benjamin, an Hebrew of the Hebrews; with respect to the law, a Pharisee; Concerning zeal, persecuting the church; with respect to the righteousness which is by the law, blameless.

Clearly Paul had been first, last, and always a Jew. He had been saved after Pentecost so he had no part in it. Then, up until his statement of Acts 28:28, according to his own words, his ministry had been confined strictly to the prophesied gospel, the promised kingdom. His first consideration was always the Jew and the hope of Israel; the Jew was first and foremost. Signs confirmed his authority to Israel, because the Jew required a sign. The Gentile was being grafted into Israel but not as an equal. Now the same gospel was being directed to the Gentile because of Israel's unwillingness to believe.

> *Acts 28:27*: For the heart of this people is become dull, and their ears are dull of hearing, and their eyes have they closed; lest they should see with their eyes, and hear with their ears, and understand with their heart, and should be converted, and I should heal them.

Then Paul told the Nation that God had sent His salvation to the Gentiles. The Nation had been set aside (temporarily) but not the gospel. The stewards had been changed and God, at that time, declared a new stewardship, but more had to happen and it did. Paul was at the centre of it, but before we go into what did happen there is one more matter to consider.

Christ

Jesus is our Creator, Saviour, and Lord, under all conditions and circumstances. He is God incarnate. This can never change. The Lord He is our God. He has revealed Himself in different ways to different people at different times.

In Eden God walked with man in the cool of the evening. He spoke to men in dreams and gave His will in tablets of stone. He spoke through prophets and led men with signs. He wrought vengeance and punished. He forgave and protected. He became a baby, the Son of God, and as King He was the Son of David. He lived as the Son of Man. He died willingly on Calvary as God's sacrifice for our sin. He rose as God's conqueror and ascended as victor.

Each revelation He gives, each name He has, each relationship He provides, each stewardship He grants, adds to His majesty. We ought therefore to look with great reverence at each aspect of Holy Scripture to learn what God would have us know of Himself.

In the New Testament Jesus is called "Master", "Lord",

"Rabboni", "Christ", "Messiah", and by other names. Of interest to us at this point in this study is the designation of "King".

It is necessary to refine further some of the definitions and terms noted earlier in this work. I have spoken of the "Body" as the "Church which is the Body of Christ", and listed the "Body Truth" as being contained in the Pauline books written *after* Acts 28:28, which are Philippians, Philemon, Colossians, Ephesians, 1 Timothy, Titus, and 2 Timothy. All the rest of the New Testament, by exclusion, falls under the heading of "Kingdom Truth".

There is a problem. Given some statements in the Bible, it may seem that my division of the Bible into "Body truth" and "Kingdom truth" is arbitrary and wrong division. We cannot divide God's word properly if we only consider what is convenient to our own purpose. The problem lies in the fact that the term "body" referring to God's assembled people or church occurs in two passages in what I have called "kingdom truth". The naming of the two portions is arbitrary just as the dividing of the Bible into two "testaments" or the division into chapter and verse of the Greek text is arbitrary but I believe that the division itself can be shown to be justified on the basis of internal evidence.

The word "body" is used for the Greek word *soma*, which is used 146 times in the New Testament. In general it means just what we would expect, the collective corporate substance of men, animals, plants, or stars, (heavenly bodies) whether living or dead. It is also used of a large or small number of people closely united into one society; a social, ethical or mystical body. In some cases it is used to refer to a church as the instances under consideration. The symbolism is obvious. What is not so obvious is the fact that just as there is more than one church of Christ there may also be more than one body of Christ. A single word or phrase repeated does not necessarily refer to the same entity but must be looked at carefully in context.

In Ephesians and Colossians the "Body of Christ" is referred to and, speaking of Christ, Colossians 1:18 says, "And He is the Head of the body, the church". The importance is the relationship between the "Head" (Christ) and the members, the believers. This relationship that I have labelled "Body Truth" will be investigated in more detail later.

Now look into what I have called "Kingdom Truth" in the books of Romans and 1 Corinthians. In Romans 12 it is written:

Romans 12:4-5: For as we have many members in one body,

and all members have not the same office: So we, being many, are one body in Christ, and every one members one of another.

In 1 Corinthians 12 Paul writes in verse 27, "Now ye are the body of Christ, and members in particular", but notice some of the things that are said in this chapter of this "body".

> *1 Corinthians 12:12,14,16,20-21,25*: For as the body is one, and hath many members, and all the members of that one body, being many, are one body: so also is Christ ... For the body is not one member, but many ... And if the ear shall say, Because I am not the eye, I am not of the body; is it therefore not of the body? ... But now are they many members, yet but one body. And the eye cannot say to the hand, I have no need of thee: nor again the head to the feet, I have no need of you ... That there should be no schism in the body; but that the members should have the same care one for another.

In these instances the subject is not the relationship between Christ as head and the believers as members, but *between* believers as co-members of the body. Notice also that in these passages the believers themselves, and not Christ, are depicted as the head or parts of the head. The picture of a body is being used to instruct Christians as to how they should behave towards each other.

Romans and 1 Corinthians were both written during the time described in the Book of Acts and therefore form part of the message of that period. Since the predominant message of that time was the salvation through the restored kingdom it follows that this "body" is an assembly of Jews and Gentiles bonded together under Israel's hope. They look to Christ as King and Messiah, not as "Head of the Body" as in Ephesians and Colossians.

The question may still be posed as to the appropriateness of calling the one set of truth "Kingdom Truth", and the other "Body Truth" when the expression "Body of Christ" is mentioned in both portions. It is as I have stated, arbitrary and a matter of convenience. There is one overarching difference that indicates many other differences. This difference is that the primary focus in one case is Christ's identity as the Messiah, the "King Saviour" of Israel, and in the other as "personal Saviour", Head of the Body. Thus it is possible to simply identify two stewardships without always using elaborate structures such as "the church, which is his body, the fullness of him that filleth all in all" (Ephesians 1:22-23).

One way used to study the Bible is to look at the frequency with which a word or words are used in a portion and make comparisons with another portion. This is not conclusive evidence but it often serves to highlight themes. A more exhaustive study in which each occurrence is examined in context will render greater understanding but for our purposes the following statistics may be helpful.

Comparison of Frequency in the New Testament

	Kingdom Truth	Body Truth
Law	215	8
King	89	2
Kingdom	153	5
Total	457	15

Frequency of "Kingdom" in combination with "Heaven" and "God":

Kingdom of Heaven	32	1
Kingdom of God	69	1

These numbers represent occurrences in the *KJV*. They will vary in other translations. They do not correspond to the Greek words that are often translated with different English words. In addition to this it should be noted that the books comprising the "Body Truth" are much smaller in volume than the books of "Kingdom Truth". Therefore, a simple direct unit for unit comparison is difficult. However, added to the preponderance of words related to the Messianic status of Christ in the Kingdom Truth is the fact that He is never called "the head of the Body" in the Kingdom Truth books, but only is in the later letters of Paul.

Through all this one thing should be clear, during the Acts period Christ was presented as King of Israel and was king over *that body* which is spoken of before Acts 28:28, with the message being the Messianic Kingdom. That body's structure would seem to be indistinguishable from things prophesied in the New Covenant. Its members' purpose is to prepare the way for the King and bring the Gentiles under His loving and absolute rule. Their message is that the kingdom is at hand, but only if the Nation receives their Lord. That

Nation of Israel is the primary administrator of the gospel as a royal priesthood. Their hope is to rule with Him.

Conclusion

The evidence so far indicates that the church of today, "the church, Which is his body, the fullness of him that filleth all in all." (Ephesians 1:23) "And he is the head of the body, the church" (Colossians 1:18)], did not and could not have begun at Pentecost. The reason is that the church (*ekklesia*) of the Acts period after Pentecost was the same church that was in existence before Pentecost. Pentecost did not begin a new work. It was simply the empowering of God's Stewards, Abraham's seed. The Gentiles were brought in to provoke and stimulate Israel so that the Nation would carry out the work that they were called to by the New Covenant.

The purpose had not changed. The message had not changed. The Stewards had not changed. The hope had not changed. Their hope was an earth bound hope of resurrection and the restoration of God's rule over His own corporate creation. Conclusively, God did not call what happened at Pentecost a New Stewardship!

Chapter 12
PAUL AND THE CHURCH TODAY
(The Body of Christ)
The Jew; The Gentile; The Law; Paul; Christ

In the introduction to this book I mentioned that a comparison is made between the teaching of Christ in the Gospels and the things spoken of by Paul in his epistles. The conclusion often arrived at is that Paul, for all his good intentions, made some mistakes. Alternatively, differences are often spiritualised out of existence. The "Church" becomes spiritual Israel; the "Kingdom" becomes Heaven, and so on with an infinite variety of possibilities. There is a third way of approaching the problem. That is that the differences are real, important, and in accordance with God's will. "Test the things that differ" (*KJV* margin, Philippians 1:10).

In the material presented up to now, I am aware that I have tended to be repetitive, but have done so with the aim of emphasising the substantial unity in teaching of the Old Testament, with that portion of the New Testament that I have labelled "Kingdom Truth". However, after the events of Acts 28:25-27, Paul is given a new message that is dramatically different. This new message is the foundation of the 'Church of today'.

Under house arrest in Rome, Paul called the Jews together and spoke of "the hope of Israel". However, a little while later he wrote that "the salvation of God" was sent to the Gentiles. It was the same message of salvation for he spent two further years "preaching the kingdom of God". The identity of the steward of God had changed but the message of salvation had not. At some point, after that time, and we do not know exactly when, Paul received a new gospel, a message of good news that was radically different to what had been known up to this point.

That message was contained in the seven letters written by Paul after the end of the events recorded in Acts 28:25-28. All the rest of the Old Testament and the "Kingdom Truth" has its foundation in the Pentateuch, the five Mosaic books of the Law. All the rest are in effect an elaboration and a fulfilment of God's promises and covenants of that first oracle. In the same manner the books of Ephesians and Colossians are the oracles of the new administration.

In one sense we could say that Ephesians and Colossians are

the books of 'the law' for 'the Church today'. The sense in which they are 'the law' is the same as when we speak of a law of nature. A law of nature is not a regulation or an ordinance that must be obeyed, but rather it is a simple observation of the way things are. When we speak of the law of gravity, we simply are saying that we observe that apples fall to the ground unless something else prevents it happening. In the same way, when Ephesians 2:8 says "For by grace are ye saved through faith; and that not of yourselves: it is the gift of God", it is a simple statement of fact. Other than in this very special context the word "Law" in Bible study refers to the Law of Moses and is usually contrasted with "Grace".

We do not know the manner in which God gave this new revelation to Paul, but then we do not know much about how He spoke to any of the men who penned the Scriptures, other than in a few instances such as at Sinai and some dreams and visions. As to the time, it must have come shortly after the end of the book of Acts, possibly after the two years mentioned. Many consider the destruction of Jerusalem with the temple in A.D. 70 to be the final setting aside of the Nation but the message had probably been issued earlier and from the Scriptures, we can see that the Jew had lost his first place earlier than A.D. 70. At any rate a whole new era had begun between God and man.

Let us look at some of the specific statements that make it clear that something new is being presented.

> *Ephesians 3:1-9*: For this cause I Paul, *the prisoner of Jesus Christ for you Gentiles,* If ye have heard of *the dispensation of the grace of God* which is given me on your account: That by revelation he made known to me the mystery; as I wrote before in few words, By which, when ye read, ye may understand my knowledge in *the mystery of Christ Which in other ages was not made known to the sons of men,* as it is now revealed to his holy apostles and prophets by the Spirit; *That the Gentiles should be joint heirs, and of the same body, and joint partakers of his promise in Christ by the gospel*: Of which I was made a minister, according to the gift of the grace of God given to me by the effectual working of his power.
>
> To me, who am less than the least of all saints, is this grace given, that I should preach among the Gentiles *the unsearchable riches of Christ*; And to make all men see what is the fellowship of the *mystery, which from the beginning of*

the world hath been hid in God, who created all things by Jesus Christ:

These statements are very explicit. They are the kind of statements that must either be taken at face value or rejected outright. Paul was either the recipient of a new revelation or he was a fake. The statements are so contrary to all the rest of the Bible that we must reasonably accept them as they stand or reject Paul's entire later ministry, that is, his *last seven letters*! If we reject these books then why should we accept any of his writings, and if the Bible can be so flawed then why not reject the Bible itself?

Would any one care to suggest that Paul became so enraged at the Jews for their refusal to accept Jesus as Messiah that he simply invented this later teaching to degrade them? These last sentences lead us into such a downward spiral of doubt and weakened faith that it is necessary to stop and say, "Is this Bible God's Word or just cunningly devised fables?" For my part I believe that it is God's infallible Word in its original manuscripts and I will follow its teachings wherever they lead me, even contrary to man's tradition.

Look at Ephesians 3:1. In Acts Paul had been "bound" for the hope of *Israel*. Now he is "the prisoner of Jesus Christ for *you Gentiles*". He sees himself one with the Gentiles, but remember that the term Gentile (Gr. *ethnos*) means people or nations. No longer is it a matter of the Jew first and also the Greek (*hellenos*) i.e. the Gentiles who had adopted Greek culture. The Nation has been set aside and now is only one nation amongst all the nations. It was the Nation of Israel as such that was set aside as God's stewards not the individual Jew. Paul was still a Jew and he began setting out a new set of teaching and a new stewardship.

The next few verses make statements that are breathtaking in scope and implication. In the second chapter of this book I mentioned that the Greek word *oikonomia* was used in Ephesians and Colossians but that I would discuss those uses later for they were central to the theme of this book. I would ask you to remember that there *is* reason to reject its use as meaning "a time period" and substitute the word "stewardship" or a calling to responsibility.

The Book of Ephesians is addressed in this manner: "Paul, an apostle of Jesus Christ by the will of God, to the saints who are at Ephesus, and to the faithful in Christ Jesus". No longer is it to the "Hebrews" or to the "twelve tribes scattered among the nations"; it is to the "saints" and "the faithful in Christ Jesus". The epistle may have been a circular letter, sent to all the churches, since the name Ephesus does not appear in the earliest manuscripts. A space presumably was left so that the various church names could be entered as it was passed about. The copy to Ephesus was the one that survived.

In the third chapter Paul told these Gentile saints that God has given him a stewardship (dispensation) for them. He claims that this "mystery", or secret, was made known to him by revelation. It was clearly not something that came out of what had been taught up to then. Statements in the next few verses declare in the strongest possible terms that *"the mystery of Christ"* is something completely new and unique! Its very uniqueness is the reason why it had to come by revelation. The teaching was different from anything in the Old or New Testaments. It was still based on the sacrifice of Christ for the sins of man.

These last two sentences appear to be contradictory but they are not. The basis of God's redemption of man always and under all circumstances rests on His irrevocable decision at the time of the expulsion from Eden that the seed of the woman would bruise the head of the serpent. How, or in what ways, was not told at that time. 1 Timothy 2:5 states it clearly, "For there is one God, and one mediator between God and men, the man Christ Jesus". These two ideas, God's omnipotence, and Christ's mediatorship, are not dispensational in nature but are the determination of eternal God, and are therefore the foundation of all stewardships.

The details of the "stewardships", on the other hand, must be revealed to the stewards in order for them to act as stewards, but this at such a time as pleases God. The timing of the revelation is the critical point. What Paul was making known to the Ephesians at that time, was new and unique because God, in His wisdom, had chosen to keep it secret in Himself until that time. It is written in Ephesians 3:9; "the mystery, which from the beginning of the world hath been hid in God, who created all things by Jesus Christ".

Remember that the word "mystery" means "secret". God had planned this stewardship from the start. It was only a "secret" to man because man had not been told about it. This means that it was not hidden in the Old Testament Scriptures, or the earlier parts of the New Testament, since it states that it was "hid in God" not "hid in the promises" or "hid in prophecy". There were many things in the Old Testament that the believers did not understand, but that was their own failure. Those things were there to see, for people of faith.

The "secret" was one "which in other ages *was not made*

known to the sons of men". Compare this with what Paul had openly stated before Agrippa, "I continue to this day, testifying both to small and great, saying *no other things than those which the prophets and Moses did say should come"*. Those things that were prophesied were made known to the sons of men, even if the men did not understand or believe them. Clearly, that which had been revealed to Paul between the end of Acts and the writing of the Book of Ephesians, "the mystery hid in God", was not the subject of prophecy. It could not be traced in the Old Testament nor was it the fulfilment of the promises unto the fathers.

Indeed, in the verse immediately before, saying that the mystery was hid in God, Paul tells the saints, "To me ..... is this grace given, that I should preach among the Gentiles the unsearchable riches of Christ" (Ephesians 3:8). The word "unsearchable" is equivalent to "untraceable". The same Greek word is used only one other time in the Bible, in Romans 11:33, and is translated "past finding out". Our first reaction to the word "unsearchable" is to think of it as meaning that the "riches of Christ" are so vast that they are beyond comprehension. It is true that with our finite minds we cannot begin to know in fullness all there is to know about our infinite Lord, but the subject of this passage is the gospel of the grace of God that Paul has been commissioned to preach to the Gentiles. The gospel is so simple that a child can receive Christ, for the gospel is not beyond its comprehension.

If there is a "mystery" or "secret" which was never before revealed, then we need to ask ourselves just what it was and how different it was to that which was known before. This is where the terms that have been referred to frequently before become useful. "Body Truth" is the statement of this New Stewardship as recorded by Paul, it is the "mystery of Christ". "Kingdom Truth" is all that was recorded in the rest of the Bible. Recently a friend told me of a study he was doing on the differences between these two stewardships and at that time he had discovered 60. That would be beyond the scope of this study. We need only to consider enough differences to establish the fact that the two gospels are sufficiently different as to constitute two distinct unities.

The method of presenting "Pairs to Compare" will be utilised. Some earlier material will be repeated and *Kingdom Truth*, and *Body Truth*, will be contrasted.

Point 1: oracles - stewardship

Kingdom Truth:

Romans 3:1-2: "What advantage then hath the Jew? ... Much every way: chiefly, because that to them were committed the oracles of God." The substance of the Kingdom stewardship was committed to Israel through the revelation of the Bible truth given to them.

Body Truth:

Paul said that by revelation was given him "the stewardship of the grace of God" on the account of "you Gentiles" (Ephesians 3:1-6). This is a new administration of God's message to man.

Point 2: Israel rules - all one in Christ

Kingdom Truth:

The body of believers of the Kingdom Truth is constituted of Israel, as a royal priesthood (Exodus 19:6), and the Gentiles, who are blessed through Abraham's seed (Genesis 12:3). Israel rules. Gentiles serve. There is no equality between them. Mankind is divided into Jew, believing Gentile, and non-believer.

Body Truth:

Ephesians 3:6 states "That the Gentiles should be joint heirs, and of the same body, and partakers of his promise in Christ by the gospel". This is more than equality. By this statement the Jew and the Gentile become virtually indistinguishable. It no longer matters whether one is Jew or Gentile. All are one in Christ. We are "joint heirs". Mankind is divided into believer and non-believer.

Point 3: salvation of Jews - salvation in Christ

Kingdom Truth:

Christ said in John 4:22, *"for salvation is from **the Jews**"*. He came to His own, and in the kingdom His grace was given through them. He was their King. They were His appointed mediators.

Body Truth:

In 2 Timothy 2:10 we read, "that they may also obtain the *salvation which is in Christ Jesus*". The believer is now saved "in Christ" with no mediator but Christ.

Point 4: King over Israel - Head over body

Kingdom Truth:

Christ is always presented as "King" over the Nation in Kingdom Truth, never as "Head" of the body. Christ is God incarnate, and as God He is King and Lord over all. When He was born of Mary He came as the Son of God and the Son of Man, to sit on the throne of His father David. He came as Messiah King over Israel and the Gentiles who were grafted in to the olive tree (Israel). The Apostles recognised Him as such. The church of Acts was a body of believers subject to Christ as King.

Body Truth:

In the "Mystery", Christ is Head over the church which is His Body, the fullness of Christ. Twice in Body Truth the title "king" is used of Him, but in both cases it is used in reference to eternal God, not specifically to Christ's relationship with the church.

Point 5: signs, healings - no signs

Kingdom Truth:

The Book of Acts is filled with the record of signs and wonders, just as Christ's own ministry was. It is recorded that on the journey to Rome, just before the events of Acts 28:28, people came to Paul for healing and they were healed. This is in addition to the incident of his protection from a poisonous snake. The Jew required a sign.

Body Truth:

Signs and wonders were no longer needed. It was never intended that miraculous healing should keep people alive forever. It is appointed unto man once to die. Paul, like the rest of the Apostles, had been able to exercise miraculous healing power. Now in 1 Timothy, we see him saying to his beloved son in Christ, "Drink no longer water, but use a little wine for thy stomach's sake and thy frequent infirmities" (1 Timothy 5:23). If Paul still had the power of miracles he would surely have healed Timothy by that power but he did not. A new order had come into being. Believers must now receive Christ by faith alone, without any miraculous evidence.

Point 6: legal forgiveness - grace forgiveness

Kingdom Truth:

In what is called 'The Lord's Prayer', (although it would more appropriately be called 'the apostles' prayer'), one of the statements relates to forgiveness.

> Matthew 6:12,14-15: And forgive us our debts, as we forgive our debtors ... For if ye forgive men their trespasses, your heavenly Father will also forgive you: But if ye forgive not men their trespasses, neither will your Father forgive your trespasses.

This is legal forgiveness and clearly forgiveness, under this, depends upon behaviour. If we forgive, we are forgiven. If we do not, we are not. It is a concept of Law, given by Christ to His followers while they were under the Law. It was valid as long as the Law held sway. It was not grace! Under Law economy, the individual forgives not out of pure love but at least in part in order to gain forgiveness for himself. God's favour was a matter of covenant agreement.

Body Truth:

By contrast, in Ephesians and Colossians we learn the terms of God's favour and forgiveness under grace.

> *Ephesians 4:32*: And be ye kind one to another, tenderhearted, forgiving one another, even as God for Christ's sake hath forgiven you.

> *Colossians 2:13*: And you, being dead in your sins and the un-circumcision of your flesh, hath he made alive together with

him, having forgiven you all trespasses;

This is *grace*! Under Kingdom Truth they had to forgive in order to be forgiven. We forgive *because we already have been forgiven!* When we receive Christ as Lord, we are assured that He has "forgiven you all trespasses". We love because He first loved us. We forgive because He first forgave us. The Jews worked under the terms of the covenant. We work just to please Him and thank Him for our forgiveness. Our salvation was finished at Calvary. We have been forgiven.

Point 7: grace + law - grace + nothing

Kingdom Truth:

Through the Book of Acts it is apparent that the Jews were still under the Law just as they were during Christ's earthly ministry, and just as they were during the Old Testament period. In these matters nothing had changed. Obedience to the letter of the Law without the spirit of the Law was never acceptable to God. Look at the first chapter of Isaiah for God's judgment on empty, formal ritual. Grace from God was always present, starting with the blessings of Eden and the clothing of Adam and Eve after their sin, the promise of a Saviour to the woman, the choosing of Abram, even the giving of the Mosaic Law, going right through Christ's prayer of forgiveness on the cross, and the re-offering of the Kingdom right up to the setting aside of the Nation at Acts 28:28. None of these things came because of man's worth. They came only out of the depth of God's love.

Grace was there, but so was Law! Consider again Deuteronomy 6:25: "*And this shall be our righteousness*, if we observe to do all these commandments before the Lord our God, as He hath commanded us." Cain and Abel were required to give sacrifice even before the Mosaic Law was given. Abraham and the fathers of the Nation raised altars to God. Moses had delivered to him, the formal requirements of the Law of ordinances. Christ honoured the office of high priest even though the incumbent was corrupt. At the council of Jerusalem the Jews were not released from the Law and the Gentiles were commanded to observe a limited structure of Law. Right up until Rome, Paul observed the Law personally and urged others to do likewise. The Kingdom gospel was God's *grace plus the works of the Law* for righteousness.

Body Truth:

With the setting aside of Israel many things changed, not the least of these was the works of the Law as a requirement for righteousness. The apostles had addressed Paul "but that thou thyself also walkest orderly, and keepest the law" (Acts 21:24). His own confession before Felix was, "I worship the God of my fathers, believing all things which are written in *the law* and in the prophets" (Acts 24:14). This man Paul, respected, practised, and taught the Law, right up to the point that God set aside the Kingdom gospel and the Nation.

With no previous suggestion of anything of the kind, look at what he taught in Colossians 2.

> *Colossians 2:13-17*: And you, being dead in your sins and the uncircumcision of your flesh, hath he made alive together with him, *having forgiven you all trespasses*; *Blotting out the handwriting of ordinances* that was against us, which was contrary to us, and took it out of the way, nailing it to his cross; And having overcome principalities and powers, he made a show of them openly, triumphing over them in it. *Let no man therefore judge you* in *food*, or in *drink*, or *in respect of an feast day*, or of *the new moon*, or of *the sabbaths*: Which are a shadow of things to come; but the body is of Christ.

This same man, Paul, who had clung to the ordinances of the Law, who had carefully observed each necessity lest he offend any one of the Jews, now says boldly that God was in Christ "*blotting out the handwriting of ordinances* that was against us ..... nailing it to his cross." Paul had observed each Sabbath and agreed to the imposing of the four requirements on the Gentiles and the retention of all the Law on the Jews. Now, to joint members of the Body, he says:

> *Let no man therefore judge you*
>   -in *food*,
>   -or in *drink*,
>   -or *in respect of an feast day*,
>   -or of *the new moon*,
>   -or of *the sabbaths*:

In Galatians he had told the reason for the Law:

> *Galatians 3:24-25*: Wherefore the law was our schoolmaster

to bring us to Christ, that we might be justified by faith. But after faith is come, we are no longer under a schoolmaster.

In the Galatians period Law was still in force but now Law has become "a shadow of things to come"; Christ is the reality. Now we are in Christ. All we have or need is a gift from Him. Paul states it clearly in Ephesians 2:

> *Ephesians 2:8-9*: For by grace are ye saved through faith; and that not of yourselves: it is the gift of God: Not by works, lest any man should boast.

We are saved and made righteous by His grace alone.

Point 8: hope of Israel - mystery of Christ

Kingdom Truth:

All through the Bible, right up until Acts 28:28 Israel had been promised a sure and certain hope, the kingdom upon the earth. It is the one for which Paul had considered himself bound in Acts 28:20. It was the Kingdom of the Messiah who was to sit on the throne of David. Abraham looked for it. Moses prophesied it. David was sure of it. The Apostles enquired about it. Christ guaranteed it.

The hope of the kingdom for Israel was what made the Nation the centrepiece, apart from Christ Himself, of God's plan of redemption in the Old Testament and the New, except for Paul's last seven letters.

When Paul spoke of being bound with this chain for the hope of Israel, he was speaking of the goal towards which he and all believers were then striving. Just as John the Baptist was committed to preparing the way for the Messiah, so ultimately all the fathers and the prophets had this glorious hope before them. As individuals their longing was to be united with their Lord. As a group they were committed to His glorification as the restored King of His own creation. It was their common purpose. They were prepared to be martyred in pursuit of this goal, and many gave their lives. The goal, the purpose, the "hope", is the distinguishing feature of a "stewardship".

Body Truth:

In the prison epistles of Paul, the term "kingdom" occurs 5 times out of 158 usages in the New Testament (Ephesians 5:5, Colossians 1:13, 4:11, 2 Timothy 4:1, 2 Timothy 4:18). The word "king" occurs 2 out of 91 times in the New Testament (1 Timothy 1:17, 1 Timothy 6:15). In none of these cases is the word "king" or "kingdom" used in a manner that suggests the messianic kingdom, but rather they are used in context of Christ as eternal God. This is negative evidence and while helpful it is not conclusive. There are, however, positives that show clearly that these later epistles are presenting a whole new gospel and a different "hope", a new purpose and a different "stewardship".

Whereas Paul had declared in Rome, "For this cause ..... have I called for you .... because that for the hope of Israel I am bound with this chain" (Acts 28:20), after Acts 28:20 he was "the prisoner of Jesus Christ for you Gentiles" (Ephesians 3:1). A new body of believers is being addressed. In Colossians 4 he goes further and shows that the message and purpose are also different.

> *Colossians 4:3*: At the same time praying also for us, that God would open to us a door of utterance, to speak the mystery of Christ, for which I am also in bonds.

He had been bound for "the hope" of Israel. Now he is in bonds for "the mystery of Christ". This is the same "mystery" that in other ages was not made known to the sons of men, therefore the "mystery" had to be something new and different from the "hope" of Israel. The "Mystery of Christ", this sacred secret, had within it a different "hope", one that was not dependent on Israel's restored kingdom. The nature of that hope changed the purpose and message of this new stewardship (dispensation). Keep in mind that when the word "hope" is used, it is not used in the verbal sense, that is that someone is wishing for something, but rather in the sense of a noun; the reality and certainty that has been guaranteed by God and which is the ultimate goal of the calling of every believer in the Church. If we are to determine when the Church began we must identify this new "hope" and find out when it was revealed. We have been called to God's service to make known the "mystery of Christ" and to be the beneficiaries of this "new hope" just as Paul was.

Point 9: earthly hope - heavenly hope

Kingdom Truth:

I have mentioned that it is necessary to distinguish the sequence of events and their presentation in Scripture, but it is also necessary to look at the nature of the subject under examination. "The Hope of Israel" was essentially earthly. Job's hope was "In my flesh I will see God" and "that in the end *he will stand upon the earth*" (Job 19:25-26). Clearly Job had the hope of bodily resurrection to this earth. The Nation had the hope of the restoration of the kingdom under the rule of Messiah. The Apostles showed that with their last question to Christ. They did not ask "Will you at this time take us to heaven?", "but will you at this time restore the kingdom to Israel?"

Consider Abraham, Isaac, and Jacob, also Moses. They looked for a city. Some Christians tend to spiritualise, or allegorise, that city, by interpreting it as heaven. However, look a little further at some of the evidence.

> *Hebrews 11:8-10*: By faith Abraham, when he was called to move into a place which he should afterwards receive for an inheritance, obeyed; and he went out, not knowing where he was going. By faith he sojourned in the land of promise, as in a foreign country, dwelling in tents with Isaac and Jacob, the heirs with him of the same promise: For he looked *for a city* which hath foundations, *whose builder and maker is God.*

> *Hebrews 12:21-22*: Moses said, I exceedingly fear and tremble: But ye are come to mount Zion, and to the city of *the living God*, the heavenly Jerusalem.

On the basis of these verses alone we might easily take the "city" as being a figure alluding to heaven, but look at what John says in the Book of the Revelation.

> *Revelation 3:12*: Him that overcometh will I make a pillar in the temple of my God, and he shall go out no more: and I will write upon him the name of my God, and the name of the *city of my God*, which is *new Jerusalem*, which *cometh down out of heaven* from my God: and I will write upon him my new name.

Here we have a totally different perspective on the situation. The "city" which Abraham sought, the "city of the living God, the heavenly Jerusalem", and which Moses perceived, is *the city of my God*, which is *new Jerusalem*, which cometh down *out of heaven* from my God" Far from being heaven, the new Jerusalem is something that comes down *out* of heaven according to John.

This confusion of the New Jerusalem with heaven has had some interesting results in popular myth. How often have we heard of the "pearly gates" of heaven through which we all must pass when we die, if we have been good enough to go to heaven? Of course we will be met there by Saint Peter who will know which way we are to proceed. If by great good fortune we are allowed into heaven, we will become angels and fly on our newly acquired wings from cloud to cloud playing on our harps like David, and walk on streets of gold. Exactly why we need streets of gold to walk on since we can fly does not seem clear, particularly since myth also has us coming down to earth to watch over those we have left behind. Recently one poor desperate person, sadly, was convinced that her deceased son had tilted a Lotto machine so that she would win one million dollars. Do we really want our departed loved ones to be spectators of our suffering and also the misdeeds of which we are guilty? That would seem to make heaven a far from happy place for many. Pray God that He has better plans for us than that. How much heartbreak has come about because we fail to study the Scriptures soberly, taking phrases randomly and building intricate fantasies?

I know of no Scripture that teaches that any human has ever become an angelic being. Wings are mentioned in the Revelation in connection with the beings in John's vision but they are neither humans not angels. Chapter 21 of the Revelation speaks of the gates of pearl and streets of gold but it was not heaven that possessed them.

> *Revelation 21:1-2,9-11,18,21-22*: And I saw a new heaven and a new earth: for the first heaven and the first earth had passed away; and there was no more sea. And I John saw the holy city, new Jerusalem, coming down from God out of heaven, prepared as a bride adorned for her husband ..... And there came to me one of the seven angels ..... and talked with me, saying, Come, I will show thee the bride, the Lamb's wife. And he carried me away in the spirit to a great and high mountain, and showed me that great city, the holy Jerusalem,

descending out of heaven from God, Having the glory of God: and her light was like a stone most precious, even like a jasper stone, clear as crystal ... And the building of its wall was of jasper: and the city was pure gold, like clear glass ... And the twelve gates were twelve pearls; each one of the gates was of one pearl: and the street of the city was pure gold, as it were transparent glass. And I saw no temple in it: for the Lord God Almighty and the Lamb are its temple.

These few verses, quoted from Revelation 21, give evidence that much of our thinking on the matters under discussion has been wrong. It would be a worthwhile exercise to compare the whole chapter with the presentation of the New Covenant in Jeremiah chapter 31. Verses 27 to 40 were quoted earlier in this book. The New Jerusalem is shown to be part of the fulfilment of God's promise of the New Covenant with Israel and Judah.

Note in chapter 21 above, the New Jerusalem is again coming down out of heaven. It is prepared as a bride adorned for her husband. Compare that with Jeremiah 31:32, "though I was a husband to them". John was told that he would be shown "the bride, the Lamb's wife". He was not shown the "church which is the Body of Christ", but "that great city, the holy Jerusalem, descending *out of heaven* from God". The ties between the Nation, the New Jerusalem, the bride, and the Lamb's wife, are very strong. They are so strong that it is hard to see why we often think of this present church, the Body, as being the "Bride of Christ", which it is not.

In the verses quoted the gates of the holy Jerusalem are described as "of one pearl". No such description is used of heaven or its gates. This is a city, for all its holiness, that comes down to rest on earth.

The term "pure gold" is used twice in the above quotes, once of the city itself, and once of the streets. Strangely the streets are said to be "pure gold, as it were transparent glass." This surely is a spectacular description, and not like anything that we know of. The description of the holy Jerusalem is reminiscent of the descriptions of the temple of old. One quote from the Old Testament will make the point.

1 Kings 6:20: And the inner sanctuary in the forepart was twenty cubits in length, and twenty cubits in breadth, and twenty cubits in the height of it: and he overlaid it with pure gold; and so covered the altar which was of cedar.

This verse in 1 Kings is typical of so much of the intricate description of the temple and tabernacle and of the instructions for their construction in the Old Testament. The careful measurements and elaborate ornamentation of the structures insured that they would represent the dignity and glory of the mighty, holy God. The same attention to detail is present in the description of the New Jerusalem. The comparison is anything but accidental. The temple is the place where God met His people. In the coming kingdom there will be no temple "for the Lord God Almighty and the Lamb are its temple". The holy city, however, will be the place of God's authority, the location of Messiah's throne and presumably the place where the Apostles will sit in judgement over the twelve tribes. It is therefore worthy of the same respect as the temple, which is a symbol of God's glory. It is also the subject of one of the promises of the New Covenant.

Let me quote again part of the passage from Jeremiah:

> *Jeremiah 31:38-40 (NIV)*: "The days are coming," *declares the Lord*, "when this city will be rebuilt for me from the Tower of Hananel to the Corner Gate. The measuring line will stretch from there straight to the hill of Gareb and then turn to Goah. The whole valley where dead bodies and ashes are thrown, and all the terraces out to the Kidron Valley on the east as far as the corner of the Horse Gate, will be holy to the Lord. The city will never again be uprooted or demolished."

Just as the temple of old was on the earth, even so, the New Jerusalem will be on the new earth. It must be so, for the stewardship of Israel is under David's son to restore God's sovereignty over earth. This is their calling. This is the purpose for which they were chosen. It is an earthly calling and hope. It is certain.

Body Truth:

David's kingdom was on this earth. If it is to be restored then it must be restored on this earth. Christ, in that He is God, is also King of heaven but that kingdom cannot be "restored" since His rule in the heavens is eternal, it was, is, and ever will be. Lucifer and his angels blasphemed Him in heaven, but He was never deposed. It was Lucifer who was cast out of heaven. There is a vacancy in heaven created by the loss of the fallen angels. Satan, when he tempted Christ, was trying to gain for himself Christ's place of honour and His throne in heaven. The dignity of the Son must be restored. It is perhaps our place to have a part in that restoration. Just as Israel is to be the trophy of Christ's grace on earth, even so, we, in the Body of Christ, are to be the trophy of His grace through His love in heaven.

Ephesians and Colossians teach us our part in restoring Christ's dignity and of our hope. This from the *NIV*:

> *Ephesians 3:9-10*: and to make plain to everyone the administration (stewardship) of this mystery, which for ages past was kept hidden in God, who created all things. His intent was that now, through the church, *the manifold wisdom of God should be made known to the rulers and authorities in the heavenly realms.*

Our presence as those whom Christ redeemed is to show God's wisdom and power to the heavenly beings. Christ's honour and His position as God's only begotten will be vindicated.

> *Ephesians 2:4-7*: But because of his great love for us, God, who is rich in mercy, made us alive with Christ even when we were dead in transgressions - it is by grace you have been saved. And God raised us up with Christ and seated us with him in the heavenly realms in Christ Jesus, in order that in the coming ages he might show the incomparable riches of his grace, expressed in his kindness to us in Christ Jesus.

And from the *KJV*:

> *Colossians 3:1-4*: If ye then be raised with Christ, seek those things which are above, *where Christ sitteth on the right hand of God.* Set your affection on things above, not on things on the earth. For ye are dead, and your life is hid with Christ in God. When Christ, who is our life, shall appear, then shall ye also appear with him in glory.

Our "calling" now is to preach the gospel that salvation is by grace through faith, to teach everyone about the "mystery", and so witness to His glory in the heavens, in the very abode of God. Our "hope" is that we are seated with Christ in the heavenly realms, and when Christ is made "manifest" (Gr. *phaneroo*) in glory, we will be made manifest with Him. Our calling is to tell of the grace of God and to teach that our hope is to be in heaven with Christ. It is a heavenly hope and calling. It is sure and certain.

Point 10: hope to come - present hope

Kingdom Truth:

Job looked forward to Christ's coming to this earth. Abraham dwelt as in a foreign country looking for a city. David looked forward for a coming king. The Apostles asked if it was time for the kingdom. John was carried forward to the great and wonderful day of the Lord. Always the Hope of Israel was future.

Body Truth:

We are in Christ now. Because of the timelessness of our heavenly hope we are eternally secure. By God's grace we are seated in the heavenlies. Ephesians tells us:

> *Ephesians 1:13-14*: in whom also after ye believed, ye were sealed with that Holy Spirit of promise, Which is the earnest of our inheritance until the redemption of the purchased possession, to the praise of his glory.

We have been saved. Our life is hid in Christ. He has seated us in heavenly realms. We were sealed with the Holy Spirit. We will appear with Him in glory. We have received the earnest of our inheritance. We are the Body of Christ. Christ in us, or among us, is the hope of glory. We are joined to our divine Head, Christ, and the bands of His love join us individually. We are in-dwelt by the Spirit. This is what is meant by the "earnest" of our inheritance. The word "earnest" means a deposit, something that is already in one's possession that begins the process of taking full ownership. It is not simply a guarantee of something future. We were saved. We are saved. We will appear with Him in glory. The process has begun. Our hope is present with us now! He is Christ.

Point 11: from Adam - before the foundation

Kingdom Truth:

Kingdom Truth is all founded on the Abrahamic covenant. God called Abraham out of Ur and gave him promises that will be fulfilled in Christ in the Messianic covenant. These covenants He renewed to Abraham's seed.

> *Psalm 135:4*: For the Lord hath chosen Jacob to himself, and Israel for his special treasure.

The Old Testament fathers and the prophets were continually the source of kingdom authority. Even the details of our Lord's life were affirmed by the evoking of, 'that it may be fulfilled what the prophet so-and-so said' or some similar statement. Starting from Genesis 12, there is an internal integrity to the revealed plan that God has for this world of mankind. It involves the Nation of Israel as His chosen bearers of the gospel of the kingdom. It has its roots back beyond Abraham in the fall of Adam, and has its fulfilment in the restoration of the paradise of Eden on earth. God will again walk in fellowship with man on earth, as would have been the case, had it not been for the fall.

The defeat of the tempter, and the restoration of fellowship, were inherent in God's promise to the woman. From Noah and the pre-flood saints, through Moses and the prophets, down to Malachi, and then the writers of the New Testament, God's will for man was hidden in the words of the Bible. It was not in any sense a secret or mystery. It was there for all who would believe to see. But it went back no further than Adam as far as we are told.

Body Truth:

However, Body Truth presents us with a different story. It is described in Ephesians as a "mystery, which from the beginning of the world hath been hid in God". Why was it not made known until it was made known to Paul? And, why is there the reference to the beginning of the world? Four quotes from the New Testament will help us to understand.

> *Ephesians 1:4*: According as he hath chosen [us] in him before

the foundation of the world, that we should be holy and without blame before him in love.

2 Timothy 1:9: Who hath saved us, and called [us] with an holy calling, not according to our works, but according to his own purpose and grace, which was given to us in Christ Jesus before the world began,

John 17:24: Father, I will that they also, whom thou hast given to me, be with me where I am; that they may behold my glory, which thou hast given to me: for thou didst love me before the foundation of the world.

1 Peter 1:20: Who verily was foreordained before the foundation of the world, but was revealed in these last times for you.

The first two verses refer to us. "He hath chosen [us] in him *before the foundation of the world*, and called [us] with an holy calling ..... *before the world began*."

The second two verses refer to Christ. He says, "Father ...... thou didst love me *before the foundation of the world*", and He was, "foreordained *before the foundation of the world*."

The promises of the Kingdom gospel, with the covenants, went back to Adam and were made known to men throughout that period, right up to the end of the Book of Acts. It was the subject of all the penmen of Scripture, including the apostle Paul. We, on the other hand, were chosen in Christ before Adam, before Eden, before the world began. It was at a time when Christ was with the Father, loved and chosen by the Father before the foundation of the world.

The first stewardship, the stewardship of Israel and the Kingdom, dates from the fall of man on earth and will find its hope and completion in the restored kingdom on earth. The second stewardship, the dispensation of grace, was ordained in the heavens with God. Its hope and completion is in the heavens, when we will be seated there with Christ, and by our presence the manifold wisdom of God will be made known to the authorities in those heavenly realms.

Conclusion

The "mystery" was hid in God since the beginning of the world because while God had already "foreordained" the Body of Christ, the Nation had been chosen at Adam's fall to fulfil the task of helping to restore God's rule on earth. Until the Nation had been set aside it would have been neither reasonable nor useful to make this new stewardship known to man. That could wait until the Church or group of called-out people was present and able to proceed with its calling.

God's word and truth are always presented decently and in order. There were no mistakes. The differences are there for His purpose. These 11 points are only the beginning of the differences between the Church *in* Acts and the Church *after* Acts 28:28. In the Church of today, the Nation has no special standing. Both Jew and Gentile in the flesh are saved simply by the grace of God, through faith in Christ. Being descended from Abraham plays no part in salvation. The Law of ordinances was never given to us. Paul who did observe the Law in time past, became an apostle out of due time. He taught us of God's love, as Israel should have done. Christ is our divine Head, our Saviour, our constant friend and companion.

This is a new gospel and a different Church.

Chapter 13
WHEN DID THE CHURCH START?

The Church - When did it start? That was the original question. I hope that the intervening chapters have provided enough evidence to give the basis for a reasonable answer. There is far more material that could be considered here, but to try to deal with more could easily become overwhelming. Perhaps it would be useful to go back and review some of the material that has been dealt with.

In chapter 2, "Definitions", I attempted to define five important words that would be factors in this study. They were, "Church", "Dispensation", "Mystery", "Hope", and "Calling".

In chapter 6, "Pairs to Compare", I gave the meanings that I intended to use for seven terms as they appeared in this text, recognising the fact that they could be used in other ways. They were "Old Testament" or "Old Covenant", "New Testament" or "New Covenant", "Kingdom Truth", "The Nation", "New Dispensation (Stewardship) or "Body Truth", and "The Body".

All of these various elements must be brought together in reasonable fashion if the main question of the book is to be resolved. While it was useful to consider each item separately they remain disconnected ideas until we see how together they present a complete picture of God's plan as it is revealed to man in His Word. The three key words are "church", "dispensation" or "stewardship", and "covenant". Everything else modifies these three.

A "church" is by definition a "body" or group of people "called" to a "purpose" and a "hope". There were churches in the Old Testament. The Levites were called out from Israel as a priesthood, just as Israel was called out from the nations as *the* priestly Nation. The Twelve Apostles were called out from among Christ's followers for special service. There was a "church" on the day of Pentecost, and there is a "church" today. There was "*a* body of Christ" in the Book of Acts and there is "*the* Body of Christ" today.

However, I have highlighted the events of Acts 28:25-28 and said that the Church of today did not start until after that time. I have also made a point of calling the "Church of Today" the "Church which is the Body of Christ". However, both "*a*" church and "*a*" body were known during the Acts period. This may appear to be a contradiction, especially when one considers the following two quotes. The first written during the Acts period, Romans 12:5: "So we, being many, are one body in Christ, and every one members one of another". The other written after the end of Acts, Ephesians 4:4: "There is one body, and one Spirit, even as ye are called in one hope of your calling".

How can there be one Church called "a" body before Acts 28:28, and a different Church called "the" Body after Acts 28:28, when Scriptures written during both periods state clearly that "There is one Body"? We begin to see an answer in the following statement in Christ's own words.

> *John 10:16*: And other sheep I have, which are not of this fold: them also I must bring, and they shall hear my voice; and there shall be one fold, and one shepherd.

Christ has more than one fold. Let us use the illustration of military units. Suppose an absolute monarchy, and the king is at war. He wishes to invade the enemy. He addresses his one navy. He wants them to attack the coastal defence of the enemy and reminds them of their responsibility to him and to each other as fellow members of his "called out ones", his navy. He later addresses his army in the same manner. They are two separate entities, but when he speaks to the sailors and talks of one navy he does not include the soldiers. They are of what we might call another fold. Both are loyal to the monarch. They are identified primarily not by their uniform or service name but by the function that he requires of them. It could as easily be two regiments.

This is far from a perfect illustration but the point is made that God in His wisdom can and does have more than one Church and more than one Body of believers called to serve Him for different purposes. The mere use of the same word or title does not indicate that they are one and the same group. There was one Body called during the Acts period for a particular purpose and there is one Body now called for another purpose. We are, each of us, one with those of the Acts period by having the same precious faith and purpose. We are differentiated from them by the hope, purpose, and message that have been committed to us. It is also true that the time will come when we will all become one (Ephesians 1:10).

A problem arises when we confuse the "New Covenant" with the "New Dispensation". We often mistakenly think that the "New Covenant" is directed to us, but it was given to Israel and Judah (Jeremiah 31:31; Hebrews 8:8). Remember that the word "Dispensation" is better translated "Stewardship". *The New Covenant must replace the Old, but is it the same thing as the Stewardship of the Mystery (the secret hid in God) of Ephesians and Colossians? If not, where is the division and what is the difference?*

The difference is abundantly clear. The New Covenant is a promise made by God to the Seed of Abraham for their redemption and benefit, in spite of their repeated disobedience. It did not define their "Stewardship", for that had been defined at Adam's fall and by God's covenant with Abraham (Genesis 12:1-3). The New Covenant was God's guarantee of help so that the Nation of Israel could fulfil that trust. They were to proclaim the Name of the Lord before the "nations" so that the "nations" could be blessed through the "Nation", Abraham's seed.

The New Stewardship is a commission given to "us" Gentiles for our service: "For we are his workmanship, created in Christ Jesus to good works, which God hath before ordained that 'we' should walk in them" (Ephesians 2:10). The one was the subject of prophecy. The other was an un-prophesied revelation. The one fulfils promises made to Abraham and can be traced back to the fall. The other was ordained before the foundation of the world. The one is regal; there is the royal priesthood of Israel between Gentile believers and God. The other is intimate; Gentile believers have direct access to the throne of mercy, and the Holy Spirit indwells us in a very precious way, and we are created new creatures in Christ. The one guarantees a future kingdom on earth with earthly blessing. The other gives immediate fellowship with God, and guarantees all spiritual blessings in the heavenlies.

The problem is compounded by the fact that we tend not to have a common understanding of the term "dispensation" (*oikonomia*) or, as the *NIV* translates it, "administration". Some have never considered or even heard of the term. To them some of this may be new territory, possibly even confusing. Among those who take cognisance of the word "dispensation" understanding varies widely, but this teaching of a "new dispensation" or 'New Stewardship' is one of those facts that is given in the Bible. It is not merely semantics. The way we understand this idea will largely control our understanding of His will for us, and the way in which we serve Him.

The idea of rightly dividing the Bible, along with dispensations, has a long history in Bible studies. In the second century Justin Martyr (110-165) pointed out that men of old, such as Enoch, Noah and others pleased God without the demands of the Law, while after Moses the Law of ordinance was necessary. God demanded different things of different people.

Over the centuries, particularly from the time of Miles Coverdale (1488-1569) onward, a more formalised view of dispensations evolved, with more or less acceptance. The traditional dispensationalism of today developed in the 1800s and 1900s with such men as J. N. Darby, C. I. Scofield, C. H. Welch and others. For an excellent history on the subject, see Michael Penny's book *Approaching the Bible* (published by The Open Bible Trust). In the various systems, the number of dispensations has varied from four, in the teaching of Ireanaeus (130-200), to at least eighteen, perceived by C. H. Welch (1880-1967). This rather illustrates that a true consensus is hard to come by. The concept that is common to each, is that of different and differing administrations of God's grace to and for man.

The immediate question for us is, "When did the present 'dispensation' commence?" We have already postulated that a new stewardship must have a *new and unique purpose*, a *new message*, a *new hope*, and a *new steward* or *administrator*. The new steward of this stewardship is "the *church*, which is His body, the fulness of Him that filleth all in all."

In all the discussions about how to define a 'dispensation' and how to decide when it begins and ends, one point seems to have been overlooked, ***God*** *tells us when the stewardship changes*. It is hard to see how we, on our own, can decide such matters when there are clear biblical statements to go by. I can see no justification for making stewardship divisions other than those dictated by the Holy Spirit in Scripture. Other divisions may be convenient for study purposes but they are not authoritative.

Let us think again of the seven times that the Greek word *oikonomia* is used in the Bible. The three times it is used in the parable of the unjust steward helps us understand the word and the responsibility of stewardship, but it does not help here (Luke 16). The use in 1 Corinthians 9:17, "a stewardship of the gospel", would apply to all believers in all times. This leaves only three occurrences to deal with.

The statement of Acts 28:28, "that the salvation of God is sent unto the Gentiles", would not seem particularly important in itself if it were not for the fact that a survey of Scriptures written before and after that time shows clearly that some momentous changes had indeed taken place. When we come to a signpost between two countries we may not at first see much difference in the landscape, but if we examine the laws, customs, and responsibilities of citizenship of the two jurisdictions, we will soon find out that the sign did herald important changes. No single verse can be the basis of doctrine, but it can betoken a need to rethink any doctrinal stand. We should not be blown about by every wind of doctrine, but a sober consideration of a mass of scriptural evidence in context indicates a willingness to submit our will to the correction of the Holy Spirit.

Of the three verses left two, Ephesians 3:2 and Colossians 1:25, indicate the beginning of the present stewardship. Perhaps they should be repeated here.

> *Ephesians 3:2:* If ye have heard of the *dispensation* of the grace of God which is given me on your account.

> *Colossians 1:25*: Of which I am made a minister, according to the *dispensation* of God which is given to me for you, to fulfil the word of God.

The last usage of the word *oikonomia* is also in Ephesians, but refers to a different and future dispensation. This would seem to indicate the existence of only three great stewardships. This last usage is:

> *Ephesians 1:10*: That in the *dispensation of the fulness of times* he might gather in one all things in Christ, both which are in heaven, and which are on earth; even in him.

This is a very few verses on which to formulate our understanding of some important biblical concepts. The alternative is to impose our own preconceived notion of what the Bible should say. This last is our natural tendency. In Eden, the tempter said, "Ye shall be as gods knowing good and evil". We still find it difficult to set aside our man-made traditions and submit to His Word.

Once we accept these key verses as guide to our thinking we find a grand pattern emerging. The pattern is this: there are three nested stewardships that are:

1. *The stewardship of eternity.*

The administrator is the Son. It was before time, ("for thou lovedst me before the foundation of the world" John 17:24). It was interrupted at the fall. It will be restored after the other two stewardships, which are nested between it's parts, are complete at "the dispensation of the fullness of times" when all things are gathered again in one in Christ, both which are in heaven, and which are on earth. His glory and honour before and after time is the grand purpose.

2. *The stewardship of the earth*.

It began at the fall and the chief steward is the Seed of Abraham. It was interrupted when the Nation was set-aside for a time. It will be restored when the kingdom is restored to Israel and Christ sits on the throne of David. The restoration of His glory and honour on earth is the grand purpose.

3. *The stewardship of the heavenly realms*.

The steward is the Church of today. It began after the setting aside of the Nation of Israel after the announcement of Acts 28:25-28. It will continue until Christ is made manifest (Gr. *phaneroo*) in glory, when we, also, are to be made manifest with Him. "His intent was that now, through the church, the manifold wisdom of God should be made known to the rulers and authorities in the heavenly realms." The restoration of His glory and honour in the heavenly realms is the grand purpose.

The pattern would be something like the chart on the next page. The chart is stylised and not in any way proportional or representative, therefore explanatory notes will be needed. It is intended to only visualize concepts.

RIGHT DIVISION PATTERN OF THE STEWARDSHIPS

The Steward of the Father is the Son

ETERNITY

The Body chosen in Christ before the foundation of the world

Creation
The fall

The Steward is Israel

The Covenant is entered into. **Law rules**

KINGDOM

Knowledge of the Body is hidden in God

The Cross

Acts: The kingdom offered and re-offered.

Acts 28:28   Israel set aside.

The New Stewardship to the Gentiles is revealed through Paul. The Body is the Steward of God.

Grace rules

THE BODY

No difference between Jew and Gentile.

End Times   New Covenant with Israel
Israel under Messiah is again the Steward

KINGDOM   Law in their hearts

Members of the Body seated in the Heavens with Christ.

The End   The Fullness of times – all become one in Christ

ETERNITY

Christ is the Father's Steward.

*There have been a great many charts produced attempting to give a representation of the ages as described in the Bible. They vary greatly in concept and particular content but all have merit in that they try to give a reasonable frame of reference by which the student can place the various events described in the Word, in an orderly array. This being done, we can appreciate the manner in which God works His will and the wonder of His grace to man in spite of His disobedience.

They are all virtually similar in one aspect. They trace the series of events described in the Bible, from the past to the future, in sequential and / or parallel form, as they impact mankind. They attempt to present a single picture of both history and prophecy. In one way or another, according to the perspective of the person or group presenting the chart, the time line is divided into "ages" or "dispensations". It is useful to consider these divisions for study purposes, but there is very little consensus as to how to determine where the breaks should come or of just what an "age" should consist.

As much as there is great value in many of these charts, I think that there is reason to produce a new one. I personally know of none that covers quite the same concept that I am trying to propound, although one may exist.

In the beginning of this book I quoted 2 Timothy 2:15, where we are told to study to show ourselves approved unto God and to "rightly" divide the word of truth. The Bible contains such an immense amount of information about our Lord and His will that such finite creatures as we are, must, as we study, follow only limited enquiries on specific subjects at any given time. Then after we have done this, we need to look further to see how other Scriptures alter our perception of the first matter. This is why we use cross-referencing.

There are unnumbered valuable lines of study open to us. We may look at the names of God. We may do word studies. We may do character studies. The list goes on and on. Each avenue leads to greater appreciation of God's grace. No study can, however, be allowed to become obsessive. We need to understand just what it is that we are studying and how it relates to the rest of Scripture.

The diversity of, and differences between, the charts indicates that most, if not all, must have some errors in them. This does not diminish their value. God does not expect perfection of man but only the willingness to try to obey within the limits of capability. He knows our weakness. The charts represent the thirst of their authors for knowledge of God's will.

The thrust of the charts is the history of man's experience with God. The Bible is the Book of the ages, not of eternity. Very little is said about eternity, past or future, since our inability to understand that which is infinite has left human language bereft of the capability of expressing such concepts. Most charts describe the ages of man in terms of time periods defined by different circumstances. Nowhere does the Bible call these ages, dispensations!

The chart that I am proposing is based on a different premise. I am not presenting the "ages" *per se*, but rather the "dispensations", or more accurately the "stewardships", as the revealed commissions of God to man. Obviously, since man is involved, there will be a time element that is important but it is not the overriding factor. So far as I can see, these three are the only "stewardships" (*oikonomia*) specifically named by the Holy Spirit in the Bible. What they consist of, where the breaks should come, what the purpose, message, and hope is, and who the steward is, are all made clear. The exact sequence in the future is not so clear. We know that the Kingdom will be restored to Israel. Virtually all prophetic statements are related to Israel and the Kingdom. We know that we will be seated in the heavenlies in Christ but this is about all that God has chosen to tell us. We know that all will become one in Christ in the fullness of time. Exactly when and how these events will take place is not clear. It is beyond our ability to understand. Prophecy was never given so that mankind should have a program for the future but to identify the event or person when needed. We need only rest in the knowledge that He can perform whatever He promised.

Let me refer to the chart itself. They have been called "Nested Stewardships" because as each is interrupted (note: not done away with, but only held in abeyance) another comes into force. The term parenthesis has been used to describe the situation, just as there is a parenthesis in the previous sentence. The purpose of the three has each been referred to above.

The light shaded line in the chart, Eternity, should have no beginning and no end. In that first portion you will see a note saying, "The body chosen in Christ before the beginning of the world." This can give us great comfort because it means that all during the period of the "Kingdom" when the knowledge of the 'New Stewardship' was being kept as a secret from man, we, who had not yet been born, were known and loved by God.

The stewardship of the earth began with the fall. The message is, "The King is coming. He is Jesus Christ, the Messiah!" The hope is the restored kingdom on earth through the New Covenant. In a special way, this stewardship has had more than one steward. From the promise to Eve down to Abraham God spoke to man through individuals but the Purpose, the Message, and the Hope remained the same. All during that time God was preserving the "Seed of the woman". Abraham and his seed became the chief stewards, but with the same Purpose, Message and Hope. Neither the individuals, nor the Nation, were the *object* of the stewardship. However, they were only the *instruments* used by God in the fulfilling that *object*, His grand purpose.

Christ told the apostles that the time when the kingdom would be restored to Israel, and when the New Covenant would be instituted, was a secret hid in God (Acts 1:6-7). Thus, of necessity, no chart can be clear on this point. Note that at no time in the Old or New Testaments, before Acts 28:28, did the Scriptures refer to a 'New Stewardship'. The "Ages" represented changes in man's situation, but did not bring with them a totally new message, hope or purpose.

The Kingdom stewardship was interrupted with the setting aside of Israel just *after* the events of Acts 28:28, by the introduction of the New Stewardship by the Holy Spirit through Paul. By now it should be clear that this is the point at which I believe "The Church of Today" began. Before going on, I would like to comment on a few other points. We are told that the ultimate hope of this Body of Christ is that we are to be seated with Christ as joint heirs with Him in the heavenlies. What is not made clear is, just how or when this is to take place. The end of this stewardship has been kept a secret just as its beginning was.

I have marked the end of the Body period as being in line with the resumption of the Kingdom calling. Only indirect evidence is available on this point. God apparently found it desirable to suspend the Kingdom gospel before instituting the age of grace. It would seem that He did not want the two gospels to be preached at one time; otherwise it would not have been necessary to set the Nation aside. This being so in the past, it is hard to conceive of the two callings being active on the earth at the same time in the future, but this point is far from clear.

Whatever the case, the portion marked "End Times", I have taken to represent resumption of Israel's calling; the time of Jacob's sorrow (the tribulation), the return of Christ to this world for His own People, and the establishment of His Messianic rule from His throne in the New Jerusalem. I do not believe that we, the believers of the Body, will have any portion in these events. Our Hope is in the heavenlies.

Then comes "The Fulness of Times", the point at which all things become one in Christ both in heaven and on earth (Ephesians 1:10). All distinction between the Nation and the administered nations in His kingdom, between the earthly and heavenly purposes, between the Kingdom and Body of Christ will cease to exist. Christ will be all and in all thus completing the purpose of the ages.

The periods of human history during which the various stewardships are not active in our sight are very much present in God's mind and plans. He is not bound by the strictures of time.

Summary

Much of the difficulty we have in dealing with this whole matter stems from the fact that the Greek word *oikonomia* was, in my opinion, wrongly translated as "dispensation". This suggests a dispensing of a new order of authority by God over man. This is true of the "dispensations" of the Old Testament, for instance, the giving of the Law to the Nation, the placing of them under judges and then under a monarchy and so on. On the other hand the "stewardships" of Ephesians and Colossians are something of a different order. It is not the imposition of a regime and a Law over a people, but a delegating of a responsibility to a people. The two ideas are not synonymous and should not be confused.

Throughout the Old Testament God constantly changed His relationship with man but all of those "dispensations" (if we wish to call them that) exist within the Kingdom "stewardship". Each was but a step in the eventual development of the over-all plan. Just as Israel was latent in Abraham, Abraham was latent in Noah, Noah in Seth, and Seth in Eve. Abraham and his seed were always present in God's plans. There was but one overall goal through the time from the fall to the setting aside of the Nation of Israel at Acts 28:25-28, and that was to present the seed of the woman, Christ, as King and Lord over and in this world.

There are only three stewardships named by God in the Bible. They possess all the necessary hallmarks. Each has a unique purpose. Each has a unique message. Each has a unique hope. Each has a unique steward. Each is proclaimed by God Himself and is not simply an age. This present stewardship was not proclaimed at Pentecost but later, after the events of Acts 28:25-28. It was made known by revelation through the Apostle Paul. Therefore the Steward of this gospel, the Church of today, could not have come into existence until that same time.

PART 2

WHY

DOES IT MATTER
WHEN THE CHURCH BEGAN?

Chapter 14
INTRODUCTION

The first portion of this book was devoted to answering the first of the two questions that comprise the title of the book: "The Church - When did it begin?" It is hoped that I made my view clear with reasonably convincing evidence. The second question remains unanswered and some may find this query more significant. "Why does it matter when the church began?" Again, I hope, I will be able to give some reasonable answers. Let us first consider the validity of the question itself before proceeding.

If the question "Why does it matter when the Church started?" is asked with the intent of seeking honest answers, then a profitable study can follow. If, however, it is asked simply because our minds are already made up and therefore the issue is not important, then this all becomes an exercise in futility. We are no longer dealing with an honest question but merely with an evasion designed to protect ourselves from the discomfort of testing our convictions against the hallmark of the Bible. If this latter is the case, let us remember that we are instructed to study to show ourselves approved unto God, with the implication that not to study the word of truth means that we are not approved of God. This should be a sobering thought (2 Timothy 2:15).

We must submit our opinions to the scrutiny of the Scriptures, rather than submitting the teaching of the Scriptures to the evaluation of our pre-conceived opinions. Most believers readily agree to this, but a legitimate concern is that we can become concerned about "splitting hairs". However, care needs to be taken when traditional practices in a church or denomination are contrary to biblical principles. Such debates can then turn into conflicts of personalities and are then anything but constructive. How many seekers have been turned from Christ by such unwholesome squabbles? How many believers have borne grudges against each other in such situations. In fact the underlying motivation has rapidly become pride, rather than a search for truth. I must confess that I can remember to my shame that there have been times when I have sought to win an argument, rather than seeking the truth. Probably most of us have done the same.

There is another aspect to "not splitting hairs", and it is a strange one at that. In almost any other field of study or endeavour this question would never even be considered. Excellence and the striving for perfection are admired qualities. We would never suggest to the athlete that just turning up at the playing field should be enough. We demand discipline and careful training and the best possible effort, or we do not think that he or she would be worthy to play.

In science or medicine, precision is mandatory. In law or finance, the slightest errors can see a person hanged or an economy collapse. Only in matters of faith is a vague approximation of truth acceptable. Some say that we can never learn the whole truth anyway therefore it is futile even to try, but that is not a valid argument. We continually set our goals beyond our accomplishments with full knowledge that there is always more possible. If we do not do this, growth is impaired.

There is often an unfortunate underlying assumption behind this type of question. That is the hypothesis of 'either/or'. The comparison is between 'day to day life' and 'a theological topic', the assumption being that 'day to day life' is what really matters. Theology is for those with their heads in the clouds. They are of little earthly use!

The word 'theology' comes from two Greek words; *theos* - God, and *logos* - discourse. Is it of less importance to consider the acts, nature, and the will of God for us? Is it not our 'discourse' with God through His word that controls our attitude towards others and the way we treat them? Both theology (learning about God) and the application of that theology (the way we walk in this world) are equally important in pleasing God.

Jerome, who translated the Bible into Latin so that his fellows could have the Scriptures in their own language, said, "Make knowledge of the Scripture your love and you will not love the views of the flesh". If we keep our eyes on our own striving from day to day, we will soon be discouraged, but consider Christ's words in Matthew 11:29, "take my yoke upon you, and *learn* of me ..... and ye shall find rest unto your souls".

Consider also Christ's answer in Mark 12 when one of the scribes asked Him, "Which is the first commandment of all?"

Mark 12:29-31: And Jesus answered him, The first of all the commandments is, Hear, O Israel; The Lord our God is one Lord: And thou shalt love the Lord thy God with all thy heart, and with all thy soul, and with all thy mind, and with all thy strength: this is the first commandment. And the second is like, namely this, Thou shalt love Thy neighbour as thyself. There is no other commandment greater than these.

Christ was speaking to Jews who were under the Law but the underlying principles are just as valid today as they were then. He did not select one of the Ten Commandments, as He might have done, nor did He refer to any of the rest of the Mosaic Law as such. He outlined all the basic standards necessary to man if he is truly to worship God. We are to recognise the one true God as Lord. We are to love Him and then our neighbour as ourselves.

In these two quotes, Christ does not speak only of us loving Him in an emotional sense, which is of course involved, but also in an intellectual way. He says "learn of me" and "thou shall *love* the Lord thy God ..... with all thy *mind*". Worship must be both emotional and intellectual. Our mind is a gift from God and should be used to control our emotions and actions. This is the very reason God chose to communicate to us in human language.

Let me illustrate. A building is to be built. If it is a small, simple, temporary structure, a handy man may simply buy some material and build it without plans and it may not matter. He may well have done a similar job before and in any event probably it will not be required to undergo much strain or last indefinitely. If it is a structure of importance, where safety and endurance are factors and where convenience and aesthetics are valued, then mere enthusiasm and good intentions are not enough, no matter how much experience the builder has.

Suppose that we are talking about a church building. It would have to conform to standards of physics, engineering, safety, use planning and community zoning. To do otherwise would be to court disaster. The understanding of, and adherence to, underlying principles may appear at times to be intellectual abstractions and not very relevant to those considering themselves more practical-minded. However, the ignoring of them can be disastrous. Some while ago in Asia, a department store collapsed with considerable loss of life because these abstract principles were ignored. The motivation for the shortcoming in the construction of the building was probably greed. The emotion of greed in some resulted in irreparable harm to others.

Ecclesiastes 12:13: Let us hear the conclusion of the whole matter: Fear God, and keep his commandments: for this is the whole duty of man.

Ephesians 2:10: For we are his workmanship, created in Christ Jesus to good works, which God hath before ordained that we should walk in them.

Neither of these verses, one from the Old Testament and one from "Body Truth", is teaching about the means of salvation. Both instruct the believer in obedience to God's will. As members of the fallen race of Adam, our intelligence, our will, and our emotions, have all been corrupted by sin. This sad fact severely limits our ability as believers to, of our own accord, render adequate "reasonable" service to our Lord.

The Bible is structured in such a manner that it outlines not only the obvious substance of God's will, but also the underlying principles that are to guide us in our walk. Surely we ought to take as much care in building our Christian walk as we do in erecting a church building. Even as uncontrolled emotions can cause an inferior building to be erected, so uncontrolled emotions can cause us to fail to do the good works that He desires of us.

When we ask "When did the Church start?", we are not simply asking an academic question about something that happened a long time ago and which is irrelevant to our day-to-day lives. We are seeking to understand God's will for us as it is written, and to distinguish it from His will for Israel and the Kingdom. We need to know God's over-all plan for mankind, and in particular how we, as Gentiles, fit into it. God chose various people and groups to do His will and gave each of them instructions concerning His purpose for them and just what they should do to accomplish it. We may be tempted to think that while all of this may be important in our personal studies, it is not clear just how it applies to our daily living and to our relationships with those around us. However, if we seek to please the Lord, we must do His will for the Church which is His Body, and not His will for some other group, like the people of Israel.

> *1 Peter 3:15*: But sanctify the Lord God in your hearts: and be ready always to give an answer to every man that asketh you a reason of the hope that is in you with meekness and fear (or reverence).

How can we do the good works that God has ordained for us or give answer to any man if we do not know what those good works are or what the scripturally sound answer is? The entire Bible is for our instruction but we are called to a specific stewardship. If those things taught in the Book of Acts differ from those in the Prison Epistles, we need to know that. If we say that the powers granted to the Apostles are not granted today, we need to know not only if this is true but why. We need to know what the message for today is. We need to know what the hope and calling for today is. We need to know what God's overall purpose is. If we do not understand these things then our answer will be confused and we will give comfort to those who say that the Bible contradicts itself. It would be tragic if someone were to reject Christ's offer of salvation because what we said was confusing, or someone else live a less than victorious life because we failed to study carefully.

The answer to "The Church - When did it begin?" is key to many of these questions. It allows us to rightly divide the Word of Truth in such a way that is logical. It makes it plain that the so-called contradictions of the Bible do not exist. God has taught us line upon line. He took Abraham out of a pagan land and gave him all the truth that he needed or could understand. He gave Moses the Law which taught Israel and us what sin is. He gave us, through Paul, knowledge of salvation by grace alone, in spite of man's inability to keep the Law, and reveals the good works which God wants us to do.

This in consequence is to say that asking when the Church started matters because it can affect both our walk and our witness. It can deepen our experience with Christ and give us a fuller understanding of His Word and His will. It is an act of obedience. Let us look at some of the ways that this is true.

Chapter 15
TRUTH AND INTEGRITY

"Each of us has the *right* to their own truth!"

"I have the *right* to believe whatever I want! Truth is not absolute but relative."

How often have we heard statements similar to these? One is tempted to say that these represent the attitude of today's society (compare Judges 21:25). In reality, these represent attitudes that go all the way back to Eden. There is nothing new or modern in them! In Eden Satan said, "For God doth know that in the day ye eat of it, then your eyes shall be opened, and ye shall be as gods, knowing good and evil" (Genesis 3:5).

There are problems with this whole line of reasoning. The idea that we, as created beings, could ever "be as gods" and be able, by our own wisdom, to know good and evil in particular, let alone truth in general, and to decide on our own authority what should be accepted, is preposterous. Our experience and knowledge are too finite. Our standard of reference is too restricted. Our capacity to judge reasonably is too limited by self-interest. We tend to decide not on how things are, but how we think they should be from our own perspective. What we call 'My own truth' is properly 'My own opinion'. My own opinion is indeed relative since I, and all of us, on the basis of the named restrictions are faulty recipients of knowledge. Our opinion is relative to our limited ability, emotional predisposition and our self-interest.

What can it mean to say, "I have the *right* to believe that the world is flat"? Does that make the world flat? Is it then my *truth* or just a wrong opinion? Perhaps what we need is a definition of "truth". The best that I have heard is this:

Truth is a proposition or statement that corresponds to an independently existing reality.

Truth then is absolute, specific and totally objective, even though we may often try to apply the wrong truth to a situation and imagine that we have found error. If our so-called truth does not correspond to reality then *it is not **truth***. The issue is not *who* is correct, but *what* is correct, not our *rights*, but objective truth.

This book is primarily directed to those who have accepted Christ as Lord and the Bible as the Word of Truth. The objection will come from those who are not so committed that while truth may be objective, the appeal to authority such as the Bible for direction is not. If we are to seek objective truth we must seek it in science or reason, which are by their very nature purely objective. This too is a flawed argument. Every scientific study must ultimately be based on assumptions that must be simply taken as given and cannot be further proven. Science, in the long run, is simply the observance of events as they occur. We know that there is such a force as gravity because we see the apple fall. We then say that the apple will fall because there is a force called gravity. There is an inescapable circularity in all research. History, for example, can never be repeated and while research may suggest possibilities, we were not there when those former events happened. Therefore they can never be proven in an unequivocal manner. At some point, even in the most basic things, we must accept some authority.

But what, one may ask, does this have to do with the subject of this book? Just this: one trait that we must exhibit, if we are to honour God, is 'integrity', and we should also have a love of truth. It is not good enough for one who calls him or herself a follower of Christ to hold that 'our own opinion' is 'our own truth', and simply not be interested in other views which may differ from our own. How can we, with integrity, give an answer to every man that asks, if what we have is only 'our opinion'? We have nothing to resort to if that were the case. However, we do have a final authority, the Word of God. We must always seek to test our knowledge against the Scriptures and find out the truth. Consider how improtant "truth" looms in the Bible from these few quotes:

> *John 1:14*: And the Word was made flesh, and dwelt among us, and we beheld his glory, the glory as of the only begotten of the Father, full of grace and *truth*.

> *John 14:6*: Jesus saith to him, I am the way, and the *truth*, and the life: no man cometh to the Father, but by me.

> *John 17:17*: Sanctify them through thy *truth*: thy word is *truth*.

2 Corinthians 6:7: By the word of *truth*, by the power of God, by the armour of righteousness on the right hand and on the left.

Ephesians 1:13: In whom ye also trusted, after ye heard the word of *truth*, the gospel of your salvation: in whom also after ye believed, ye were sealed with that Holy Spirit of promise.

Colossians 1:5: For the hope which is laid up for you in heaven, of which ye have heard before in the word of the *truth* of the gospel.

The living Word is full of grace and *truth*. Jesus said that He is the *truth*. We are set apart by the *truth*. We are to commend ourselves as ministers of God, "by the word of *truth*". We trusted through the word of *truth*. We heard of our hope in the *truth* of the gospel.

Christ's words of teaching were often prefaced by the words "*Amen, amen*". This same amazing phrase, transliterated from Hebrew to Greek to Latin and English texts, is rendered "*Verily, verily*" or "*Truly, truly*", to affirm His teaching. At the end of a matter it means, "so be it" or "may it be fulfilled". Christ was never satisfied with an approximation of truth. Neither can we be. Christ, being divine, knew absolute truth. We being mortal can never attain such absolute knowledge. We can strive towards truth. When we say that "hair splitting" theology is nonsense, and we ought to go about helping the hurting, we have bought into deception. We may also have bought into pride. It can feel good to be viewed as a hero of the needy. It can feel bad to admit error in our own opinions. We do not need to choose between careful study and helping others. Christ did not. He quoted the Scriptures, healed the sick, and battled the false teaching of the Pharisees.

Among other things, we need to realise that many are hurting just because partial truth has been accepted as absolutely true, and because such deception has allowed injustice to abound. An apparently good cause can blind us to the fact that in all good conscience we may do harm to the very people we intend to help. Many are confused and unable to deal with reality. They need clear teaching and quiet instruction. How many have been led into fanaticism and some to self-destruction due to teaching that appeared to be true, and was close to true, but was not true? False teaching can hurt.

False teaching is a slippery slope. Once we start being

selective about which Scripture is important (in our own opinion) we can easily justify our own misbehaviour by the misuse of the very Word of Truth. Were the Jews Christ-killers? In that case we can develop a "Final solution to the Jewish problem", and could do so by ignoring the fact that Christ Himself, while on the cross, asked for the forgiveness of the Jews.

We tend to believe that it is the emphasis on minor points of doctrine that causes all the division within the Christian community. There is no reason why this need be. There is no reason why we cannot search ever deeper into scriptural truth without rancour. The problem is that we very soon switch from "*what* is right?" to "*who* is right?". In the final analysis it is not a difference in doctrine that causes the dissension, though that difference may be present, but pride and the fact that the discussion has slipped to a matter of personalities.

All of this has to do with our relationship with other people but there is something more involved. Integrity is an internal matter. To honour Christ we must be people of honour. I must be able to look into myself and know that I am being truthful with myself and know that I am seeking His truth and not just what is expedient. Each of us is an individual and in the final test we are answerable to Christ. Can we tell Him that the details of His Word were not all that important?

> *Romans 3:4*: Not at all! Let God be true, and every man a liar. As it is written: "So that you may be proved right when you speak and prevail when you judge." (Psalm 51:4, *NIV*)

A small lie destroys credibility. An interest in convenient truth destroys integrity. We are answerable to God not man. Paul spoke of pressing towards the mark. Our first goal must be to seek His will and truth. We need not judge our fellow believers, but we should judge our own responsibilities in the light of His Word, as we understand it. His Word is the only authority in all matters of doctrine and behaviour. There is no other authority.

The word "integrity" has some interesting connotations. It means "moral uprightness" and "wholeness". It is this latter term with its synonyms that is of particular pertinence here. Wholeness, soundness, coherence and consistence express the necessary ingredients of a Christian life. The word integrity is tied to the word "integrate", or to combine parts into a whole. This is just what 'right division' is about, setting each part of God's teaching into context so that coherence is achieved. The goal is integrity of understanding *and* walk!

> *Proverbs 21:3*: To do what is right and just is more acceptable to the Lord than sacrifice.

We cannot **do** what is right in God's eyes if we do not **know** what is right in His eyes. Look at a few examples of God's teaching on wholeness:

> *Galatians 5:9*: A little leaven leaveneth the *whole* lump. (A little false teaching spreads through the whole body of truth.)

> *James 2:10*: For whoever shall keep the *whole* law, and yet offend in *one* point, he is guilty of all.

> *Ephesians 6:11*: Put on the *whole* armour of God, that ye may be able to stand against the wiles of the devil.

Galatians teaches that a small error is like mould (or an infection). It spreads throughout the host mass. James teaches that anyone under the Law must keep it perfectly or they are considered totally guilty under the Law. Now we know that we are all guilty under the Law for Romans 3:23 tells that all have sinned and come short of the glory of God. Does this imply that we are all lost then? No! We are not under any law; we are under grace. We are saved by grace, not by keeping any law. "But take heed lest by any means this liberty of yours should become a stumbling block to them that are weak" (1 Corinthians 8:9).

Ephesians speaks of the *whole* armour of God. When it goes on to describe that armour, it begins with truth, continues with righteousness, the gospel of peace, faith, salvation and ends with the "word of God". It does not present choices that we can make of either/or at our own discretion.

It is true that we are creatures of limited ability, we cannot do all things or know all things but we can press towards ever-greater knowledge of His Word of truth. It is also true that each of us, by circumstance if nothing else, is in a position to concentrate on particular ministries. The question is, "How can we faithfully carry out the responsibility that God has laid on us if we are not fully aware of the full importance of the carefully structured design of His Word of *truth*?" or if we are confused over what pertains to Israel in the Acts and what pertains to the Body of Christ after Acts.

Let us look again at one of the first verses quoted in this book.

2 Timothy 3:16: All Scripture is given by *inspiration* of God, and is profitable for doctrine, for reproof, for correction, for instruction in righteousness.

We reason that the Bible is God's love-letter to us, therefore it is natural for us to think that **all** Scripture is written **to** us. As encouraging as this idea is, it is **not** true. We cannot simply take any promise in the Bible, or any doctrine or instruction, and apply it directly to ourselves. It is all *for* us but not *to* us. It is all profitable for us. Every verse helps us learn more about Christ and the wonder of His person. They teach us about His will and love for man. They teach us about how to be righteous, and show how badly we fail. He loves us anyway. The centre of the Bible is neither you nor I, but Christ. The Book is about Him.

In order to understand each teaching we must put it into context. It soon becomes clear that all Scripture is indeed not for us to follow. Think, for example, of specific portions of Scripture. Adam and Eve were instructed not to eat of the fruit of the tree of life. This has implications for us but it could not apply to any other person except the two of them since no other person has access to that tree. Noah was told to build the Ark, not us. Moses alone received the Law. John the Baptist alone was the forerunner of Christ. Paul was given the 'New Stewardship'.

It is clear that in His wisdom God has commissioned single individuals for specific purposes. In the process each one was issued instructions as to how to proceed. For example, of the five just mentioned, John and Paul, had the whole Old Testament available and had no doubt read it. Those passages in the Torah that related to the first three, Adam, Noah and Moses, were "profitable for doctrine, for reproof, for correction, for instruction in righteousness" to John and Paul and therefore "*for* them", but they were obviously not "*to* them". Paul would not build an Ark, nor would John serve any purpose in climbing Mount Sinai to seek tablets of stone inscribed with the Law.

Similarly, only Abraham was promised that he would be the father of "the nation" through whom all the nations of the earth would be blessed. Only David would receive the promise: "Thy seed will I establish for ever, and build up thy throne to all generations" and that the Messiah would sit on that throne. What is true of individuals is also true of groups. Each tribe of Israel was appointed a place in the

Nation's calling, but no Jew could be a priest unless he was of the tribe of Levi. And the Twelve Apostles were another special group.

These are but a few instances in which God elected groups or individuals for specific tasks and gave them specific promises. God's word is true; it "corresponds to an independently existing reality". That "reality" is God's will. Let God be true! What God has ordained is certain.

God's word is not only true but it also possesses an exquisite integrity. Each part is integrated to present a complete whole. Each part modifies and illuminates each other part. Prophecy in the Old Testament finds its fulfilment in the New. Indeed, without knowledge of the Old Testament, the New would be almost unintelligible. The New Testament, for its part, completes and fulfils the Old. In modern medicine one approach that has merit is called "holism", that is the theory that the whole is to be regarded as greater than the sum of its parts. One treats the whole person rather than the symptoms. There is a parallel. We need to take a holistic approach to our faith. When we accept the Lordship of Christ, we dare not simply take what is beneficial to us as we see it. We need the whole mind of God as revealed in His Word. A mistake in our understanding of the Bible will inevitably lead to a mistake in our service.

Truth, especially scriptural truth, in so far as we are concerned, is objective. Integrity applied to us can be very subjective. It is hardly necessary to point out that as God's elect, we are responsible not only for the way we treat others, but also as stewards of God's Word. If we misrepresent scriptural truth, no matter how innocently, we may mislead others, younger and weaker believers, into folly. We will also damage our testimony before the unbeliever.

In the first line of chapter 1 of this book I mentioned the denominational divisions within the body of believers. This is a continual problem. Over the centuries many wars, hatreds and much injustice have been the result. It is easy to say that we should just ignore the differences. They don't matter anyway. The implications of this approach are not as simple as they would appear.

Some differences are very real and important. If Christ is not the only way to God then what does Christian or Christianity mean? Is salvation just a question of being good? Is there any after-life? Do we have to belong to some particular group to gain heaven if there is a heaven? The truth is that we do not have the capacity simply to wish these differences out of existence. Each of us, as individuals, start at exactly the same point. We know nothing. We build up knowledge step by step. Because we come to each problem from different viewpoints and biases, we come to different conclusions. This does not make those conclusions unimportant. What we think about Christ, our fellow humans, or such things as justice and the well being of society, are not trivial matters. What we think of our duty to our stewardship of the gospel is not trivial. Since we claim that the Bible is God's code for our behaviour we cannot, at the same time, say that its internal consistency is less than vital or of secondary importance.

The goal of this book is not to investigate the difficulties caused by denominations or suggest any solutions. In fact it may be that this book itself could be considered to add to the possible disharmony. These are strange statements to make in the light of the fact that I have spent so many words and time emphasising the need for internal harmony and consistency within God's word and by extension within the Christian community. Would it not be better to set up a committee to come to an agreement about which things are of real importance and what Christian teaching should be, and settle it once and for all?

This has been tried often, and it did not and cannot work. The reason is simple. As stated earlier, a church is a gathering of called out ones, individuals! For the reasons that I have just given, individuals differ in understanding and viewpoint. Any arbitrary statement that purports to represent the beliefs of large numbers of people accurately, will ultimately leave some of those people in the position where they must assent to things that they inwardly do not believe, or reject the statement, or be rejected by the group. The alternative is to have a statement that is so vague that it has virtually no value. It is better in the long run simply to accept the denominational system as a given and continue on with personal study. The denomination is not answerable to God, the individual is.

To make it more personal: you and I are answerable to God. Integrity is a quality that God desires from us as individuals. We have the Bible and God has given us a sound mind. If we err in our thinking, we cannot blame the system or the denomination. We must answer for ourselves. I have presented my thesis as a personal opinion and at some point I must answer for my presumption. Simple honesty is a major part of integrity. I cannot avoid the fact that I believe that the Church of today started after the end of the Book of Acts. To deny what I believe, or even to ignore it, for however noble a reason, would be dishonest. For this reason I intend to write this portion in the first person singular.

There is a price to pay for seeking to follow God's word soberly and to the best of our feeble ability. The price that I, personally, have paid has been very slight indeed. Others have paid for their faith with their lives. It would be arrogant of me to suppose that those who do not agree with my understanding of the Bible are less committed to serving Christ than I am. Without question, vast numbers of people, who would totally disagree with the principles that I have laid out, have served the Lord much more effectively than I have. When they challenge my thesis it is because they honestly believe that I am wrong. They are sincere and, unfortunately, some are offended, but all I ask is that I am granted some understanding. This is why I have undertaken to present this book. I hope to show that it is not only true that the evidence is present in Scripture to support my view, but that the reason for declaring a view that is so contrary to commonly held beliefs, is not pride or contrariness but is motivated by the desire to serve Christ in an honest way.

The church that my wife and I attend is of the Open Brethren tradition. They practise the Breaking of Bread weekly and water baptism. They also accept the idea that the Church started at Pentecost. We have attended there for over 40 years. We are the only people still attending from the first day of the assembly yet we have never taken out formal "legal" membership. Some may conclude that our actions constitute an arrogant and judgmental condemnation of our fellow believers because some of their teachings are not in agreement with our own. However, this is not so. We cannot say enough about the way that these good people have supported us through difficult as well as happy times. It has often pained us to step aside when we would rather have joined whole-heartedly with them. This is one of the slight costs that I mentioned. We hold back because we respect their beliefs and we would not expect them to give them up to suit us, nor would we give up ours simply to gain acceptance. Each of us must hold to God's truth, as we understand it, while still supporting the other and regarding the other as fellows in Christ.

I have written this study not to criticise others but simply because I believe that the conclusions are true. It would be lacking in integrity to fail to declare what I believe to be the revealed truth of God. It would be equally lacking in integrity for me to change my opinion for any other reason than because scriptural proof was presented to prove the contrary. To say that "this is what I believe", but at the same time, "what others believe is just as right", may sound grandly open-minded but it is mere evasion. It does not come to grips with reality. Others do not need my approval nor do I need theirs. We both need answers for that time when we are alone. We also need each other's understanding and support.

This book started as a result of a visit to our home by two of the elders of the Brethren Chapel I attend. It had been decided that, in order to increase fellowship among the people of the assembly, the elders would undertake to visit each family and see what they could do to encourage or help them. The discussion came around to the fact that we had fellowshipped with then for so long a time and yet had not made any specific commitment to them in the form of a formal membership. There was no pressure exerted and no suggestion that if we did not "join" we were somehow not fulfilling our Christian duty. They simply tried to understand our position and see if it were possible for us to take a fuller part in the fellowship. We did our best to explain our position. The conclusion that they came to was that, as far as they were concerned, we were members with them in the Body of Christ in the local assembly on the basis of our mutual faith in the Lord, even though we were not members in the man-made Corporation of Bendale Bible Chapel. They regarded the latter, in spite of its obvious usefulness, to be less important.

As a point of interest, in this jurisdiction, and I expect in others, the "Corporation" is a legal entity, established under the authority of the government to transact the business of the assembly. It can hold property and collect funds as a charitable organization. It must have recognised officers, hold annual meetings and submit financial reports to the Ministry of Revenue. Its existence and use by groups of believers is justified in the Scriptures on the basis of doing all things decently and in order (1 Corinthians 14:40). The Corporation is not the "local church", the assembly of the people is.

We parted warmer friends than ever. I decided to type up a few pages of scriptural references with a few explanatory notes to make clear what we believed and why. A short time later I asked one of the Elders what he thought about it. His honest answer was "Lloyd, I don't understand what you are talking about. The material did not make sense to me." To my chagrin, he was right. I knew in myself what I believed but was very poor in explaining it to others. It was at that point that I determined to put down in written form my understanding of these matters, if for no other reason than to clarify them in my own thinking. We tend to become so absorbed in our own thoughts that it never occurs to us that our words do not match our thinking. We expect others to understand our statements about things we may have studied for years when they could not possibly do it. They cannot be aware of the perspective from which we approach the Word, nor are they privy to the step-by-step development of our beliefs. Without realising it, we tend to speak in a kind of mental shorthand. We quote verses and make series of statements without showing the connecting thoughts. These all make perfect sense to us since we inwardly know what we intended to say. The final result is that we all tend to talk at cross-purposes, each having good answers to questions that the other did not ask.

By putting down on paper what I thought, I hope to be able to examine what I have written and see where I have failed to say what is needed and to see some of the points where I am just plainly wrong. To give an answer to anyone that is irrelevant, confusing or inaccurate is more likely to bring contempt to the gospel of grace than it is to bring honour to the Lord. These two men have done their duty, forcing me to swallow my pride and rethink the way that I view my own beliefs. I have probably learned more than anyone who might chance to read this book.

A visit from another elder forced me to consider another thought. After a period of discussion about the breaking of Bread, he asked me, "Then do you think that we are doing wrong in this practice?" I could not give a good answer. Faced directly with the question I realised that I had been placed in a quandary. On the one hand, I do not accept Water Baptism or The Lord's Supper as legitimate ordinances for the believer of today. On the other hand I regard these people as believers dedicated to serving God and who accept these ordinances as acts of obedience to the Lord. They do not impart to these acts any value as a means of salvation.

If I say that it is all right to take the Lord's Supper, then it could appear to contradict my convictions on the matter. If I say that they are doing wrong, which was my first reaction, then I am suggesting that they go against their own convictions and act rebelliously to what they believe the Lord has instructed them to do.

I have come to the conclusion that the answer may lie in the Book of Romans.

> *Romans 14:12-14*: So then every one of us shall give account of himself to God. Let us not therefore judge one another any more: but judge this rather, that no man put a stumblingblock or an occasion to fall in his brother's way. I know, and am persuaded by the Lord Jesus, that there is nothing unclean by

itself: but to him that esteemeth any thing to be unclean, to him it is unclean.

It is written that all have come short of the glory of God. With our finite knowledge we *all* have errors in our understanding of the Bible. On the cross Christ asked forgiveness for Israel on the basis of their lack of understanding. This passage in Romans indicates that God judges on the basis of motivation and understanding. When a person deliberately does something that they believe to be contrary to God's will, then they are in rebellion to God.

Obviously, I believe that the "Lord's Supper" is not the will of God for me since I believe it was a sign for Israel; therefore it would be an act of rebellion towards God for me to partake. Equally, since the people at Bendale have never considered this idea, nor probably ever heard of it, they would be acting in rebellion if they did not partake.

Right from the first none of the elders, and there have been many different ones, has ever acted as if we were not fellow believers just because we differed from them in some points. They were chosen to be elders on the premise that they were mature and not given to rash or excessive judgment. That is not true of all the congregants. Some are new believers and, as in any group of people, some will not be entirely mature. To the weaker person we would be a stumbling block. If we were to loudly proclaim a contrary view, or take membership even although we did not accept the ordinances that are so much a part of the Brethren tradition, we could be the cause of much pain and confusion to these our brothers and sisters in the Lord. Better to fellowship quietly. For us, it is better not to have official membership of the assembly. It is not worth hurting others for.

Consider the case of Ananias and Sapphira (Acts 5:1-11). They sold what they had and gave into the common purse. The disciples were living in a communal fashion. The pair did not give all that they realised from the sale but pretended that they did. Peter condemned them with the words, "Thou hast not lied unto men, but unto God." They were free to give or keep whatever they wanted. Peter made it clear that what they did was entirely voluntary. Had they spoken the truth there would have been no problem or criticism. They had lied in order to gain acceptance and this was unacceptable. With the power given to him by the Lord, and as one to sit on one of the twelve thrones of the twelve tribes, Peter judged them and God confirmed that authority by striking them dead.

No one today has such power over any member of the Body of Christ. I would not be stricken dead if I lied or took the Lord's Supper. The point of quoting this story is to emphasise God's attitude towards truth and towards integrity. There is no deception in God. Christ said, "I am the way, the *truth*, and the life". Above all, Christ had integrity, wholeness (John 14:6). Any who seek to follow Him and be His witnesses on this earth must also seek to emulate Him in spurning even the appearance of falsehood.

We can and must respect the views of others. They are accountable to God not us. In time past there have been many attempts to impose a teaching by coercion of one kind or another. It does not work. You can force a person to say that they believe something but that does not mean they do, or even that they even understand what the issue is. Often the result has been reaction to an opposite view simply for defiance's sake with no real appreciation of the issue involved. This simply heaps division upon division.

Summary

In the last chapter, I dealt with the title question and concluded that it is legitimate and important to ask when the Church started on the grounds that we were commanded to study the Bible and this is a vital part of obedience. In this chapter, I have pointed out that truth is objective and not subject to how we rate its importance. Because of our fallibility, we can never expect to achieve complete knowledge of God's word but that is no excuse for failing to try. We also considered the idea that not only is truth in general objective and specific but Biblical truth is objective and specific. God spoke to specific people with specific instructions in a context that is a complete interrelated whole. Each part perccived adds to and modifies each other. There can be no teaching of the Bible that is unimportant, only parts that we have failed to understand.

God has called on us to be His witnesses on earth. Therefore when we are called on to give an answer to men, that answer must be as close to the truth as we sinful creatures are capable of. I became personal in one portion in order to illustrate that what we believe will have implications for our walk and testimony and the way others react towards us. If we cling to integrity and consistency, and avoid compromising scriptural truth because of social pressure, then our witness will be more effective. The beginning of the Church, which is the Body of Christ, is a part of God's word, and we need to study those last seven letters of Paul which proclaim it. These letters are important because they are the one part of the Bible which was directed specifically to us. Since we are members of the Church which is the fullness of His Body, it follows that the portions of Scripture which reveal the teaching concerning the Body is directed to us. We must study that portion, as we need to know His will for us today. "If ye love me, keep my commandments" (John 14:15).

Chapter 16

WALK WORTHY

There are two verses in Body Truth, (the last seven Pauline Epistles), that help put this study in proper context.

> *Ephesians 4:1*: I therefore, the prisoner of the Lord, beseech you that ye *walk worthy of the vocation* by which ye are called,

> *Colossians 1:10*: That ye may *walk worthy of the Lord* to all pleasing, being fruitful in every good work, and increasing in the knowledge of God;

The *worthy walk* is a reasonably clear concept and includes the merit of truth and integrity. Twice before we have mentioned Ephesians 2:10, which states that we are created unto good works "which God hath before ordained *that we should walk in them*". This is a subject that warrants an extensive study but all I intend to do now is deal with a special facet of the issue that relates to the thesis of this book.

In the two verses quoted, one must ask if there is a difference between walking worthy, "*of the Lord*", and walking worthy "*of the vocation* by which ye are called*". At first glance it could be that they are just different ways of saying essentially the same thing.

In some ways this is true. If you are walking worthy of the Lord then it follows that you will walk worthy of your vocation. As we mentioned in the last chapter, the Lord expects integrity from us so that we cannot do other than try to do all things as unto the Lord. Still, there is a difference. Walking worthy of the Lord is all-inclusive; no matter what the circumstances or what the calling. All who are redeemed by the blood of Christ are required to honour God by their life as a matter of gratefulness to the Lord. This was true of those people who lived before the choosing of Abraham. It was true of the Nation of Israel. It is true of us today. Remember again, Ecclesiastes 12:13, "Fear God, and keep His commandments."

The phrase from Ephesians, "walk worthy of the vocation by which ye are called", is different. It will require different things from different people. Consider Jonah.

> *Jonah 1:1-3*: Now the word of the Lord came to Jonah the son

of Amittai, saying, Arise, go to Nineveh, that great city, and cry against it; for their wickedness is come up before me. But Jonah arose to flee to Tarshish from the presence of the Lord.

Again we have an individual instructed to perform a task for the Lord just as others we have mentioned before. He was told to go to Nineveh. However, because he did not think it was right that Nineveh should benefit from the mercy of God (as they were Israel's enemies), we find him fleeing to Tarshish from the presence of God. We know his feelings because when he was forced to go to Nineveh and preach to them, and God forgave them, we read:

> *Jonah 4:1*: But it displeased Jonah exceedingly, and he was very angry.

He had actually decided that God was wrong and these people were not worthy of mercy. "Ye shall be as gods knowing good and evil". The point is that he was called to do something and he refused to do it until God made him do it. Before we judge Jonah too harshly let us remember that we also have a calling. Let us understand the nature of our "vocation" and just what it is that God wants us to do.

As God's servant Jonah was under the admonition to walk worthy of the Lord, whether by those exact words or not, but he also had a specific "vocation". The word "vocation" in Ephesians is the Greek "*klesis*" which is otherwise translated "calling". So it is with us. We are called to walk worthy of the Lord, but we are also enjoined to "*walk worthy of the vocation* by which ye are called".

Let us bring together some of the components of the thesis. Perhaps the best way is to step back and view the broad sweep of Scripture. It is always useful to look at chapter and verse evidence to understand any particular teaching in the Bible, just as it is necessary to examine detail of any scientific or practical study. A microscope will teach us how plants and animals function, but beauty is perceived by gazing across the fields to see spring colour, the world with the everlasting hills in the background. There is something more in the whole, than in the parts.

The Bible is "the book of the times". Eternity is beyond our ken. I have spoken of three "stewardships" or "dispensations". The first is eternity, which is the abode of God, and very little is said about it. The other two exist in time and are the abode of man, who is temporal. None the less, there are some things that are vital to man that are eternal. We know that God has given us eternal life through His Son. We know that we were created out of eternity and that our stewardship was "an holy calling ... before the world began" (2 Timothy 1:9). Some of the great questions are:

1. Why did God create man with the ability to sin?

2. Why would God send His Son to save sinful man?

3. Why would God call sinners to such a stewardship as ours?

4. In the light of these questions, what are the purposes of the two great temporal stewardships? This question is of critical importance to the study.

Definitive answers may only be ours in eternity, when we are with the Lord, but the Bible does contain some clues that can give us insights that are helpful.

1. Why did God create man and allow him the ability to sin?

Concerning man

> *Genesis 1:27*: So God created man in *his own image.*

Concerning Christ

> *Philippians 2:6*: Who, being in the *form of God*, thought it not robbery to be *equal with God.*

> *Hebrews 1:3-4*: Who being the *brightness of [his] glory*, and the *express image* of his person ..... sat down on the right hand of the *Majesty on high;* Being made so much *better than the angels.*

Christ's incarnation

> *Psalm 8:5*: For thou hast made him a little *lower than the angels.*

Hebrews 2:7,9: Thou madest him a little *lower than the angels*; (lower: or, inferior to) ..... But we see Jesus, who was made a little *lower than the angels* for the suffering of death, crowned with glory and honour; that he by the grace of God should taste death for every man.

Romans 8:3: For what the law could not do, in that it was weak through the flesh, God sending his own Son *in the likeness of sinful flesh*, and for sin, condemned sin in the flesh.

In this small sampling of verses several things are evident. First, among the beings represented there is a hierarchy. At the top clearly is God, who is the divine, immortal, pure being (I am). Below God there are two created kinds, the angels and mankind, with mankind at the bottom. Christ is "equal with God", and "the express image ... of the Majesty on high", "much better than the angels". He is God. In His incarnation He became "a little lower than the angels", for He was sent "in the likeness of sinful flesh".

How can it be that man was created in the image of God yet is mortal and sinful, while Christ was in the image of God and is immortal and sinless? There is a great difference. Man was created as an image or possibly a reflection of God. He has aspects that are similar to aspects of God. He is not the same as God. Christ is in His being the "form of God". He is the "express image of God". In Gethsemane (John 18:5) He used the words *"I am He"* referring to Himself, thereby claiming the title that God used of Himself, when speaking to Moses from the burning bush (Exodus 3:14). "I am", that is "I exist", but not in the contingent sense as in our case, for "In Him we live, and move, and have our being" (Acts 17:28). And Paul declares in Colossians 1:17, "And he is before all things, and by him all things consist." His existence is contingent on nothing and no-one but Himself.

Now, sin is anything that falls short of the glory of God (Romans 3:23). It follows that all human beings fall short of God's glory and therefore are included under sin. God did not grant man the ability to sin any more than He granted angels the ability to sin, yet both are under condemnation as sinners; all men, and Satan and his followers, have sinned. God could only bring into being sinless creatures by reproducing Himself.

The original question was - Why did God create man with the ability to sin? A better question is - How is it that man, of all creatures on this earth, understands what sin is? The answer is one of grace and love.

Of all the earthly creatures, God created man with freedom of choice. Only man is rational. He can distinguish abstract ideas and he was able to classify and name the beasts under him. In this at least man is a pale reflection of God. Adam chose to disobey God when he was tempted and ate of the tree of the knowledge of good and evil. Adam thought that this would make him equal with God. It did not. Still, the strange part is that it is this very quality of choice that makes us God's highest being on earth. Freedom, which we value so much, is the very quality that makes us able to knowingly sin. Had God made us without the capability of good and evil then all of our functions would have been purely mechanical. Love, in its highest sense, would have not existed in us. We would not have been worth saving, yet He loved us and valued us so much that He "gave Himself for our sins" (Galatians 1:4).

The brute beast does neither good nor evil, it merely reacts. Like us it falls short of the glory of God but it is not judged to be sinful, nor does it understand such a concept, for God has made only mankind moral beings. This does not mean that we act in a moral manner. It means that we are capable of distinguishing those values that we call morality from their opposites. It is this very gift of God that allows us even to question the existence of sin. We sin because God gave us the very thing that we demand the most, our own way. Then we blame God for granting us our wish.

Why did God grant us our wish? He granted us our wish because without the twin knowledge of good and evil, conflict and peace, greed and compassion, hate and love, we could neither appreciate His love for us nor show love to others. He wishes us to grow in love and grace. We sin because we choose to. This is the price we must pay for the honour of carrying in us the image of Christ without His perfection.

2. Why would God send His Son to save sinful man?

John 3:16: For God so loved the world, that he gave his only begotten Son, that whoever believeth in him should not perish, but have everlasting life.

In this most beloved verse we have an answer that is so clear and simple that it leaves us speechless. I know that He loved the world, but why would He love me? Perhaps, because of grace, I have both the image of Christ in me and the love of God. Let His words stand-alone. There is another reason. He loves the Son.

> *Ephesians 1:6,12,14*: *To the praise of the glory of his grace*, in which he hath made us accepted in the beloved ... That we should be *to the praise of his glory*, who first trusted in Christ ... Which is the earnest of our inheritance until the redemption of the purchased possession, *to the praise of his glory*.

Because we were created in His image, whom the Father loves, our redemption will bring praise and honour to Christ.

3. Why would God call sinners to such a stewardship as ours?

Romans 3:23 tells us, "For all have sinned, and come short of the glory of God", making it clear that there is no-one else to call but sinners. He is God. He can and does use even the rebel and unbeliever to do His good purpose; the pagan nations to chastise Israel; Herod, Caiaphas, Pilot and Judas all served God in spite of themselves. To us, as His redeemed, He has granted by grace the privilege of serving Him as His ambassadors. He does not need us. He simply loves us.

4. In the light of these questions, what are the purposes of the two great temporal stewardships?
(This question is of critical importance to the study.)

One may wonder why this question arises now, considering that I have already given reasons for their existence. I said that God's intent was that through each dispensation or stewardship Christ was to be exalted in a different setting. Through Israel He was to be exalted on earth and through us in the heavens. This is true, but there is another aspect of the issue that I intend to explore now. It should be remembered that the names that I assigned to the two great temporal stewardships are arbitrary. This was done for identification purposes.

The names parallel the terms "Kingdom truth" and "Body truth", when we seek to rightly divide the Bible into two great complementary gospels. I chose those names, "The stewardship of the earth" and "The stewardship of the heavenly realms", in order to indicate the "Hope" of each steward. Each steward has been promised that in resurrection life they will be granted the privilege of a unique place of service by God's grace. I would like now to examine them in terms of the great identifying feature of each stewardship, and consider God's purpose in connection with each.

Law

The stewardship that I have labelled "Earth", with its promise of the Kingdom, has always had *Law* written across it. In its fullest form "law" was given at Sinai and was called the Law of Moses. That was not the beginning of law however. Law was present in Eden. The prohibition against eating of the tree of knowledge was a law, however rudimentary. The first man broke it.

There was a law of ordinance for Cain and Abel to make sacrifice. Abel pleased God by his obedience. Cain's sacrifice must have been contrary to some instructions that they were given since it was rejected. And so it was through the centuries. Abraham and the fathers built altars, gave sacrifice, worshipped God, and followed some code of conduct that was intended to please God; all of this before the Mosaic Law was given.

As we have seen, the Mosaic Law was binding on Israel. They prospered whenever they were obedient. When they fell away from it they suffered the consequences. God gave them sign after sign. Miracles were theirs. The Lord delivered them from Egypt. Manna fed them in the wilderness. They were given the land. Invaders were turned away. They backslid and were carried into exile. Under Ezra and Nehemiah they were given another chance. Still they failed. They killed the prophets and rejected the Son!

God's mercy is great. On the cross Christ forgave them. During the Acts God still offered the Nation the promised kingdom, through the ministry of the apostles including Paul, right up until Paul was in Rome, when they were then set-aside for a season. Appropriately, even after the cross, as we have seen, the Nation was under the Law of Moses, right up until the New Stewardship was offered. During the Acts the Gentiles were also under law, albeit a very limited form (Acts 15:19-20), and signs and wonders abounded, but then came Acts 28:28, and after that change!

Grace

The Holy Spirit through the apostle Paul made known this second great stewardship, "the stewardship of the *grace* of God". This was a mystery that was hidden in God from before the beginning of the world and was not made known to man until this point. There were no more signs and wonders. The *Law* of ordinance had been blotted out. These last epistles of Paul completed the oracles of God. There was no more revelation only illumination. The Bible was complete.

The hope of this stewardship is to be seated in the heavenlies as joint heirs with Christ. The message is "For by grace are ye saved through faith; and that not of yourselves: it is the gift of God: not by works, lest any man should boast." It is *grace unadorned*. No law! No feasts! No new revelation! And there is no priesthood to stand between God and us! No signs and no wonders! No works of merit on our part. Just His love and His free gift of eternal life. For salvation we need only believe Him!

When we compare the two Stewardships there are a number of issues that need consideration. First, is it true that we are saved by grace and they of the earlier stewardship are saved by obedience to the Law? It would appear to be so when we remember again the verse in Deuteronomy:

> *Deuteronomy 6:25*: And this shall be our *righteousness*, if we observe to do all these commandments before the Lord our God, as He hath commanded us.

However, it is not so. This verse does not suggest that keeping the Law will be a means of obtaining eternal life. It only says that it will be their *righteousness*. They, like us, were created unto good works. The difference is that their good works were to be guided by the Law, but we have been told in Romans 6:18 "Being then made free from sin, ye became the servants of righteousness." We are to be guided by the examples given to us by Israel's experience. Eternal life is the gift of God. His gift is free so let us freely give obedience, not for gain but out of a grateful heart.

Even if they were able to perfectly fulfill the Law, there is no suggestion that it would do more than give them a worthy temporal life. Law deals with the quality of life on this earth and submission to God as Lord. They were only able to fulfil the Law through God's provision of a sacrificial component foreshadowing Christ's own sacrifice. This, too, was an act of grace on God's part. When they failed to obey the Law, God gave them prescribed sacrifices, rituals, and holy days to remind them of His provision, protection and love for them, and a priesthood to act on their behalf to seek forgiveness.

In spite of the fact that it was God Himself who gave these ordinances, remember what the prophet Isaiah wrote about those very things.

> *Isaiah 1:11-14*: To what purpose is the multitude of your sacrifices to me? saith the Lord: I am full of the burnt offerings of rams, and the fat of fed beasts; and I delight not in the blood of bulls, or of lambs, or of male goats. When ye come to appear before me, who hath required this at your hand, to tread my courts? Bring no more vain oblations; incense is an abomination to me; the new moons and sabbaths, the calling of assemblies, I cannot endure; it is iniquity, even the solemn meeting. Your new moons and your appointed feasts my soul hateth: they are a trouble to me; I am weary of bearing them.

This prophecy was written between six and seven hundred years before the setting aside of Israel. The Mosaic Law was still to be in authority over them for centuries. God had good reason to be exasperated with them at this point since they had repeatedly accepted God's benefits and at the same time allowed the sacrifices of the Law to become mere meaningless ritual. They went about living their lives to suit themselves and using formula prayers and offerings as a hypocritical veneer to cover inward rebellion. They were much like people today who profess to accept the teaching of eternal security but inwardly rebel against real obedience to God's Lordship. About 500 years before Isaiah the word had come through: "Behold, to obey is better than sacrifice, and to harken than the fat of rams" (1 Samuel 15:22). Yet still, through it all, they did not heed.

It would seem that God had given law to man, in one form or another, right from the time He created him, yet man remained in sin. Had God failed? No! He had not. We assume that law was given to make man good. Let us look at some of the many surprising verses that deal with the true purpose of *Law* and show its relationship to *Grace*.

> *Romans 3:20*: Therefore by the deeds of the *law* there shall no

flesh be justified in his sight: for by the *law* is the knowledge of sin.

Romans 4:15: Because the *law* worketh wrath: for where no *law* is, there is no transgression.

Romans 5:13: For until the *law* sin was in the world: but sin is not imputed when there is no *law*.

Galatians 2:16: Knowing that a man is not justified by the works of the *law* ...... for by the works of the *law* shall no flesh be justified.

But surely Abraham and his seed, Israel, must have benefited from the Law since they received the promise of the kingdom.

Romans 4:3,13: For what saith the Scripture? Abraham believed God, and it was counted to him for righteousness ... For the promise, that he should be the heir of the world, was *not* to Abraham, or to his seed, through the *law*, but through the righteousness of faith.

The statement of Ephesians 2:8, "For by grace are ye saved through faith; and that not of yourselves: it is the gift of God" was as true in Eden, at Sinai, and at the time of the apostles as it is today. Only by God's grace can any person receive eternal life. Why then did God give the Law if no one could live by it anyway and it could not give resurrection life? If God is omnipotent, could He not just make us immortal? The answer begins with Galatians.

Galatians 3:24: Wherefore the *law* was our *schoolmaster* to bring us to Christ, that we might be justified by faith.

The quote from Ephesians was not complete. It should have continued with verse 9, thus "it is the gift of God: not by works, lest any man should boast". Let us review some points.

- God created mankind.

- Man was created last so that he could not claim that he had a part in creation.

- Man is mortal, because of Adam's sin, and so is subject to death without access to the tree of life, or a special act of God's grace.

- Man is lower than the angels and short of the glory of God, therefore he is unfit to reside with God.

- God loves man.

- God made man rational so that he could comprehend God even though he could not see Him.

- God made man emotional so that he could love, and return God's love.

- Rationality provides the means of doing things.

- Emotion provides the incentive needed for motivation.

- Man is born knowing nothing. He lacks the instinctive ability of brute beasts. He must be taught.

- Man was made a moral being. When taught, he can choose right from wrong.

- It is these abilities, to knowingly choose and to be able to love, that make man the highest and most loved of God's creatures.

- Eternal life is a gift of God so that it can be a pure act of God's love towards His beloved creatures.

- Eternal life is not of works so that man cannot claim a part in his own salvation.

- Without instinctive knowledge, man needs a teacher.

- The *Law* is that teacher.

The beasts of the earth kill and do many things to satisfy their appetites, but they are not considered to have committed sin, for where there is no law there is no transgression. Without the gift of language they could not receive law therefore they are innocent. They are incapable of sin, but they also are not offered eternal life. They know fear when imminent danger is present but they do not understand that they will die.

With man it is different. From the first, God has communed with man in human language. God spoke to Adam and Eve. He conversed with the great men of old. He told Noah to build an ark, instructed Abraham to leave Ur, and gave Moses the Law in man's written language. Thus we have the oracles of God committed to the seed of Abraham.

There is justice here. Man was given things not offered to the beasts but along with them came responsibilities. With knowledge, reason, emotion, and law, man was given all that he needed to live a perfect life and know boundless joy.

Christ had all these things and did live a perfect life, wholly pleasing to God, for Christ was God the Son. One thing was missing for man; man was not God. His life was dependent upon God and his nature was flawed. Law failed, due to the weakness of man's nature, and could not make man good, but man does not recognise nor admit that. If, by chance, man sees his own failure he blames God.

Usually man is self-satisfied. He thinks that he is as good as anyone else and maybe a bit better. He thinks that given a decent chance he can be good enough to merit the best, and that God really owes it to him to give man the best! It does not occur to man that he has been created mortal and no matter how good he is, his nature is not compatible with eternal life in heaven. Man must, by God's grace, literally be re-created as a new creature able to sustain existence in a totally new dimension.

When we think of being made a new creature in Christ, we generally think in a rather limited way of the observed change in a person's life when that person becomes a Christian. This is part of it. We do gain a completely new perspective on life and a new set of values. We are told that we are given life from on high and that the Spirit of God resides within us. This and much more is true. Our life on this earth is changed radically, but there is more.

Life as we have it now ends. Christ has granted us new, resurrection life in the heavens. For this we are totally ill equipped. This body is already dying when we are born. Corruption is with us every moment. To use a crude illustration, suppose we compare our lives to a damaged car. We tend to think of salvation in terms of taking the wreck to a body shop to get the fenders straitened out. It may look different but the weakened rusty frame is still there underneath. Its usefulness is still limited. What God does can be compared to melting it down and rebuilding it completely, as a new strong flawless vehicle. Salvation is a literal miracle on a grand scale, not just a make over. Perhaps this is why it is necessary for believers to die and be resurrected. God made us from the dust of the earth. To the dust we must return so that He can clothe us with a new body fit for our new eternal life.

> *1 Corinthians 15:53-54*: For this corruptible must put on incorruption, and this mortal must put on immortality. So when this corruptible shall have put on incorruption, and this mortal shall have put on immortality, then shall be brought to pass the saying that is written, Death is swallowed up in victory.

God's plan is far beyond separating the good people from the bad people. His plan is nothing less than to take those individuals from the two stewardships who accept His Lordship and, in the words of Ephesians 1:10, "bring all things in heaven and on earth together under one head, even Christ".

God's creation, and the creatures in it, are bound to obey the laws of nature that God Himself ordained. His Lordship over them is absolute, so they do not *voluntarily* obey Him. His Lordship over us is absolute but to us he granted a free will. He can command us but His calling to us is not dictatorial. He desires our voluntary, intelligent, and willing love. John 3:16 gives us His motive. John 12:32 gives us His method.

> *John 12:32*: And I, if I be lifted up from the earth, will draw all men to me.

God could have prevented Adam from his disobedience but He did not. He wants man to learn and grow. Adam's disobedience arose from his desire to gain the knowledge of good and evil. He believed that this would make him to be as God, but it did not. Amazingly God not only allowed him to disobey, but also in an act of grace granted man his wish by the giving of the Law, for by the *law* is the knowledge of good and evil. If man was to learn and grow, not just the individual but mankind, he had to be given the opportunity to try to do things his own way. He had to understand his own limitations. He had to see that he could not earn Gods love, but that God loved him in spite of man's own failings.

> *Romans 8:3*: For what the *law* could not do, in that it was weak through the flesh, God sending his own Son in the likeness of sinful flesh, and for sin, condemned sin in the flesh:

This is God's great purpose in the stewardship of *Law*. By it, He showed mankind that no matter how man tried, he could not be worthy of God by his own efforts; he must rely on God's grace in Christ. It is often said that God has no mouth but our mouth, and no hands but our hands to do His work. This is not true. He is God, omnipotent, almighty. He is perfectly able to speak to each person and command that person if He so chooses. He could command obedience. The difficulty with that is that doing so would frustrate His original objective in creating a being with free will. God is all-powerful but gentle.

Man, on his part, is not exactly what you would call a "quick study". God, on His part, gave mankind century after century to learn but man still rejected God's grace. So that man could find out for himself, God chose to speak to man through his own kind. This implies stewards and a stewardship. God's household was to be administered by individuals and groups of people. God walked with man in the Garden so that man could see the wonders of God's love. God gave the Law so that man could recognise sin and avoid it. God called the prophets to speak for Him and tell of His love and when necessary to pronounce judgement on them. God chose a typical people, the Nation of Israel, and granted them the privilege of receiving His written word so that mankind could learn from their experience. God acted miraculously to validate His message and His messengers. God gave His Son and man crucified Him. Christ arose from the dead, and His stewards continued to offer the Messianic Kingdom to the people. They rejected Him and it. God had spoken to mankind in man's own language yet it is written:

> *Luke 16:31*: If they hear not Moses and the prophets, neither will they be persuaded, though one shall rise from the dead.

All this time the message of grace was to all of mankind. The prophets and the Nation were simply God's stewards. The miracles teach of Christ's power. The Law teaches us of His goodness and holiness. The repeated opportunities teach of Christ's forgiveness. Christ's rejection of Satan's temptation, and His refusal to act with overwhelming power, show that Christ's way is gentle persuasiveness. Yet it is also written:

> *Genesis 6:3*: My spirit shall not always strive with man, for that he also is flesh:

Through all this time, God was preparing man for the great message of John 14:6:

> *John 14:6*: Jesus saith to him, I am the way, and the truth, and the life: no man cometh to the Father, but by me.

Then God the Holy Spirit, through Paul, set aside the stewardship of Israel. That message was complete. He did not set aside the Jews as individuals but rather he instigated a new stewardship and called a new set of stewards; us! We, both Jew and Gentile together, form one new Body of believers and are called to a vocation. He has given us a complete Bible. The Old Testament, the Gospels, and the books written during the Acts period, show that man, even given the truth, does not believe. Law shows that given enlightenment of good and evil, man will not admit his failing. It also shows that God is a just God and also a forgiving one, for He ordained sacrifices to give man a way out that should not be too difficult for him and to point to God's ultimate perfect sacrifice. The history of the Nation shows, because they are a typical people, that no matter how often God forgives, man rejects His grace and goes his own way.

God has called us to proclaim that God does not owe us eternal life. There is none righteous, no not one. We are not fit for heaven. We have no claim through genetics on His grace. The Nation has been set aside so even the Jew has no faint claim. God would be justified on the basis of His repeated offers of grace that have been rejected, simply to write off mankind as a failed creature. The wonder of it is that in spite of it all Christ died for the ungodly. His love is pure and without cost on our part. *Agape*, Godly love, is spontaneous love, irrespective of "rights".

The great purpose of the stewardship of *Grace* is to tell man that even after man's failures under *Law*, God still loves him. We have no *inheritance* through Israel but God has promised to seat us in the heavenlies as *joint heirs with Christ*. Grace is revealed in its fullest by knowledge of man's failure under Law. Law finds its fulfilment in Grace, Christ's sacrifice of Himself for us on the cross. Our calling is to declare grace unadorned by law or works, and to yield to the Lordship of Christ.

> *Ephesians 2:8-9*: For by grace are ye saved through faith; and that not of yourselves: it is the gift of God: Not by works, lest any man should boast.

God knows mankind's flaws so He promised Israel in the New Covenant (Jeremiah 31:31-34) that in the Kingdom:

> I will put my law in their minds and write it on their hearts.
> I will be their God, and they will be my people.

His strength for their weakness. Even so He has promised us the indwelling of the Holy Spirit, as well as the gift of life from on high. His strength for our weakness!

The Vocation

> *1 John 4:19*: We love him, because he first loved us.

With this elegant statement John sums up what should be the testimony of every child of God who ever lived. The parent loves the child long before the child knows what love is or even what a parent is. A child soon understands and returns that love, and when they are grown and no longer under the parent's protection and authority, they will still seek to please and honour the parent for the sake of that love. A child who does not do so is looked on with contempt. A person of honour will not willingly dishonour their parent.

Christ died for us before we were born. He loved us when we were yet sinners. God is our loving father who gave His own Son to redeem us. We ought not to need the penalties of law to motivate us to seek to walk in a manner that is worthy of the Lord, to honour Him. This is as true under *Law* as it is under *Grace*. We are all equally in debt to Him and all equally unable to pay that debt. We have nothing to offer but our faith, love, and obedience in return for what He gave us.

Our walk refers to our manner of conduct, the way in which we live. It is not only what we say and do, but also the way we think and feel within ourselves, the attitude we have towards others and God. All of it should be worthy of our Lord, yet we fail, but He knows our weakness and forgives us. This too is part of salvation, a salvation that was finished on the cross. He asks us to strive towards the mark, even though that old nature, the Adamic nature, is still in us, at war with us.

We are entreated also to walk worthy of the vocation, or calling, by which we are called. This is something that is more specific and more intimate. Each person or group is called to service that only they can perform. On a general level, each person is born in a specific place and time with specific knowledge and talent. Within these parameters they are bound to strive to be worthy of the service committed to them.

I have mentioned before a number of the many stewardships that there are in the Bible that are peculiar to individuals or groups; only Noah could build the Ark, only Jonah was called to Nineveh, only Daniel could walk in the den of lions. Each prophet and king had a service to give. To the tribe of Levi was given the priesthood. To the Nation was committed the oracles of God, the *Law*. This was their stewardship, their calling. They were to make known to the Nations through the Law that God had seen fit to stoop down to mankind in mercy and love, offering to reconcile them to Himself. All the nations of the earth were to be blessed through their faithfulness. How worthy they walked their vocation is something between them and Him who called them. Ultimately, through the New Covenant by the power and authority of Christ, they will fulfill their due service. We too have been granted a unique *stewardship*. That is our special responsibility.

Ephesians 3:2: If ye have heard of the *dispensation* of the grace of God which is given me to you wards (on your account).

Colossians 1:24-28: Who now rejoice in my sufferings for you ... for his body's sake, which is the church: Of which I am made a minister, according to the *dispensation* of God which is given to me for you, to fulfil the word of God; Even the mystery which hath been hid from ages and from generations, but now is revealed to his saints: To whom God would make known what is the riches of the glory of this mystery among the Gentiles; which is Christ in you, the hope of glory: Whom we preach, warning every man, and teaching every man in all wisdom; that we may present every man perfect in Christ Jesus.

All too frequently, when we see the word, "dispensation", we think of a time period during which God acted in a certain way towards us, an administration. This in part is true. There is a difficulty however. We tend to look at it in a passive manner. It is as if we were simply spectators watching what God was going to do next. This is perhaps why the idea of "dispensation" became so associated with prophecy. We want to know what is going to happen next. Am I being too harsh when I suggest that we want to know, "What's in it for me?" This seemed to be the case with the apostles. They wanted to know which of the Twelve Apostles would be the greatest in the kingdom when Christ established His rule. Again, James and John came with their mother who petitioned Christ to allow her sons to be seated on His right side and left side in His kingdom. We still have not understood that our place is that of a servant.

This is why it is better to translate the Greek word *oikonomia* as "stewardship" rather than "dispensation". Stewardship is clearly a call to service. As ones who have been redeemed by God's grace, it is our commission to make known to all who will receive the gospel of that grace. To do so is the "vocation" by which we have been called.

Let me make it clear. In no way do these "good works" earn us merit towards our salvation. It is a privilege that God grants us as His joint heirs *after* He has made us His own. They do not "keep us saved" either. Our security is a product of His finished work, not ours.

Jonah walked worthy of the Lord in that he worshipped God, yet he did not want the people of Nineveh to receive God's forgiveness. Israel worshipped God, (at least a portion of them) and they thought that the Gentiles were unworthy of God's love. Jonah was called to Nineveh, but he refused. Israel was called to make the righteousness of God's Law known to the Gentiles so that every nation should be blessed, but they did not do so. Jonah was made to walk worthy of his calling and Nineveh was blessed. Israel failed to walk worthy of their calling so Paul was sent as an apostle "born out of due time" to do a service that Israel should have done.

If we are to walk worthy of our calling, we must know what that calling is. We must be able to differentiate between what things were committed to Israel, and what things they needed to accomplish their task, and what things apply to us, and what the difference is, otherwise our testimony will be confusion and our walk ineffectual. We tend to regard each blessing in the Bible as ours to claim, but each failure or punishment we are glad to assign to Israel. If we do this, we will not be able to discharge our duty as outlined in Colossians. Look again at the words.

> *Colossians 1:27-28*: To whom God would make known what is the riches of the glory of this mystery among the Gentiles; which is Christ in you, the hope of glory: Whom we preach, warning every man, and teaching every man in all wisdom; that we may present every man perfect in Christ Jesus.

We need not only to walk worthy of the Lord, which is obvious, but we also need to "walk worthy of the vocation", which means carrying out our appointed task. He will never fail us. Let us not fail Him.

There is a special relationship between these two admonitions to "Walk worthy". They are not independent of each other. If we are to be faithful to the Lord we need to practise both. We need to consider what this means in practical terms.

We are not born with equal abilities so that it is not possible to state a series of "things" that each person should do but just that they should do the best within the limits of their ability. Some can evangelise. Some can pastor. Some can teach. Some can be theologians and there are many other possibilities. We tend to rate these functions on a sliding scale, a kind of "top ten", but consider for a moment. Some without special abilities can only strive to live a consistent loving witness with truth and integrity. In God's eyes, they will be called "good and faithful servants".

Dr. Billy Graham is admired as the leading evangelist of our generation. He has the God-given ability to sway great numbers of people and through him thousands have been touched by the Holy Spirit and accepted Christ as Saviour. Surely we might say that this is a man who is "walking worthy of his vocation". He has been called to declare the gospel of the grace of God and is doing so. The trouble is that there are men of equal ability whose ministry has turned out to be a disaster. They have been an embarrassment to other believers and a disgrace to God's name. The difference is just this. Dr. Graham has over the years striven not only to remain faithful to his calling but also to make sure that his walk was worthy of Christ. He has taken extreme measures to insure that no hint of scandal would compromise his witness. Your actions in day-to-day life can shout louder than your words.

There was a pastor in the early days of the Associated Gospel Churches of Canada named Revelation A. W. Roffe. I never saw him or heard any of his sermons nor do I know whether he ever wrote anything. All I know of him is from my mother's recollections. Mr. Roffe was always dependable and always there for people when they needed him. He was a quiet man unlike others of the same period who demanded attention by their charisma. They often faded away and some in disgrace. Mr. Roffe has in some ways been my role model. As much as I want to testify to the matters expressed in this book, it would all be in vain if I cannot live a life of honour and love before my family and those around me. The influence of Mr. Roffe's life has outlasted his words.

As important as I have insisted that knowledge is, and it is, to be committed to a walk that is worthy of Him is just as important. The one without the other can be empty words. There are unfortunately theologians who have allowed the pride of their knowledge to lead them to reject Christ in favour of worship of their own vain proclamations and to the condemnation of those who do not agree with them. The only sign that we can give to affirm our declaration of teaching is a Christ-honouring life.

Chapter 17
WHAT DIFFERENCE DOES IT MAKE?

I have given some answers as to why it matters when the Church started. Generally the answers given have been rather abstract but perhaps important. Chapter 14, "Introduction", deals with such a detailed meditation as is needful to God's command to study, and also to prepare oneself to answer any man who asks a reason for the hope that is in us. Chapter 15 raises the question of "Truth and Integrity". Given the fact that a "new stewardship" is given to us, we cannot with integrity simply ignore it. Chapter 16 points out that the "vocation" to which we are called is one of making known the gospel of *grace*. If we are to fulfil that calling, we need to know just what is included in that gospel and what is not, and to act in light of that knowledge.

There are three questions that must now be asked.

1. How do we differentiate between those things that apply to all believers of all dispensations and those that are peculiar to us who live in an age of grace; i.e. universal Biblical truth as compared to Stewardship truth? The difference between *for us* and *to us*.
2. How does knowledge of when the Church started, help us to decide this?
3. What impact is there on our stand as believers if we discern these matters? May there be a cost to us?

As has been mentioned before, all Scripture is for us. 2 Timothy 3:16 makes this clear. It is also clear that each verse or portion has a specific use. Not every verse is for doctrine, or reproof, or correction, or instruction in righteousness. Each has its own unique value. It appears evident that every word is not directed *to* every person. As we have previously pointed out, Noah alone received instructions to build the ark. The temple dimensions were *to* Israel only. Yet while these and similar passages were *to* those people, they taught all men in every age something about God and His will. They were *for* us though not *to* us.

The repeated use of "to us", and "for us", very quickly becomes confusing. A more direct approach is to follow the phrasing of the first part of question one. We need to know "those things that are to all believers of all dispensations and those that are peculiar to us who live in an age of grace; i.e. universal Biblical truth as compared to dispensational truth". I offer these definitions:

> **Universal truth:** those portions of scripture that define God and the individual's relationship to God, and their responsibility before God regardless of any special calling.

> **Stewardship truth:** those portions of scripture given by God as a means of calling an individual or group to particular service, and defining that service, and method of fulfilling that service. All that is unique to the chosen persons and calling.

By observing the former, we walk worthy of the Lord. By observing the latter, we walk worthy of our vocation.

When we speak of the nature of God as almighty, holy, un-surpassing good, omnipresent, and any other superlatives that we can imagine, this is universally true. The love and grace of God is universal. The sinfulness and failure of man is universal. All men are mortal. The gift of God, eternal life, is offered to all who believe Him. All who believe are called to be His servants. They are called to love and serve Him and their fellow man.

Regardless of Stewardship, it is true that "every one shall give an account of himself to God", and equally true that, "by the deeds of the *law* there shall no flesh be justified in his sight: for by the *law* is the knowledge of sin". God's moral and ethical standards as shown in the Law apply to all mankind as individuals. Ultimately all are to be made one in Christ (Ephesians 1:10).

Why therefore is there a need for these two great temporal Stewardships? The need stems from God's grace. He created us and therefore He knows our weakness. He knew that being mortal and limited in our ability to perceive great truths, we would be quite unable to understand or appreciate the acts of love and sacrifice that He had planned for our benefit. It was necessary for Him to lead us into knowledge step by step. We needed to be given what, in effect, we might call a great object lesson.

The first Great Stewardship was designed to tell us what righteousness and sin were, and to show man that however much he tried he could not succeed. It gave man the freedom to try to live up to God's standard. Opportunity after opportunity was given. Failures were forgiven. Priesthoods were established. Social structure was detailed in the form of a Nation. Signs and wonders were performed, to establish the validity of those through whom revelation was given. On this point we might note that all those who were healed or raised from the dead eventually sickened and died again so that these demonstrations of power were not executed for their own sake but as part of a higher purpose. For example, had Christ wanted to, He could just as easily have raised all the dead in the land but He raised only Lazarus.

But why a Stewardship at all? If Christ could raise all the dead, if God by the exercise of His will could bring worlds into being, if God could walk with Adam and Eve in the cool of the evening and talk with them, why could he not also speak with all men directly and exact their obedience? He could if He so wished. By His sovereign will He chose to grant man the opportunity to find out for himself just how far below the mark he was, and by that, come to realise just how much love Christ exhibited for us when He gave Himself for us on Calvary. When we read of Jesus' childhood in the Gospels a marvellous statement is made.

> *Luke 2:52*: And Jesus increased in wisdom and stature, and in favour with God and man.

God made us in His own image and it was His wish that by grace we experience something of the same growth.

When He cast Adam from the garden He distanced man from Himself and spoke only through chosen servants. Still, while He distanced Himself from man, He did not abandon him. Before the Law of Ordinance was given, man could know God and His will.

> *Romans 1:18-20*: For the wrath of God is revealed from heaven against all ungodliness and unrighteousness of men, who hold the truth in unrighteousness; Because that which may be known of God is revealed in them; for God hath shown it to them. For the invisible things of him from the creation of the world are clearly seen, being understood by the things that are made, even his eternal power and Godhead; so that they are without excuse.

God did not stop there. He chose to contact man through individuals. In spite of man's repeated disobedience, or perhaps because of it, God called a Nation and through them gave us His written word and His code of law in human language.

Let us understand what was included. At the base were the Ten Commandments. Then there were the details of the Law. These told man just what was good and what was evil. Laws of ordinance do not force anyone to act appropriately, whereas Laws of nature do. Laws of ordinance say, "Do that and this will be the consequence." There follows a list of penalties and sacrifices to compensate for the offence. This is where "An eye for an eye", comes in, "Let the punishment fit the crime". The Bible is not backwards in teaching both explicitly and implicitly, (by way of historical record) what the direct results of sin are to man's own well-being in this life.

God knew that man could not live up to the Law. It was man who had to find this out. Christ came and as a minister unto the Circumcision made the demands of the Law more stringent. After the resurrection God allowed the apostles to preach the same message up until the time when God decided to end this lesson. All during this time, since God was not personally contacting mankind, there had to be substitutes or stewards to act on His behalf, thus a Stewardship.

Since God knew that man could not live up to the Law, had that been the end, one would be tempted to say that there was some injustice involved, but it was not. The Law was weak because of the weakness of the flesh but it was also weak because the blood sacrifices of animals and the memorial Sabbaths could not make man fit to live in the presence of God. These were only shadows pointing to Christ. He is the reality. Only He can atone for sin. This is what is meant when Paul writes in Colossians 2:14, "Blotting out the handwriting of ordinances that was against us, which was contrary to us, and took it out of the way, nailing it to His cross." He did not destroy the Law, He fulfilled it. He did not remove that portion of the Law that taught us what is right and what is wrong. The righteousness of the Law is as valid as ever. It is those portions of the Law that represented sacrifice and provided symbolic memorial to God's grace that were nailed to the cross. Christ, Himself, is the just sacrifice. His death on Calvary is the only memorial to God's grace that we need. It is not symbolic but real.

Had Israel learned the lessons of that first great Stewardship and accepted their Messiah, it is conceivable that the New Covenant would have been enacted at that time. They did not. God, knowing this in advance since He knew their nature (how like ourselves they were), chose a new group of people to be the Stewards of this new gospel. He chose us in Him from before the foundation of the world. He called us the Body of Christ.

The great hope of this present Stewardship is to glorify Christ while we are still present here, and in the life to come, to love and glorify Him in the heavens, even as Israel's hope is the Messianic kingdom on earth. Our great purpose is that we might be the instruments through which God's message is carried to a world needing His love and to believers who need His guidance.

One lesson we may learn from the experience of Israel is this: that Nation became proud of its position and considered that the blessings and kingdom of God were their exclusive possession, just as some of the Apostles were keen for the position of glory in Christ's kingdom. In fact they were called to be *servants* of the realm so that all nations should be blessed. Paul addressed their pride in Romans.

> *Romans 2:25-27*: For circumcision verily profiteth, if thou keepest the law: but if thou art a breaker of the law, thy circumcision is made uncircumcision. Therefore if the uncircumcision keepeth the righteousness of the law, shall not his uncircumcision be counted for circumcision? And shall not uncircumcision which is by nature, if it keepeth the law, judge thee, who by the letter and circumcision dost transgress the law?

> *Romans 3:30*: Seeing it is one God, who shall justify the circumcision by faith, and uncircumcision through faith.

They failed in their Stewardship in part because they failed to recognise that God had marked them by circumcision to identify them as His servants through whom His blessing was to flow to all men. This passage indicates that Gentiles who honoured God in their lives would be considered by God to be equally blessed with believing Israel. God alone justifies. In like manner, we Christians will fail in our Stewardship if we do not realise that we are called to be His servants through whom His blessing is to flow to all men in our own age. Those who accept the Lordship of Christ are to be joint heirs with us, even as we are to be joint heirs with Christ.

Let me rephrase again the definition of "Stewardship" as used in scriptural context. A "Stewardship" is a commission or calling to an individual or group to serve as God's agent when God chooses not to intervene directly. The service constitutes the delivery to the rest of mankind, knowledge of God's plan for them, and God's love for them.

Just as the Gentile was to have a place in the Kingdom through the Abrahamic covenant, even so, through the New Stewardship, all who come to God in faith will have their part in the Heavenlies. It is one God who justifies all by faith.

The Stewardship Truths for the Kingdom are all things necessary to those called to that vocation that enable them to fulfil their trust. This includes those things relating to the *Law*, the prophetic basis needed to identify the Messiah, the structure and administration of the Nation, the signs and wonders granted to the people to confirm their faith, the unusual powers granted the Apostles to rule as just judges, and the promises to do with the ultimate destiny of any under that administration. In general anything needed to prove to man, from an examination of all those centuries, that he could not, on his own, live worthy of God's Christ. These kinds of things were unique to that stewardship and came through the Nation, and some described the Nation's position in the Stewardship, but the message was for all who came to God in faith.

The Body Truths are those amazing things that are proclaimed by Paul in Ephesians and Colossians as part of "the stewardship of the grace of God which is given me to you ward (on your account)", "you Gentiles", (also in the 5 associated books Philippians, 1 & 2 Timothy, Titus and Philemon). The things "which in other ages were not made known to the sons of men". There are no signs, no wonders, no law of ordinance, no priesthood, no sacrifice, no holy days, no earthly kingdom to come, and no covenant. Both our salvation and our walk are only through His sacrifice and by His grace. We have the complete word to teach us. We have the Holy Spirit to guide us. We have forgiveness and strength in Him and blessings beyond our comprehension. No summary or paraphrasing of those two books can begin to tell the wonders available to us in Christ. Please read them and meditate upon them for yourself.

I have spoken of three great masses of truth, Universal truth, Kingdom truth, and Body truth. The latter two constitute Stewardship (Gr. *oiknomia*) truth. The question still remains, "How does knowledge of when the Church started, help us to decide which truth belongs to which Stewardship?"

A rather obvious fact is that the beginning of "the Church which is the fulness of the Body of Christ" must coincide with the introduction of the new *oikonomia*. Just as the *Law* was not given in the absence of the Nation, even so New Stewardship truth was not given until the Nation was set aside. The "New Covenant", which was for Israel, and the 'New Stewardship' which is for us, are not the same thing. This has been established earlier. Since the Holy Spirit stated that Israel was to be set aside by the statements of Paul in Rome in Acts 28:28 it follows that all those elements of truth that constitute our Stewardship must be in those Scriptures written after that time. Universal truths will not be affected.

What impact is there on our stand as believers if we discern these matters? May there be a cost to us? Every person's life is formed by what that person believes, not by what they say they believe, but what they hold in their deepest being to be true. The fool has said in his heart, "There is no God," and lives accordingly. The materialist gives possessions and fame the place of honour in his life and acts accordingly. At every level and in every way, whatever a person holds to be prime, controls that person's life, and it is no different for us; (note our Lord's words in Matthew 6:21; "For where your treasure is there will your heart be also".).

Most readers who follow through on this book will agree with the general conclusions above, but they will want a more precise answer that will address their special needs as believers. They will want to know how all this will affect what stand they will take on matters of faith and teaching within the Christian community. We should not judge our fellow believers but we must judge the various opinions so that we can give reason for our hope. We dishonour God if we are blown about by every wind of doctrine or if we take insupportable stands.

As we all know, and as was referred to in the first sentence of this book, there are dozens of denominations dividing Christians. As individuals we need some way to decide where we stand. I am about to compare a few denominational stances in order to see how knowing when the Church started alters our understanding.

Before I start let me make three points. Firstly, I am **not** doing this to criticise the people involved. Every one of these groups were started by people with the best of intentions. There are within every group on earth some who are there for dishonourable motives, but most are honest, sincere people with the best of motives. We are all still learning and we ought to treat each other with great respect. Still, when we differ, we cannot all be right. Only those who have perfect knowledge can afford to stop learning, and I am not one.

Secondly, these are only sample groups. They do not begin to cover the possible variation of doctrine that exists. Let me say plainly that I consider each group mentioned to be Christians with a different understanding of the Bible to ours. There is one exception that will be made clear.

Thirdly, there is a great danger in this kind of exercise. We tend to think that if we can only prove the other fellow wrong then that is the same as proving *ourselves* right. That is not true. We may both be wrong. I am examining these few other possibilities so that readers can follow the reasoning and study for themselves. Each group has some distinction that represents a way of thinking. Other possibilities are infinite.

In these comparisons I will treat as proven the following, since they are the subject of the first part of the book. To do otherwise would be needlessly repetitive.

- The contention that the Church did not come into being until after the events of Acts 28:28.

- That the New Stewardship constitutes a new message entrusted to us of the Body of Christ, as Stewards, to make known to mankind, for their benefit as well as ours.

- That the Apostles are Stewards of the New Covenant which is to replace the Mosaic Covenant and institute the Messianic Kingdom with the people of Israel as a royal priesthood.

- That the powers and signs granted during the Acts period were to enable the apostles and the Nation to fulfil their vocation.

- That since we have the complete revelation of God's will in the Bible, we have all that we need to fulfil our vocation.

- That since our Calling and Hope is to the heavenlies in the presence of Christ, we have no need of that which is a shadow or in part. We as individuals have direct access to God through His Spirit and through His Word and not through any form of priesthood.

- That the Apostle Paul was the apostle to the Gentiles and that he was given this New Stewardship for us which was never made known to men before it was made known through him after Acts 28:28.

- That while there are numerous differences in doctrine between all of us, I will only deal with those directly affected by the above points. If these contentions are correct then there will be a domino affect on other issues but that will be the duty of the reader to consider.

The Roman Catholic Church

Catholic doctrine is based on the concept of Apostolic Succession. In the very early years after the death of the Apostles there arose a great number of false teachers within the Christian community. Even during the writing of the Bible there is record of people claiming superior knowledge and leading people astray. Some were Judaisers; others were just plain frauds. Look back at Chapter 3, "Canonical Order", to see some of the problems that had to be faced. The early Christians decided that the Apostles, who had actually walked with Christ, and those who had been taught by the Apostles were more reliable than people who came with what they claimed was "further revelation". During the compiling of the Bible this had a good deal of merit.

What developed afterwards was not so good. Those in authority evolved a power structure. The traditions that they established gained authority equal with the Bible itself. The very error they were trying to avoid became institutionalised. If there was a discrepancy between the Bible and what the "Church" said, then the "Church" could simply "re-interpret" the Bible. (Inwardly we all tend to do the same thing and it is just as wrong for us as them.) The priesthood claimed for itself powers that equalled those granted to the Apostles, thus "Apostolic Succession" through the laying on of hands. The authority to forgive sins is part of the confessional. Particularly pious individuals, usually ones having taken holy orders, are said to have miraculous powers. They are referred to as saints. New doctrines are proclaimed by Papal decrees.

Any good Protestant will know immediately that this is just Catholic heresy. But hold on. Did not the apostles have miraculous powers? Were they not told that they should have the power to bind things on earth and that they would be bound in heaven? Were they not granted the authority to forgive sins? Were they not granted revelation? It is not good enough to reject a teaching just because it is someone else's tradition rather than our own. Our stand, whatever it is, must be positive rather than negative. It must be based on Scripture not prejudice.

On the basis of Scripture we need to consider what the evidence is. Suppose that the Church began at Pentecost, which is the view of most Christians. Judas was gone. By God's authority Matthias was chosen in his place by the eleven to keep the leadership intact. That would appear to set a precedent. Apostolic Succession would seem reasonable.

If on the other hand the thesis of this book is true, then the problem is immediately solved. The teaching of Apostolic Succession is not valid. The Body represents a New Stewardship. There is no priesthood needed and the powers and signs that accompanied the Apostles' ministry became redundant after Acts 28:28. Peter was not the Pope, the first of a line, but a ruler of Israel. The Apostles are the leaders of the Messianic Kingdom and the powers were for Kingdom purposes. Twelve were needed for the twelve tribal thrones. Change was required. With the completed Bible we all as individuals answer for our own actions in the light of His Word. We as individuals have access to God and His mercy with no mediator but Christ Himself. This does not make Catholics less Christian, but simply misinformed Christians, which we all are by virtue of our Adamic nature. All have fallen short of the glory of God.

Jehovah's Witnesses

While many Catholics are believers in Christ as Saviour, it is doubtful if many of the next group are. The Jehovah's Witnesses claim roots to a Judaeo-Christian heritage, but the name that they chose for themselves says it all. They do not accept Christ as their divine Lord but are the "Witnesses of Jehovah". They do, however, accept the Bible as valid, though as interpreted by their own leaders. On that basis the Witnesses' teaching is subject to comparison in this study.

Strangely enough, while the Witnesses and the Catholic Church tend to think of themselves as being very different, there is a remarkable similarity in some of their underlying doctrines and structures. Both possess an authoritarian leadership. The Catholic papacy finds justification in the Apostles. The Witnesses find structure and doctrine in the belief that they have replaced Israel as God's chosen people. This is akin to Apostolic Succession but goes much further.

Salvation becomes very much a matter of works. Laws are important, such as the forbidding of blood transfusions on the basis that it amounts to eating blood and they state that the soul of an individual is in the blood. I know of no explanation why the entire Law, including the whole Law of sacrifices, should also not be followed once one part has been accepted. Be that as it may, the underlying doctrine is more relevant here.

The Jehovah's Witnesses claim that Israel the Nation has been replaced by the Witnesses since the Nation failed due to disobedience. The modern leadership replaces the Apostles in authority and the Witnesses are inheritors of the covenants. The rationale of this stand is invalid since the Old Covenant was doomed. God's full knowledge saw that Israel would fail, and the New Covenant was made with the same people (Jeremiah 31:31-34). Had they not failed there would have been no need for such a New Covenant. To say that God having made such a commitment would then disinherit those to whom He gave that commitment, is to call God a liar. Let God be true! Their view is certainly not intentional blasphemy, but intent is God's to judge. Nevertheless, the view is still erroneous.

One outcome of this view is that the Witnesses, having placed themselves in the place of Israel, see only the one calling with its attendant hope. This is why they expect to spend eternity on a cleansed earth and reject the very idea of the heavenly hope. Just as Job expected to be resurrected to earth, even so Israel's hope is on earth. If believers today are the inheritors of Israel and there is no New Stewardship to the heavenlies, then the Witnesses may be right. Clear knowledge of our hope in the heavenlies is only shown in the later Pauline Epistles. What these people have failed to understand is that after Israel was set aside, God gave a new message that was never told to the sons of men before. There is a New Stewardship, a new hope in the heavens, a new purpose that is to be to the praise of His glory up there, and a new message, the gospel of grace.

Since the validity of the foundation doctrine of the Jehovah Witness movement comes into question, (their position as inheritors of Israel's blessings), all other of their teaching is brought into doubt. A Witness may well argue that my understanding is wrong, and that their leadership has the true understanding. Good, then I would refer anyone to the Berean principle of Acts 17:11: "These were more noble than those at Thessalonica, in that they received the word with all readiness of mind, and searched the Scriptures daily, whether these things were so." By all means *do not* take my word for anything but also do not take anyone else's word. Rather go to the Scriptures and find out for yourself. We cannot hide behind anyone to avoid our own responsibility.

Seventh Day Adventists

The following are excerpts from the *Seventh-day Adventist Church Manual*, from the Chapter 2 marked "Fundamental Beliefs of Seventh-day Adventists". I have chosen portions from 4 of 27 propositions listed. They have been chosen because they are comparable to the thesis of this book.

11. The Church

> The Church is a community of believers who confess Jesus Christ as Lord and Saviour. *In continuity with the people of God of the Old Testament times*, we are called out from the world ...

12. The Remnant and Its Mission

> *The universal church* is composed of all who truly believe in Christ, but in the last days, a time of apostasy, *a remnant has been called out* to keep the commandments of God and the faith of Jesus. This remnant announces the arrival of the judgment hour ...

18. The Law of God

> The great principles of God's law are embodied in the *Ten Commandments* ... These precepts are the basis of *God's covenant with His people* and the standard of God's judgement ...

19. The Sabbath

> The fourth commandment of God's *unchangeable law* requires the observance of this *seventh-day Sabbath* as a day of rest, worship, and ministry in harmony with the teaching and practice of Jesus, the Lord of the Sabbath ... The Sabbath is *God's perpetual sign of His eternal covenant between Him and His people* ...

The Adventists speak of a universal church that exists "in continuity with the people of God of the Old Testament time". Because of this, since their standing rests on the same foundation as Israel, it is necessary for them to be very legalistic in their outlook. They state that "The Ten Commandments" are the basis of "God's covenant with His people". They go further and focus on the fourth commandment, and speak of "God's unchangeable law," of the "seventh-day Sabbath". They speak of Jesus' practice concerning the Sabbath, and also declare, "The Sabbath is *God's perpetual sign of His eternal covenant between Him and His people.*"

There are a series of errors in this thinking. There is no indication in the Bible that there is such a thing as the "Universal Church". It may well be, "in the dispensation of the fulness of times he might gather in one all things in Christ" (Ephesians 1:10), that a universal "Church" will come into being, but until that time the "churches" must be separate if they are to be gathered. We have already seen that the Bible uses the Greek *ekklesia* and the Hebrew *kahal* to indicate various groups called for various purposes. During His earthly ministry Christ spoke of having "sheep" of other "folds". A church is a group of believers called together for a particular purpose. The Church which is the Body of Christ was not called until after Israel was set aside. God can and does subject each "called assembly" to different purposes and different disciplines. It is obvious that all believers are subject to the Lordship of God, and all fall short of His glory, but each has a unique position before Him.

Interestingly, the "Church Manual" also states that a remnant has been called out for a special purpose. This "remnant" is of course The Adventist Church. Called out from what, the Universal Church? Since the Adventist Church considers itself to be one with the Nation of Israel, this would make sense from their viewpoint but if there is a new calling to a New Stewardship for today then it does not. The "remnant" referred to is always identified as being "the remnant of Judah" or "the remnant of Israel".

A point is made about the fourth commandment of God's unchanging law. This sounds very impressive but it is not as compelling an argument as it would appear. The righteousness of the Law of God is absolute, but its terms and application can and do change. Man cannot alter them but God can and does. Remember again Christ's parable about the workers in the vineyard and the answer to their complaints, Matthew 20:15, "Is it not lawful for me to do what I will with my own?"

The Ten Commandments were an integral part of the Law of Moses delivered to the Nation in the Pentateuch. Christ fulfilled the

Law and confirmed it. As we have noted, in some instances He even made it more stringent when teaching the Apostles. However, we find out in Colossians that Christ nailed the "Law of Ordinance" to the Cross. These most surely were changes. In His earthly ministry He declared that if we put ourselves under one part of the Law, we are under all the Law. If we insist on laws pertaining to blood or the Sabbath day, are we not also bound to fulfil all ceremonial and dietary laws, and laws of sacrifice also? The Council of Jerusalem (Acts 15) did not put the Gentiles under the strict Mosaic code that was applicable to the Jews. Without some guidance we would appear to have confusion in the matter.

All of the Mosaic Law does not apply to all people, at all times, under all circumstances. The Law of Moses was the substance of the "Old Covenant" and by God's solemn promise through Jeremiah was to be replaced by the "New Covenant" for Israel and Judah. As has been repeatedly pointed out, the New Covenant is *not* the New Stewardship. The "Nation" is not the "Body". There were two special signs that were peculiar to the "Nation" that marked them out as God's chosen "People", not simply as a gathering of individuals, but as a nation among the nations. We are called out as individuals from among the unbelievers.

The one sign is of course circumcision. The other sign is clearly stated in Exodus but its status as such is almost universally ignored.

> *Exodus 31:12-17:* And the Lord spoke to Moses, saying, Speak thou also to the children of Israel, saying, Verily my *sabbaths* ye shall keep: for it is a sign between me and you throughout your generations; that ye may know that I am the Lord that doth sanctify you. Ye shall keep the *sabbath* therefore; for it is holy to you ... for whoever doeth any work in it, that soul shall be cut off from among his people. Six days may work be done ... Wherefore the children of Israel shall keep the sabbath, to observe the sabbath throughout their generations, for a perpetual covenant. It is a sign between me and the children of Israel for ever.

It is abundantly clear that the only weekly Sabbath taught in the Bible was the seventh day Sabbath. It is just as clear from the above passage that it is a sign between God and the children of Israel. The weekly Sabbath is an integral part of the Mosaic Covenant. It is the only one of the Ten Commandments that is symbolic and commemorative in nature. All the others deal with matters of righteousness. Only this one comes under the heading of ordinance. Not only did the Council of Jerusalem not impose it on the Gentiles, but also, after the New Stewardship was given, Paul in Colossians explicitly writes:

> *Colossians 2:16-17*: Let no man therefore judge you in food, or in drink, or in respect of an feast day, or of the new moon, or of *the sabbaths*: Which are a shadow of things to come; but the body is of Christ.

As a rule, observing the principle of Sabbath rest is of benefit to any society. A day set apart from the insane materialistic rush of life for worship, or in the very least contemplation, a day spent with family and friends, cannot help but enhance society. We truly need time aside to appreciate the wonder of our existence. This is typical of all the Law. God gave it all for our benefit. Christ said that the Sabbath was made for man not man for the Sabbath.

Let us bear in mind, when we note Jesus' practice with regard to the Sabbath. He was not only the Christ of God, the Saviour of the world. He was in His earthly ministry, the Messiah of Israel. He came unto His own, Israel. Remember again:

> *Romans 15:8:* Now I say that Jesus Christ was a minister of the circumcision for the truth of God, to confirm the promises made to the fathers.

The error lies in the failure to recognise that the law of ordinance and the covenants were given to Israel as the oracles of God for their obedience and that we have a new commission that does not include them. By following this error we are failing to fully acknowledge the Gospel of Grace that is ours to proclaim. Let us walk worthy of the vocation wherein we are called.

When we allow ourselves to become legalistic, we fall into the same error that was exhibited in Antioch in Acts 15, when men came from Judaea and tried to impose the Mosaic Law on the Gentiles. The Council of Jerusalem was called together to address the matter, and the very men whom Christ had empowered to deal with just such matters rejected the notion that the Gentiles should keep the Law of Moses.

The Pentecostal Movement

In time past I regularly attended Pentecostal churches and have had many years of wonderful fellowship with these devoted Christians. Please do not consider this a personal attack on Pentecostals or their churches. What I wish to deal with is their *raison d'être* as a movement.

The Pentecostal movement is part of the Holiness group of churches. They all believe, to one extent or another, that the individual's salvation and security is based partly on works. Christ's sacrifice is viewed as the ultimate cause of our redemption but we must work to remain faithful if we are to be acceptable followers and retain our salvation. We can lose our salvation if we stray or are away from God at the time of our death. They also believe that the Church began at Pentecost.

What differentiates the Pentecostals as such, is a very firm conviction that whatever was available to the church during the period of the Book of Acts is available to the Christian today. This includes all the powers, miracles, signs and authorities granted to the Apostles. Clearly, if the Body did not come into being until after Acts 28:28, and a completely new Stewardship was introduced that did not include these items and was not even made known until after that time, then this very basic pillar of the movement is unsound.

One criticism of the Pentecostals that is not acceptable is that their teaching is basically just emotionalism. There are too many earnest, level-headed, Pentecostal teachers who are committed to God's Word to accept that. They simply teach the Word, as they understand it. It may well be that certain individuals and groups have become too emotional, and that emotionalism has led to extreme behaviour to the detriment of the Christian community. Sober Pentecostal groups have had to deal with such situations and correct them, but so have others who have been in such unfortunate positions. Understanding is needed rather than censure. One would suggest that if the sign gifts, tongues and miraculous healings, etc., are present, then there is ample reason to be emotional. In any event, judging people is not only unjust, it brings us no closer to discerning whether a teaching is scriptural or not. Again, truth is objective not subjective.

If the Church did in fact begin at Pentecost then we surely must expect such signs and wonders to be present. Again we must compare this stance to that of the Roman Church. Both views constitute an acceptance of the idea that there is a kind of Apostolic

Succession in operation. Without some clear point of demarcation, separating the Church of today from the Church in Acts, it is hard to argue against this. It becomes a matter of sorting, little by little, which things are to the Jews, and which are to us. If we accept the idea that the Church of today is the same one that existed in Acts, there would seem no reason to doubt that whatever God expected of them, and granted them, should also apply to us. It would then bring into doubt the statements in Ephesians that there is a New Stewardship given by the Holy Spirit for us Gentiles, one that had never been revealed to the sons of men before. Paul's writing would be of questionable reliability. Since it is through Paul's writings that we learn of the gospel of grace we are in trouble. Again, if Paul's letters are unreliable, then is the Bible truly God's word or just a collection of man's works? This is far from an unimportant set of abstractions. If Acts 28:28 is a clear point of demarcation, if the Nation of Israel was set aside by God, and if the New Stewardship of Ephesians and Colossians was given, this, of necessity, changes the picture. Our faith is based on our acceptance of God's completed Word alone without the need of signs and wonders. To phrase it succinctly, the Church in Acts was chosen for one purpose and given what they needed to fulfil their task, and we were chosen for another purpose and given what we need to fulfil ours. They are not the same.

Conservative, Evangelical, Fundamental

The last group to consider at this time, as being typical, is those churches often referred to as Conservative, Evangelical and Fundamental. Among them are the Associated Gospel, The Baptist, and the Open Brethren. My grandparents and my aunts and uncles were involved in the church that was I believe the first of the Associated Gospel denomination, pastored by P. W. Philpott the founder. My uncle was a Baptist minister, and we helped, as I mentioned before, commence the work of Bendale, an Open Brethren Assembly. My roots are deep in this movement. The Salvation Army, my wife's, Olive's, background, shares some of the views of both the Pentecostals and the Conservatives. We have no desire to hurt or offend any of these dear people. However, honesty and devotion to the principle of the ultimate authority of the Bible, requires us to make plain the differences of opinion that we have with them and just how this affects the way we look at scriptural truth.

The Conservatives, ourselves included, hold to the doctrine of salvation by grace alone and not of works. They teach eternal security through Christ's work on Calvary. In all essentials they are sound. As a reminder, the essentials are, the sole authority and accuracy of the Bible, the Divine nature of the person of Christ as God the Son, equal with and co-existent with God the Father and God the Holy Spirit, and the complete efficacy of Christ's sacrifice on the Cross as the only means of man's salvation. In most points we are at one with the Conservative Christians. In many instances we confess that their knowledge of the Word is superior to ours. We have a staggering amount to learn from them.

There are, however, some weaknesses in their teaching. This stems from the fact that Conservatives also consider that the Church of today started at Pentecost, yet identify no clear point at which "Kingdom Truth" ceased and "Body Truth" commenced. Each item is treated on an ad hoc basis, often on a personal preference manner rather than a clear biblical principle. This leads to some confusion.

- -They reject apostolic succession and the power of church leaders to forgive sin, yet the Apostles were empowered by Christ to forgive sin, pass a death sentence for sin bound by the authority of heaven, and to replace fallen Judas.

- -They reject the Jehovah's Witnesses' contention that they have replaced Israel as God's chosen people, yet often claim the New Covenant, the royal priesthood, and the Millennial kingdom of Messiah on earth for themselves, in spite of the fact that the Bible clearly states that these things are promised to literal Israel and Judah as the seed of Abraham.

- -They reject the Adventists legalism yet the seventh-day Sabbath was still practised during the Acts period and they seldom perceive that the Sabbath was stated to be a sign between God and Israel. During that period Israel were under the Law. Remember Paul's claim before Festus, "no other things than those which the prophets and Moses did say should come". At that time he still kept the Law and only after Acts 28:28 was the Law of Ordinance declared to be set aside.

- -They reject the Pentecostal's emphasis on signs and wonders and the expectation of miraculous healings and gift of tongues, yet right up until Paul's voyage to Rome all those signs were there. If the Church started at Pentecost they surely would be present today as they were in the New Testament times, unless some dramatic change took place. Such a change did take place. The signs were always identified with Israel and in Acts 28, Israel was set aside!

Note that I have been more detailed in dealing with the Conservative position than with the other groups. This is because as Conservative Christians ourselves, these are the kind of matters that we have had to consider in our own quest to search the Scriptures to see if things are of God. It follows that we have had to change our stand accordingly.

There is a cost. As much as we would like to, we cannot easily join formally most churches since it would in effect require us, at least apparently, to give assent to teachings that we do not believe. It is not the appearance that matters. It is the fact that to pretend to believe something that you do not believe is to lie. Most churches produce a statement of faith that outlines their beliefs. When you formally join a church their statement becomes, *de facto*, your statement. It is better therefore to fellowship without membership, but it does create a sense of isolation that is painful.

It is obvious that I have not in any way dealt with the bulk of the teaching of any of these groups. This is not an exposé. There are some things that they teach that I thoroughly oppose, and there are a vast number of things I thoroughly agree with. What was chosen to test was done so in order to illustrate how the question raised by this book impacts our stand as believers, and what wide results there can be.

In most cases the issue has been key to the existence of the group involved. The Catholics like most Protestants tend to begin the Church at Pentecost, but take the Apostles as the beginning the Papacy. The Witnesses look on themselves as replacing Israel but retain Israel's Stewardship and hope of an earthly kingdom. The Adventists on the other hand tend to see Israel and themselves as having a seamless continuity with the change being more in form than in substance. The Pentecostals also start the church at Pentecost but fail to note the vast change after Acts 28:28. The Conservatives recognise the changes but still start the Church at Pentecost.

One of the obvious effects on the whole Christian community of when the Church started, and which teachings relate to the New Stewardship, is denominationalism. One is forced to conclude that the thesis of this book is important. It also has great impact on our stand as believers and also on our walk.

18. Why does it matter?

We do not know exactly when, in terms of date, God gave Paul the New Stewardship for us Gentiles, but it was after Acts 28:25-27 and we do know which books of the Bible contain the knowledge of that great truth. We know also from the scriptural evidence examined in this book that by this New Stewardship, God has entrusted to us a distinct message and a distinct hope. We are to proclaim these to the world around us. Just as Israel was chosen to declare the Gospel of the Kingdom of the Messiah on earth, with its base as the Law, even so, we have been chosen to declare the Gospel of Grace, with its base as Paul's last seven letters. Paul gloried in the grace that he was given in these words:

> *Ephesians 3:9-11*: And to make all men see what is the fellowship of the mystery, *which from the beginning of the world hath been hid in God*, who created all things by Jesus Christ: To the intent that now to the principalities and powers in heavenly places might be known by the church the manifold wisdom of God, According to the *eternal purpose* which he purposed in Christ Jesus our Lord.

Now we know that we have been chosen in Christ from before the foundation of the world. We were chosen and instructed in the words Paul wrote to Timothy:

> *2 Timothy 2:2*: And the things that thou hast heard from me among many witnesses, the same commit thou to faithful men, who shall be able to teach others also.

The disciples were instructed to go into all the world to preach the gospel of the Kingdom. We are "to make all men see what is the fellowship of the mystery". This means all those values and teachings related to the New Stewardship or "dispensation". If we are to commit to faithful men what we have heard from Paul, we must be sure that we understand just what he did say and just what is appropriate to us as stewards of this New Stewardship. We also are not given the option of either/or. We are to take Christ as Lord of our life and treat others with love and respect, *and* we are to study to show ourselves approved and teach others the fellowship of the Mystery that was hid in God.

This is why we are told to 'rightly divide' the word of truth and "test things that differ". It is so that when we study, we will be able to place each verse and idea in its pertinent context. Whatever we teach we must first understand! This is more difficult than we might expect.

In the last chapter I looked at some of the teachings of five denominations or movements which take the Bible most seriously. The list could have been larger, but I dealt only with a very few matters that illustrate how the thesis of this book could reflect the way we could look on these teachings. This was not intended as an exposé of these groups. Had that been the case there are some doctrines that some groups hold that I find very disturbing, for instance, the denial of Christ as being divine. Such an approach would not have been helpful. The point here is that these and many other assemblies of people have in all honesty and integrity, taken the same Bible and after great deliberation come to startlingly different conclusions.

At first this appears odd. One would think that given the same book with the same words, providing we are willing to accept what is written as it appears, we would all, after reasonable consideration, come to the same conclusions. One world wide church with a unified statement of faith would result. Alas, there are unavoidable factors acting against such a result.

To begin with, we start life knowing nothing. We each learn within the context of a given environment and culture. Because we must function within that environment, of necessity words and ideas tend to gain special meanings. Sometimes the result is the formation of figures of speech unique to a geographic area or culture. Dialects develop. People speaking the same language often cannot understand each other because while they are using the same words, and they both understand the words themselves, the connotation of those words may be radically different. Many, if not most, words have alternative meanings. Recently I looked up the word "right" in the *Reader's Digest Oxford Dictionary*. To my amazement the entry for that one little word, extended to more than one large page of small type.

We commence with words that have differing connotations to people of different backgrounds and a variety of possible alternative correct meanings. The simple answer is that the correct meaning is set by the context, but that is not so simple. It is the context that we are trying to understand in the first place. Then we say that it is the one intended by the person who wrote the book. However, 2,000 years or more separates us from the people who penned the Bible. They lived in a completely different society to ours and they wrote in a different language to ours. Is there any wonder that God encourages us to study?

Problems are compounded by the fact that few of us are able to study the original Hebrew and Greek texts, so it is necessary to depend on translations in our own language. I could not even hazard a guess as to how many translations there are in English alone. Most translations are done by honest men, who sincerely want to give people the opportunity to study for themselves. It is virtually impossible for anyone to undertake the task without, at some place or other, personal or denominational bias creeping in. Every time we try to learn a new thing, we have to build on knowledge that we already have and time alone prevents us from thoroughly examining each item individually. We must and do take many things for granted, otherwise we could accomplish very little.

Add to this the fact that language itself is dynamic, continually changing in meaning from year to year, from generation to generation. For example consider the word, "propaganda". Originally this carried a good connotation. It simply indicated the means to teach or disseminate an idea or doctrine with no negative inference, as in mission work (to propagate the Gospel). With the advent of the Fascist Ministries of Propaganda, it took on a sinister meaning and now infers lying, quite different from its original usage. We all know words that have made such changes though not many with as negative a result. Some words simply fall out of use and become obsolete. Some words and phrases in older translations are almost unintelligible to new generations who speak the same language.

So far we have only dealt with individual words, and the Bible has many of them. The words form sentences. The sentences are interlinked to develop teachings on individual subjects. The teachings are woven together to form major doctrines. Each doctrine that we consider we find to be influenced by our understanding of other doctrines. Taken together with other items not mentioned, the possible combinations of the ideas involved, and considering the number of places where error can enter our thinking, the wonder is not that we find it so difficult to find unanimity in doctrine, but rather that we find so much unanimity. Added to the purely objective problems that we must face, there are many subjective ones as well. We all look at the world of necessity through our own eyes. When we study or learn anything, we first ask the questions that appear to us to matter the most. We may ask the wrong questions because we have a preconceived notion about the item to be considered. In addition to this, the Bible packs an immense amount of information into comparatively few words. One is amazed at the economy of words used to express powerful and far reaching truths. The language of Scripture is as elegant as mathematical formulas. There are often several layers of truth in a few phrases.

The list of difficulties could go on and on but there are two that are most difficult to deal with. The one is pride; the other is denominational bias. The two tend to reinforce each other. Love, trust, and respect, on the other hand, work against pride and bias.

We are now talking of motivation, why we accept or reject an idea, especially a view that is different from that which we have already accepted. Reason and emotion are both actively involved. The snap answer is that we need to be broad-minded rather than narrow or bigoted. Honesty demands that we be somewhat narrow in our thinking if we are seeking truth. Others do not need our approval to believe what they do; patronising the views of another is condescending. Neither do we need their permission for our thinking. If our motivation is self-centred pride then it is wrong. When our motive is to prove our superiority to others or simply to compete with others, we are in error. The only motive that is acceptable is the desire to obey God as our Lord and to seek His will.

When one considers all the violence done by people in the past to those of other persuasions, from burning at the stake to all kinds of legal sanctions, one is tempted to turn aside denominationalism as an unqualified evil. It is not quite that simple. Denominations are communities of people who interact and support each other. In times of crisis or sorrow we turn to those around us for comfort, advice, and help. We feel secure amongst these folk. The sense of love and respect engenders a trust in their opinions that is not easily set aside. We may be led into faith in Christ through a family member, a friend, a pastor or other church worker. Step by step they teach us all we know and they seldom deliberately deceive us. We cannot lightly reject their views.

The Apostle Paul warns us of the opposite case in Ephesians 4:14; *"That we henceforth be no more children, tossed to and fro, and carried about with every wind of doctrine, by the sleight of men, and cunning craftiness, by which they lie in wait to deceive"*. Satan is the lord of this world and opposition to Christ is abundant, but whether the error is deliberate or innocent, we must always search the Scriptures to see if what is said is of God, no matter who says it. The final responsibility for learning and witnessing to the truth rests on our own shoulders.

We are told to avoid being "tossed to and fro, and carried about with every wind of doctrine". In the same chapter we are counselled to, "keep the unity of the Spirit in the bond of peace" (Ephesians 4:3). Taken together these instructions would appear to indicate that a single great church with a fixed body of beliefs is what we should seek. Ecumenicalism has been a theme through the centuries for Christians. As fine a concept as this is, it is an impossible goal. Only under the direct and personal rule of Christ at the "Stewardship of the fulness of times", will there be such unanimity.

We are told, however, to keep the "unity" of the spirit, not to seek 'uniformity' of organization or doctrine. The two words and ideas are not synonymous or interchangeable. Unity implies mutual respect and support for one another as Christians, not abrogation of our individual responsibility as Stewards of His Word. For now, uniformity of doctrine would only be a possibility if either we all have perfect knowledge or are willing to set aside things that within ourselves we actually believe in order to placate others. This is neither honest nor honourable. We do not need to agree in order to view each other as fellow-Christians or to love one another as Christ commanded. Mutual respect is more apt to exist between those who openly disagree without rancour and who treat each other with civility.

We now come to the central theme of the argument of this book. The underlying purpose and message of the two great Stewardships contrast with each other. I have throughout this book referred to Acts 28:28, and the events at Rome when the Holy Spirit through the Apostle Paul set aside the Nation of Israel for a season, as the point of demarcation between the Gospel of the Kingdom and the Gospel of Grace. Grace was always present but it was not always openly expressed as it is now. It is appropriate to repeat this crucial verse now, along with the 29th verse so that there can be no confusion.

> *Acts 28:28-29*: Be it known therefore to you, that the salvation of God is sent to the Gentiles, and they will hear it. And when he had said these words, the Jews departed, and had great disputing among themselves.

The twenty-eighth verse has at times been referred to as a "Dispensational barrier" between the two bodies of truth. I find this to be somewhat awkward in that it appears to suggest that the two gospels are totally separate, as if having accepted the one, the other could be ignored. In fact they are very interdependent. They explain and complement each other. I prefer to think of the verse as a kind of prism that allows us to bring the two into focus, overlaying "Kingdom truth" with "Body truth" and in the process enhancing our understanding and appreciation of both.

No teaching can be based on a single verse and it is no different in this case. The passage is simply a marker between two great bodies of truth. In the first it is as if God said to man:

> "Child, I will give you every chance to work to be good enough to be worthy of eternal life but you will always fail! I will give you the Law so that you will know what is right and what is wrong and because of this you will understand the extent and the value of the love and grace that I have extended to you."

Israel, as a typical people, acted as a surrogate for mankind in general. Their history of constant failure is exactly what would have occurred no matter to what people God had committed His message.

The Law of Moses was Israel's charter, the Kingdom the hope. No-one has ever had a better opportunity. In the long run the Kingdom will be theirs but not because of their merit, but by His grace through the giving of the "New Covenant", which is His work alone. They may have failed but He will not. His love is great. Christ wept for Jerusalem even though it rejected Him. His love for them will triumph ultimately.

The second great message might be paraphrased:

> "You are sinners and just as flawed as Israel but I love you. I have set the Law aside because it has served its purpose. Now just come to me and receive eternal life as My free gift. My grace alone is sufficient. I want you here with me in the heavenlies as my joint heirs. I want you to fulfil the stewardship that I have called you to, not for selfish reasons, because you want to get to heaven or win a reward, but just because you love Me and your neighbours, whom I love dearly also. I will dwell in you in the person of the Holy Spirit so that you only need to ask and I will give you the strength to do My will."

In the Old Stewardship we see a picture of blackness, man's continual rejection of God. God gave man a wonderful world in which to live, and man became so corrupt that the flood was necessary. Sodom and Gomorrah despised the righteousness of God. God freed the Nation of Israel from bondage in Egypt. They built a golden calf to worship. Abraham lied. David murdered. Christ was crucified. Even after the cross Christ sent the Apostles to offer the Kingdom to the Nation but they would receive neither Him nor the Kingdom. Then comes the change. A "new people" is called and *grace* is proclaimed! To this new Body of believers, to us, is committed the new message. It is the message of Ephesians 2, which has been repeated before in this book.

> *Ephesians 2:8-10*: For by grace are ye saved through faith; and that not of yourselves: it is the gift of God: Not by works, lest any man should boast. For we are his workmanship, created in Christ Jesus to good works, which God hath before ordained that we should walk in them.

It is the message of God's *agape* love. It is unqualified love. While we were yet sinners Christ died for us. Against the backdrop of man's unending failure is set the dazzling brilliance of God's love. It is like a diamond on black velvet.

Only when we come to appreciate the sharp contrast between the two Stewardships can we come to understand the total interdependence of the two. One gospel of love expressed to mankind through two Stewardships, one for the Jews in the past, and one for us today. We must be faithful to our own calling.

Still, after all these great matters have been considered, one may yet ask, "Why does this apparently minor matter of when the Church started rate serious thought?" The question, "Why does it matter?" is essentially a matter of personal evaluation. We mean, "Why does it matter to me, and why should I bother about it?" These are the kinds of questions we need to ask. We need to know how we should act and react in any important relationship in life, whether it is with those around us or, more important, with our Saviour.

We have dedicated this book to our children and grandchildren. The thesis has been presented as a personal opinion. It could be no other way. No matter how much evidence we may present or how much we insist that it is scripturally correct, the fact remains that each individual must decide for himself what to believe. With this in mind I will try to approach this from a personal viewpoint and try to explain how we feel about our stand.

Let me repeat, and I can scarcely do it strongly enough, we are saved by Christ's finished work on Calvary alone. Knowing when the Church started will not add one thing to our redemption, nor will it help to keep us saved. We are complete in Christ alone. He is our redemption.

God did not have to save us. He did not owe it to us to save us. He would have been perfectly justified in simply destroying mankind either as an interesting experiment gone wrong, or in judgement of our failure to respond to His grace. Let us understand that He is God and we are just created objects of no more importance than any other created object, apart from the fact that He chose to love us.

One is tempted to think that since our salvation and our eternal security is dependent on God alone, we are free to do just whatever we like, and that will be all right. After all if God is omnipotent it would seem to follow that everything is out of our hands and in some way it is up to Him to make things right. On a basis of such thinking we may indulge ourselves in disgraceful and selfish behaviour and justify our actions in our own minds, thinking that God has promised forgiveness so that it makes no difference what we do.

Such thinking is utterly false. It is virtually spitting in the face of God. God's grace is the active force that brings about our salvation. His power alone creates us as "new creatures in Christ". He requires one thing of us, "*faith*". Faith means a number of things. In this context it includes not only believing "in" or "on" God, that is trusting Him for our redemption, but also "believing Him". What can it mean if we say that we believe that God has saved us but ignore it when we are told in Scripture that we were "created in Christ Jesus to good works ... that we should walk in them"? This is not faith; it is greed.

We are told to believe God, and we are told to love God. On both of these counts a selfish attitude fails. God took centuries and put the Nation through endless trials so that mankind could grow in knowledge of God's will. The Law taught what is good, and what is evil. The whole Bible instructs us in righteousness. We are not vindicated in casting all that aside for our own selfish desires.

The response of love is the desire to please and do good for the person who is the object of that love. We ought to strive to do the good works that God desires of us, not to improve our own position but simply as an act of gratefulness to the loving God who has loved us. Good works as a means of improving our own position smacks of selfishness. Our motivation matters.

Does a man who loves his wife stop trying to make her happy once they are married? Does a loving child act properly towards his parents just to secure his inheritance? We all recognise such behaviour as contemptible. However, this is how some tend to act towards God when they suppose that once we are saved we are free to do just as *we* please and they think that everything will be alright. One is reminded of those who say that they have done things in the Lord's name and have the Lord say to them, "I never knew you."

The issue becomes one of "priorities". This is often taken as ranking issues in order of importance. The idea being that if we get the important things right then the rest does not matter. In some ways it would be better to say, "If we don't accept the essentials of salvation, that is faith in Christ's finished work, then the rest becomes redundant, no matter how important it is."

For us, priority is quite different. In any series of events some must precede, others even though they are all of equal importance in bringing about a true conclusion. For example, in a mathematical formula any wrong component will result in a wrong answer but some functions must precede others. If we are to serve God we must first submit to Him. If we are to be His ambassadors and witness to his grace we must study and learn of Him. And so it goes, step by step. For example, if Christ is not raised then the whole gospel is meaningless.

Everything in the Bible is of equal importance *in its own context* and for the purpose for which it is given. That is what right division is all about. It is not just a catch phrase, but is a means of accomplishing a useful purpose. That is so that we can know God and learn His will for us.

A person need not know when the Church of today started in order to be "saved". Salvation is not based on knowledge or merit. A person is not a better Christian because he or she knows when the Church started. We all fall short of the glory of God and we all lack understanding of most of what is taught in His word. We are finite creatures trying to comprehend infinite God. It follows that we cannot justly judge one another on such matters. However, let us keep in mind that salvation, as important as it is, is just the first step in our walk with God.

On the other hand God does not need us as His witnesses. He has the power to accomplish all things on His own. By His grace and omnipotence He has granted us the privilege to be co-workers with Him in His redemption plan. Through Paul He has given us the calling of the New Stewardship, the gospel of grace. How can we do less than consider service to Him a sacred privilege?

Israel and the Old Stewardship are there in the Bible for our learning. One clear way in which Israel failed, lies in the fact that as time went on they became more and more egocentric. They had been called to make known to mankind the will of God. They will yet dispense His justice and mercy in the Messianic kingdom. In time past it was not so. They thought in their pride that they, as God's chosen people, were superior and worthy and all the other nations were inferior and unworthy. They forgot the fact that they were called to be servants of those very people that they despised.

We too have been called to be servants. We too, as Israel of old, are called to serve God and those around us. We have been given the great honour of making known the gospel of God's grace to man. We have been instructed to teach His truth. If we fail to try, then we are guilty of the same sin as they with even less excuse. They had only the Old Testament. We have both Old and New Testaments, including the revelation specifically given to us about the New Stewardship, and grace as the free gift of God through Christ.

Please look at some of the points that have been covered before, but perhaps in a different light. The administrations that we choose to call dispensations from Eden to Acts 28:28 have a common factor. They all have a common purpose. It is best summed up in the words of John the Baptist. "Repent; for the kingdom of heaven is at hand ... Prepare ye the way of the Lord, make his paths straight" (Matthew 3:2-3). They form one stewardship. They all relate to the establishment of the Messianic kingdom of Christ. They must still be taken into account when gaining an understanding of Scripture. We must be wary of reading back into an earlier period, things that were not revealed until later. The people who are being addressed could not know or understand these later things.

A case in point mentioned before would be the baptism of Jesus. Those watching could not possibly think of John's baptism as representing Christ's death, burial, and resurrection, which is the way baptism is viewed today. However, it must have had great importance to them, or the Pharisees and Sadducees would not have been present and, according to John, wanting to take part. The interpretation of any Scripture must take into account the people who are being addressed at the time. The Christian faith, as has been indicated, is not mystical but historical. God entered into time and space. He made Himself subject to their restraints. Similarly all Scriptures are subject to the same restrictions for in them the Holy Spirit is dealing with real people with their limitations.

In time past it has been custom to treat the New Stewardship as simply one more administration and call it the "dispensation of grace." Indeed in terms of study, the principals outlined above of the time line are equally applicable. The basic difference between what I have just agreed to term "dispensations" and the great "stewardships" that have been outlined in this book might be usefully defined in this way:

> **Dispensations** - represent changes in man's circumstance before God. These are *not* specifically delineated in Scripture but are arbitrarily established by us so that we may understand God's step-by-step revelation to us. Each change adds to the total of our understanding of His message to us. The steps are progressive, and cumulative, ranging from a simple instruction to Adam, to the immensely complicated Law of Moses and the history of the rejection of Christ by the Nation.

> **Stewardships** - are specifically delineated in the Scriptures. They represent the changes in Christ's position before God. In the Old Stewardship He is presented as the Word with God in the beginning, as the Messiah of Israel, and as the Son of David. In our Stewardship Christ is the Head of the Church which is the fulness of His Body, and He is our Saviour. In the third Stewardship, eternity, Christ is All and in all, with the Father and the Holy Spirit. For those who believe, each Stewardship defines their relationship to Christ, the hope towards which they look, and the gift of responsibility that they are granted as God's servants, and particularly the message committed to them for others. We are not saved *by* works but *unto* good works. As believers we must live according to our message, or we are false witnesses.

In all things our faith demands consistency. Let us return therefore to some of the issues raised in the beginning of this book. Why not concentrate on the really important issues and not bother with the rest. After all, some might say, "When the Church started is not of prime importance." No-one is apt to be saved or lost just because of this issue. However, there are some flaws in this thinking. It behoves Christians to act in a loving manner, but such behaviour is not restricted to Christians, so more than this is needed on our part. Second, asking which are the ten most important issues is not sound thinking. The various matters are not in competition with each other but rather complement each other. Some issues relate to salvation. Some relate to growth. Some relate to service, and so on. Paul rebuked the Hebrews (Hebrews 5:11-14) because they were not mature and needed milk and not solid food. We need to ask, "What purposes are served by each teaching?" and "How can they add to my service to Christ and my fellows?"

Asking the question, "What purpose?" is the same as asking, "Why is it important?" Consider the different denominations that were mentioned earlier. The manner in which each of them dealt with the very issues put forward in this book, and the manner they consequently applied the Scriptures, to a large extent defined them as denominations. They failed to answer the question of when the Church started, and its effect on their understanding of Scriptures is the source of much of the very disunity that we decried in the opening pages. The problem will not go away just because we ignore it. The truth is that we all tend to come to some kind of a determination about these issues, in spite of our protestations about how unimportant they are. It is better to face openly any problem. What is presented here attempts to let the Scriptures rationally interpret themselves, often at the cost of turning from long held beliefs, which are often the product of our own faulty thinking. Make no mistake. No matter how hard we try, we will never achieve one seamless Church. Our fallible human nature will prevent that, but we can try.

The question arises, "Why bother striving towards goals that we do not believe we can achieve?" The answer is simple. Just as Paul pressed "toward the mark of the prize of the high calling of God in Christ" (Philippians 3:14), even so we must strive towards goals that are beyond our reach, otherwise the goals will serve little purpose. If we aim for perfection, even though we don't achieve it, we will come closer to the truth and we may even be able to overcome some of our own partisan thinking.

We can never do away with "denominationalism", but we can lessen some of its effects. By letting the Scriptures interpret themselves, instead of blindly following our own prejudices, we will not only come to a more accurate understanding of God's will but we will be able to understand why others think as they do and be more tolerant of them. Our own need to change will make other's "errors" seem less blameful. It is more difficult to be judgmental of others when we realise that we too have feet of clay. This is tolerance without the need to compromise our basic principles.

Right division of the Scriptures matters on two main counts. First, because we have a better understanding of the will of God for us, we can serve him better and glory in His grace more fully. Second, because we have had committed to us the gospel of grace, as His stewards we can be more loving towards our fellow believers. Remember Christ told us that the greatest commandments were to love God *and* to love our neighbour! There should be no thought of "doctrine" *or* "help for the hurting". It should be both. If we fail in either, it will not alter God's plan nor, in the long run, will it be others who lose. God's will is immutable. Just as His plan for the Kingdom will be accomplished in spite of Israel's failure, even so His plan of grace will be accomplished in spite of our failure to obey. It is we who will have lost; lost the chance to serve.

I have covered a great many things in this book. Most of them have been covered only fleetingly. They all deserve thorough study. The most important for us in this context is the Gospel of Grace. To truly understand it we must be able to compare and contrast it with the Gospel of the Kingdom. The differences are great and illuminate each other. This is why we need to be able to place each part into its correct context, not only its immediate context but also its overall context.

The marker of Acts 28:28 is of immeasurable value in this effort. When God gave a new calling it was to a new people (a called out people; a new Church, the Church of today), and the details are in Ephesians and Colossians. It was for us and to us. We are not called to fulfil Israel's calling but our own. Our service will reflect our understanding and beliefs. We are what we believe. Our deepest held beliefs control all our values and actions.

To any who might read these lines, especially those who are dear to us, let me say this: we have not stood aside from our fellow believers through any sense of pride or in any way to criticise those who do not see our view of God's word. We are only too painfully aware of our own shortcomings for that. We are simply dazzled by the beauty of the gospel of God's grace to us in Christ as expressed in the New Stewardship that has been committed to us. Our desire is to make it known to men so that He may be honoured, and thus we seek to walk worthy of the vocation wherein we are called. We would urge you to do likewise.

To the best of your ability, in the clearest way you know how, be witnesses before men to the redemption through Christ, and the gospel of Grace as the free gift of His love! You need not choose between doctrine and charity towards those around you. The doctrine is the doctrine of love.

Chapter 19
SUMMARY

The church in Acts, the Pentecostal or Apostolic church, had as its base the covenant with Abraham, and Israel had a central role. In the future they are to be a royal priesthood and all the nations (Gentiles) will be blessed through them. The hope is to be a redeemed earth through the restored kingdom. Job expected to stand on the earth and see his Redeemer and the Messiah is to sit on David's throne. All this, and more, will yet come to pass.

If the Church at Pentecost is the beginning of today's Church, we are hard pressed to explain why we do not have *all* the sign gifts or the power to forgive sins, clearly granted to the Apostles. The Pentecostal movement is based on just such a claim. So is the Roman doctrine of apostolic succession. Barring a change of stewardship (dispensation) between Acts 2 and now, there is no clear reason why these ideas should not be true.

Israel's hope, even during the Book of Acts, was the Kingdom of the Heavens, that is the rule of the heavens over the earth with the Nation acting in God's name as priests, standing between God and the redeemed Gentiles. The signs, the special powers, and the ceremonial water baptism (cleansing), were all in preparation for their role as priests of God. It is an earth-bound hope.

The terms "bride" and "bridegroom" are always used in relation to the "Nation" and the "new Jerusalem". The specific idea of "going to heaven" was foreign to the Jew. Like Job, Israel looked for physical resurrection to this earth (Job 19:25-27). However, at Acts 28:28 the Kingdom hope was set-aside for a time, until this present age is complete, and then it will be restored.

Just before Christ's ascension, He gave His disciples what is considered to be "The great commission" in the following passage:

> *Matthew 28:18-20*: Jesus came and spake unto them, saying, All power is given unto me in heaven and in earth. Go ye therefore, and teach all nations, baptising them in the name of the Father, and of the Son, and of the Holy Ghost: Teaching them to observe all things whatsoever I have commanded you: and, lo, I am with you alway, *even* unto the end of the world. Amen.

This clearly was a commission or parting instructions to the Apostles and the Nation. They were to rule the earth under Christ, but this commission was not to us. What He had taught them related to the restoration of His rule on earth - the *kingdom. This was their Stewardship!* They were to make known those things that had been taught to them by the Lord.

We have been given a new commission, *a new Stewardship.* It is similar but not the same as theirs. God, through the Apostle Paul, taught us all things particular and special to the gospel of grace and our hope in the heavenlies. This is the *mystery* of Ephesians and Colossians. We are to teach others the things that we have been taught. Consider again:

> *Colossians 1:26-28*: Even the mystery which hath been hid from ages and from generations, but now is revealed to his saints: To whom God would make known what is the riches of the glory of this mystery among the Gentiles; which is Christ in (or, among) you, the hope of glory. Whom we preach, warning every man, and teaching every man in all wisdom; that we may present every man perfect in Christ Jesus.

Viewed simply as a historic event, the beginning of the Church is something that happened a very long time ago. Indeed, apart from scriptural revelation, some might view it as a kind of development that evolved at that period as a resistance movement to the injustices of the society of the time. Humanists consider Christ as simply a reformer. If that were true then the point of beginning would be of no great importance but it is not true.

The beginning of the Church was coincident with the revelation of the Stewardship of Grace. It is a matter of revelation from God, as is the Gospel for today, and the Church for today, the Body of Christ, was created to fulfill the stewardship. We must know the point of it's beginning for only then will we be able to proclaim faithfully through our lives, actions, and words, God's Grace. Only then will we have a clear knowledge and understanding of the message that God has committed to us.

The Body of Christ was part of the "mystery" revealed by the Holy Spirit through Paul after Israel had been set aside at Acts 28:28. Unlike kingdom truth, it did not go back to Abraham and the fathers and was not the subject of prophecy. It was a part of the secret "which from the beginning of the world hath been hid in God" (Ephesians

3:9), we will not find it in the Scriptures until Paul penned it under the inspiration of the Holy Spirit in his last seven letters.

Like the Nation we are ambassadors for Christ, witnessing to His glory and grace to the unsaved, but we in no way stand between Christ and His redeemed as priests, for we are all complete in Him. The Nation's hope was based on the promises unto Abraham, but of us it is written, "According as he hath chosen us in Him (Christ) *before the foundation of the world,* that we should be holy and without blame before Him in love" (Ephesians 1:4).

They were saved by grace, through faith, but works and the law were added for our and their instruction. We are saved by grace through faith, not of works lest any man should boast, "For we are His workmanship, created *unto good works*, which God hath before ordained that we should walk in them" (Ephesians 2:10).

Adam's race on earth fell, but the Kingdom will glorify the Lord through the display of His grace on this earth, the place where He was blasphemed by Adam's race. Our hope is that we are, even now in His will, seated in *heavenly places* in Christ. There we will glorify God before the heavenly hosts by being displayed as trophies of His grace. This was where He was blasphemed by the disobedience of Satan and his angels.

Our Position

> *Ephesians 4:4-6*: There is one body, and one Spirit, even as ye are called in one hope of your calling; One Lord, one faith, one baptism, One God and Father of all, who is above all, and through all, and in you all.

> *Colossians 2:10-14*: And ye are complete in him, who is the head of all principality and power: In whom also ye are circumcised with the circumcision made without hands, in putting off the body of the sins of the flesh by the circumcision of Christ: Buried with him in baptism, in which also ye are raised with him through the faith of the operation of God, who hath raised him from the dead. And you, being dead in your sins and the uncircumcision of your flesh, hath he made alive together with him, having forgiven you all trespasses; Blotting out the handwriting of ordinances that was against us, which was contrary to us, and took it out of the way, nailing it to his cross.

Grace, before the "mystery" was revealed, was separated from believers by a "priesthood", and was administered by a "nation" through a "conditional covenant". *The mystery is **unconditional grace**!* Both the Kingdom and the Body are but steps towards His final revealed will, which I understand to be shown in Ephesians 1:9-10.

> "Having made known unto us the mystery of His will, according to his good pleasure which He hath purposed in Himself;
>
> That in the stewardship of the fullness of times He might gather together in one all things in Christ, both which are in heaven [us], and which are on earth [them]; even in Him."

There are two stewardships ... but only one Lord!

Index of Bible References

Bibliography

Approaching the Bible; Michael Penny; The Open Bible Trust, England.
(See page 236 for details.)
Christian History – Issue 43 (Vol. XIII, No. 3); Christianity Today, Carol
Stream, Illinois, USA.
The Companion Bible; E. W. Bullinger; Kregel Publications, Grand Rapids,Michigan, USA.
Evolution or Creation?; Arthur C Custance; Acaedemie Books (Zondervan
Publishing House), Grand Rapids, Michigan, USA.
The Interlinear Greek-English New Testament (Nestle Text); Rev. Arthur
Marshall; Zondervan Publishing House, Grand Rapids, Michigan, USA.
Seventh Day Adventist Church Manual; General Conference of Seventh
DayAdventists.
Think on these Things; Ernest Streets, The Open Bible Trust, England.

Approaching the Bible
by Michael Penny

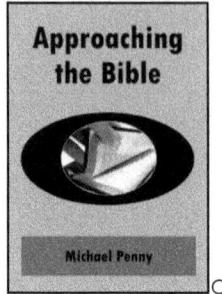

With many interesting examples, Michael Penny provides the rationale for the view that before we try to *apply* any passage in the Bible to ourselves, we should discover first what it meant to those to whom its words were initially addressed. The book advocates that this is best done by considering the passage under the following headings:

1) **W**ho said or wrote it;

2) to **W**hom was it said or written, or concerning **W**hom was it said or written;

3) **W**here it was said or written, or concerning **W**here was it said or written;

4) **W**hat was said or written;

5) **W**hen was it said or written, or concerning **W**hen was it said or written;

6) **W**hy was it said or written.

Applying these six **"W"** rules puts the passage into its proper context and gives us the right perspective on it. Only after doing this can we determine:

7) **W**hether the passage applies to our situation and what the correct application is.

It is the *consistent* use of these **Seven Ws** which helps us discover the right and relevant application of any passage to our lives.

Published by The Open Bible Trust and available as a book or an eBook.

www.obt.org.uk

www.ingramcontent.com/pod-product-compliance
Lightning Source LLC
Chambersburg PA
CBHW071524040426

42452CB00008B/880